CARE AND MANAGEMENT OF EXCEPTIONAL CHILDREN

CARE AND MANAGEMENT OF EXCEPTIONAL CHILDREN

JUANITA W. FLEMING, R.N., Ph.D.

Associate Professor and Director
Maternal-Child Nursing Division
College of Nursing
University of Kentucky
Lexington, Kentucky

APPLETON-CENTURY-CROFTS
Educational Division
MEREDITH CORPORATION
New York

Library of Congress Catalog Card Number: 72-90438

PRINTED IN THE UNITED STATES OF AMERICA
390-31999-6

To

Bill, Billy, Bobby, and Bertha

Contributors

LORETTA DENMAN, R.N., PH.D.
Professor of Clinical Nursing, College of Nursing, University of Kentucky, Lexington, Kentucky

BARBARA HAUS, R.N., M.A.
Instructor of Clinical Nursing, College of Nursing, University of Kentucky, Lexington, Kentucky

PEARL ROSSER, M.D.
Medical Director, Child Development Center, Department of Pediatrics, College of Medicine, Howard University, Washington, D.C.

DAVID SABATINO, PH.D.
Associate Professor, Department of Special Education, School Psychology Program, Pennsylvania State University, Hershey, Pennsylvania

SHIRLEY SCALES, R.N., M.A.
Public Health Nursing Consultant, Child Development Center, Department of Pediatrics, College of Medicine, Howard University, Washington, D.C.

CAROLYN STEWART, M.A.
Speech Pathologist, Child Development Center, Department of Pediatrics, College of Medicine, Howard University, Washington, D.C.

SHARON THOMPSON, R.N., M.A.
College of Nursing, University of Kentucky, Lexington, Kentucky

Preface

This is not a text or necessarily a reference book, but one designed to stimulate the nurse to look at exceptional children in terms of their behavior and to try to help their parents manage them so that they can be accepted in society and function at their maximum potentials. An approach that lends itself to understanding mankind is important in working effectively with exceptional children. The contents of this book are based on what the editor has chosen to call a humanistic scientific approach.

Certain basic premises have been considered in preparing this book. They are:

1. Exceptional children require satisfaction of their basic needs. This includes their survival needs as well as their esteem needs.
2. Exceptional children are in a state of continual adjustment. They do not ever completely adjust to their environment. Consequently, they continue to order their lives so that they will, with some degree of accuracy, know how to behave.
3. Exceptional children have a desire to do something that will bring them a sense of accomplishment.
4. Exceptional children have worth and some capacity for self-realization through reasoning. The aim should not be so much toward cure as toward assisting each child to reach his maximum potential.
5. Exceptional children should be handled with dignity.
6. Exceptional children must be viewed as a whole. Forces within them as well as forces without affect their behavior.
7. Exceptional children should be viewed objectively. Assessing, planning, and managing problems, if done systematically and objectively, are in the long run more effective.

This book does not cover all the relevant information about exceptionality. There are textbooks and other references available for this purpose. Rather, it is a guide that is general in some instances and more specific in others.

The authors acknowledge the following persons:

Dr. Doris Payne, Department of Pediatrics, College of Nursing, University of Florida, Gainesville, Florida, and Dr. Sally O'Neil, Assistant Professor of Nursing, University of Washington, Seattle, Washington, for reading and commenting on the chapter, "Children with Social Disability."

Dr. Ouida Westney, Coordinator, Maternal and Child Nursing, School of Nursing, Howard University, Washington, D.C., and Dr. Lisa Barkley, College of Home Economics, Department of Human Development and Family Relations, University of Kentucky, Lexington, Kentucky, for reading and commenting on the chapter, "Family Dynamics and The Exceptional Child."

Mrs. Gretchen LaGodna, R.N., Doctoral Candidate, Department of Educational Psychology, College of Education, University of Kentucky, Lexington, Kentucky, for reading and commenting on the chapter, "Changing Behavior of Exceptional Children."

Dr. William Green, Director, Speech and Hearing Clinic, University of Kentucky, Lexington, Kentucky, for reading and commenting on the chapter, "Children with Speech and Hearing Disorders."

Miss Naomi Mason, Miss Betty Nordholm, University of Kentucky, and Miss Sandy Harshbarger, University of Nebraska, Lincoln, Nebraska, for their help in obtaining materials.

Mrs. Judith Tuthill for secretarial and editorial assistance.

Finally, Deans Marcia A. Dake and Marion E. McKenna, for their support and ecouragement during the time-consuming process of writing and assembling this material.

Contents

Foreword

Although our society values its children above all else, it has long been apparent that children who deviate from the capabilities and activities of the normal healthy child are penalized in many ways. The authors of this book address themselves to the specific types of problems encountered by exceptional children. The use of the term "exceptional child" sets the educative tone of this volume, an innovative departure from nursing approaches adapted to the traditional medical model.

Of further importance is the fact that the authors address themselves to the role of professional nurses in the management of the exceptional child. Nurses are among those professionals most likely to encounter exceptional children and their families. In some situations the exceptionality is of primary concern and in others it is secondary; but if we believe in the concept of promotion of optimal potential, exceptionality is inherently significant regardless of the presenting situation.

While this book is the result of specialized study and work, it is not written exclusively for the specialist in pediatric nursing, but should be helpful to any nurse who deals with children and families. Throughout the volume the exceptional child is viewed as an individual, one of a family, a member of society, and, perhaps most important, as a child. Emphasis is placed upon normal growth and development as a basis for identification of disturbances. Interventions are directed at maximizing the potential of the individual toward normal achievements. Chapters include discussions of types of problems common to many exceptional children and elaborate upon some disabilities which present specific behavioral manifestations. Biological, psychological, and social factors are taken into account as both primary and secondary effects upon normal growth and development.

The authors do not pretend to erase disability by a wave of the magic wand of knowledge, but they do present research and practice findings that encourage optimism about the capability of each of us to become more effective in the management of exceptional children.

Eleanor Repp, Ed.D.
Dean, College of Nursing
Creighton University
Omaha, Nebraska

Introduction

The term "exceptional child" refers to children who are either gifted or limited. The exceptional child is defined as the child who deviates from the average child in mental, physical, or social characteristics to such an extent that he requires a modification of services in order to develop his maximum potential.

The initial disability in those children who are limited may be mild and hardly noticeable or it may involve several areas of function which may result in life-long impairment. The goal for children with limitations is to prevent them from becoming handicapped.

Some use disability in the same context as handicapped. Not everyone who has a disability needs to be classified as having a handicap. Objectively, a disability may be defined as an impairment of either structure or function. Wright (1960) has defined a handicap as a cumulative effect resulting from a disability and the personal and social consequences which have a detrimental effect on the person's functional level.

A child may be considered handicapped if he cannot, within limits, play, learn, work or do those things that children his age are expected to do, therefore hindering him from achieving his full physical, mental, and social potential. Hamilton (1950) proposes a distinction between the terms "handicap" and "disability." A disability is a condition of impairment, physical or mental, having an objective aspect that can be described medically. A handicap is the cumulative result of the obstacles which disability interposes between the individual and his maximum functional level.

This work will deal primarily with children who have intellectual limitations, physical defects, and social deviations, since they comprise the largest number of exceptional children. Exclusive of the material concerning gifted children, the discussion will deal with children who have limitations. The term "exceptional children" will be used throughout as the reference term for all such children when the specific disability or deviance is less significant than the fact of disability or deviance.

Children with characteristics which place them in a position of being considered exceptional often pose problems to those responsible for their care. Exceptionality may present obstacles that will prevent the child from developing his maximum potential. The obstacles that may emerge from the source in which the child has his initial and primary contacts — the family — are perhaps the most significant in preventing maximum development.

The child who is exceptional has, like any other child, the problem of growing up. It is essential that those working with families who have an exceptional child understand and appreciate family dynamics and the normal processes and stages of human development, as these will aid the worker in helping the family guide the child to as high a level of independence as is possible for him.

The exceptional child has to be looked at first of all as a child. He, like any other child, is a person going through developmental stages which are indicative of his level of maturity. He has aspirations and needs in tune with his level of development.

The exceptional child also has to be looked upon as an individual. He has a uniqueness that is exclusively his and should be considered based on his individual differences. He is doubly unique. He is unique or different because he has an exceptionality as well as being unique or different from any other human being because of his genetic endowment.

The exceptional child, like any other growing child, must learn of the dangers that exist in his environment. He must learn that a hot stove burns, that a sharp knife cuts, and that certain liquids and solids are not fit for human consumption. He must learn to walk, to talk, to feed, and to dress himself. These lessons, plus many others, are learned in the early stages of development, primarily in the family circle. Teaching these lessons to a normal child can be a mammoth task for a family. Parents of exceptional children are not excused from this task of translating the norms of society to their children. If the task for parents of average children is tremendous, consider what it must be for the parents of an exceptional child. And yet, it is perhaps even more important for the exceptional child than for the average child to learn these tasks well at an early age.

Parents of exceptional children, like any other, are expected to begin the translation of the norms of society to their young. However, there are a number of factors that should be considered in expecting these parents to meet this goal. First, few, if any, parents are actually prepared to rear an exceptional child. An infinite number of reactions of parents of children who have disabilities or intellectual limitations have been described in the literature. Some will be discussed in the section dealing with the needs of the exceptional child. Second, there are many psycho-social considerations, such as educational level of parents, socio-economic status, background, number of children in the family, parental values, personality characteristics, attitudes of parents, and the like. We are not sure, for example, how the exceptional child views the world. We have some evidence through drawings as to how he sees himself in relation to significant others.

As the child grows older, he depends on peers for determination of his attractiveness; but during his early childhood, he looks to his parents for approval and status. He is able to maintain a desirable self-image if he is intrinsically valued by his parents.

We are learning more about perceptual disabilities and believe that many exceptional children perceive their world differently than other children. Responses to stimuli depend on how the stimuli are perceived. Some exceptional children behave in what may be described as an atypical manner. The behavior responses seem different from those of the average child. This brings us to our third consideration, which is a consideration of the nature of the exceptionality. Evidence shows that the personalities of blind children and deaf children are basically different from those of the average child. The difference may be attributed to their special limitation. Deaf children are said to absorb influences that have to do with many feelings and experiences except the experiences of speech. These are reflected in their behavior. Many congenitally blind children have behavior problems in addition to their blindness.

From a growth and development point of view, it is perhaps safe to say that the exceptional child needs the stimulation from the family to move through the developmental milestones adequately. He may not reach milestones at the rate of a normal child because of his disability; but from a purely biological point of view, he will grow from a child to an adult if he is nurtured. Therefore, he needs to reach the various milestones — even if belatedly.

The nurse will need to have some understanding of family situations, as much of what she will do with families will depend on what type of family she finds for each case she works with. Role obligations in families will depend on the type of family.

The nurse who works with families who have exceptional children is in an enviable position. She can observe the family in both the home and the institutional setting. She is in a position to relate as a knowledgeable friend and step into the void that so many families who have exceptional children seem to experience. If any professional is able to view the exceptional child and his family from a holistic point of view, it is the nurse.

The nurse should be careful to maintain objectivity and not to impose her own ideas and feelings on the families with whom she will work. The nurse, because of her own experiences, is likely to view families from her point of view. The story is told about two medical specialists who were on vacation in Florida. They were walking along the beach when the orthopedist remarked, "These girls in Florida have beautiful legs, don't they." "I hadn't noticed," his companion replied. "I am a chest man myself." Nurses, like others, have their own special interests and concerns and may tend to overlook or overemphasize aspects of the family because of this. The plea for objectivity is pertinent and necessary.

Nurses need to practice being good listeners, as many parents who have exceptional children have much that is valuable to say about their care. In order to be a good listener, the nurse must concentrate solely on the other person's conversation without introducing any thoughts or questions of her own. If the nurse nods slightly and waits as the person talks, and looks at the speaker expectantly without saying or doing anything more, this will encourage the speaker and perhaps reassure him that she is staying with the conversation. Casual remarks, such as, "I see," "Is that so," "That is interesting," will let the speaker know she's sticking with him and is interested in hearing more. Repeating back the last few words the speaker said is referred to as echoing his thoughts back. Finally, to listen more effectively, the nurse should mirror or reflect back to the speaker her understanding of what he has just said, such as, "You believe that . . ."

The nurse should try very hard not to assume the role of a parent to parents of exceptional children. Assuming a parental role may be reflected in words such as, "should," "ought," "right," and "wrong." She should make every attempt to maintain an adult-to-adult relationship. Parents of exceptional children are sometimes likely to revert to responding as a child. In such cases, the nurse should become sensitive to why the parents need to respond in such a manner. The nurse should do what she can to strengthen the parent so that adult responses are made. The parent may be having difficulty in making decisions. A wise nurse would spend time with the parent(s) and provide the necessary support that would enable her (them) to make a responsible decision.

A 10-month-old infant was admitted to the hospital and diagnosed as having pneumonia. The child appeared to be about three months old. Two days before discharge the parents were advised to bring the child to the developmental clinic for a diagnostic "work-up." The father asked, "Is that where they take retarded children?" Before an answer was given the father broke into a temper tantrum — shrieking and shouting. He once said he'd kill the child before he'd bring her to that clinic. The wife told a nurse several months later that her husband just couldn't decide what to do because he thought the child was retarded and he didn't believe the child could be helped.

REFERENCES

Berman, S. I. The Closed Mind. San Francisco, International Society for General Semantics, 1965.
——How to Lessen Misunderstandings. San Francisco, International Society for General Semantics, 1969.
——Understanding and Being Understood. San Francisco, International Society for General Semantics, 1969.
Berne, E. Transactional Analysis in Psychotherapy. New York, Grove Press, 1961.
Hamilton, K. W. Counseling the Handicapped in the Rehabilitation Process. New York, Ronald, 1950.
Harris, T. A. I'm OK — You're OK: A Practical Guide to Transactional Analysis. New York, Harper & Row, 1967.
Wright, B. A. Physical Disability: A Psychological Approach. New York, Harper & Row, 1960.

SPECIAL NEEDS OF EXCEPTIONAL CHILDREN

To consider seriously the needs of exceptional children, one must attempt to be honest in one's bias and beliefs about exceptional people. One's emotional attitudes, socio-economic standing, and values may unconsciously affect feelings. This may result in attitudes toward exceptional people that will either help us be more cognizant of their special needs or help us deny that they have them.

✶ Exceptional children have the same basic needs as other children. However, in addition to these basic needs, their exceptionality may cause them to have intensified problems in some areas. The discussion that follows is general and is not geared just to exceptional children but tries to put into perspective some of the needs of exceptional children that relate primarily to problems they may encounter.

SOCIAL NEEDS

Exceptional children need to engage in social behavior that does not put them at a disadvantage or others in a state of undue discomfort. Social behavior is the crux of being accepted or rejected in a society that puts emphasis on how people behave. Children learn early that they say please and thank you, eat with a spoon and fork and not with their fingers, wear clothes, use the toilet, and act in certain other specific ways. The social niceties are an ingrained part of the culture; to be out of tune with the society in which one lives, all one has to do is violate the code of dress and/or the code of manners.

Conformity to social norms is difficult for the average child. Parents, no matter how permissive they are, still expect that their child will not be at odds with the social norms. If one exhibits behavior that is at odds with social expectations one should be prepared to accept the consequences of such behavior. A young child is likely not able to accept the consequences so it is important that he be taught the social mores of his culture.

The child must be recognized as a unique individual as he becomes socialized. Recognition that the child's biologic and psycho-social needs are tied together is a first step. Secondly, it must be understood that his functional or biologic needs undergo transformations as he grows and develops. The child experiences socialization and enculturation. For example, hunger becomes a desire for specific foods, eaten at prescribed times, utilizing various eating tools, and accompanied by certain forms of etiquette. Social gratification will result only if the process is successful.

Exceptional children, like all children, need to have the feeling that they have the benevolent guidance of someone who is interested in them. Without this from a parent or a parent surrogate, socialization may be very difficult. It will not be possible for exceptional children to meet the mounting tasks of life without a caring individual who gives them wise direction.

LEARNING

Like all other children, exceptional children need to learn as quickly as they can how to be human beings. Human behavior is learned behavior. Simply put, certain cues and responses must become connected. The connection between the cue and the response can either be strengthened or weakened dependent upon the conditions. Exceptional children must be conditioned to make responses that will bring rewards for having responded in a socially acceptable manner.

Too often, children with disabilities are restricted. They are not allowed to explore their world as other children are. Expectations of them may be grossly different from those of other children their own age. They may not be allowed to experiment with their senses and their muscles because their actions appear more crude and awkward than those of their more normal peers. Sometimes the length of time it takes them to perform an activity may mitigate against permitting them to do it.

Learning can only take place according to definite psychologic principles. These learning principles can operate only under certain specific conditions. For the child, learning appropriate social behavior begins in his family.

DISCIPLINE

Exceptional children need to be disciplined just as normal children are. It is important to discuss discipline as a need critical to exceptional children for two reasons:

1. Many live in a more permissive atmosphere than do their more normal peers and siblings.
2. When they become adults they will be expected to do as well or better in order to obtain employment.

Too often, exceptional children are pitied, given more sympathy and less responsibility than their more normal peers. This does not foster growth as a self-sufficient, independent person but perpetuates a weak, dependent person and sometimes a demanding, overbearing person. Such persons would not be ready for the competitive life one must face as an adult. Those individuals who have a limitation already have a strike against them. Individuals with disabilities are likened to minority group members. Having a disability often places a person in an inferior status position. Our society seems to be geared toward the "whole person" and sees individuals with disabilities as lacking in wholeness.

Studies (Barker, 1948; Rusk and Taylor, 1946; Cowen, Vortenberg, and Verillo, 1956) have shown that disabled individuals have less than full status in our society in that their disabilities preclude them from the better job opportunities and marriage; and, further, attitudes toward them correlated significantly with antiminority, anti-Negro, and pro-authoritarian attitudes.

Wright (1960) points out that individuals with disabilities are in the same position as minority group members. But, unlike minority racial groups — which are continuous from generation to generation through genetic inheritance — and minority religious groups — which are socially inherited — disabled individuals are likely to be the only member of their family with such a problem. As children they may have no awareness of other persons like themselves and consequently have no identification with a minority group as such.

Exceptional children need to learn early to accept authority. They must learn to control the behavior that gets them into conflict and causes them unhappiness and sometimes fear. Parents should begin early teaching these children how to behave towards persons and things. Private property is sanctified in our society and is to be protected. Exceptional children must learn early that they cannot violate the property of others. Further, they cannot be constantly excused if they do not know how to behave towards others. Reinforcing desirable ways of behavior towards others and things will help these children move a long way toward success in their society.

SELF-CONCEPT

An awareness of one's self is an essential need of exceptional children. Gordon (1964) states:

> The body image is no built-in model to be found in some specific part of the brain, but has to be laboriously acquired. Failure in its normal development, due to defects in afferent sensory pathways or to impairment of integration with the cerebrum, may be an important contribution to the total disability of a handicapped child.

Individuals with disabilities are likely to devalue themselves because others devalue them. In preparing these children for life, one may not be able to do much about others, but these children can be taught to value themselves.

A healthy concept of self must emerge if the child is to go on developing in an acceptable way — that is, from dependence to greater independence.

Some exceptional children have physical stigma and some have limitations such as difficulties in visuo-spatial perception or deficits in language development or motor development. Their lack of motor development may be manifested in clumsiness, awkward movement, and difficulty in buttoning clothes and lacing shoes. Difficulties in visuo-spatial perception may be manifested in inabilities in copying, matching, and recognizing position. Koppitz (1968) concludes that what distinguishes the brain-injured child from the non-brain-injured child is "primarily a malfunctioning of his integration capacity . . ."

These difficulties may mitigate against these children having healthy self-concepts. In some cases, such as the brain-injured child, the lowered self-image may be associated with impairment in the brain. An intense effort to aid these children in developing desirable self-images is crucial.

SELF-CONFIDENCE

Children who are exceptional need to develop confidence in themselves. Lack of self-confidence can be more defeating than many other deterrents that block the paths of exceptional children. One of the initial steps in developing confidence lies in accepting oneself and believing that one is valuable.

Exceptional children need to learn to accept their exceptionality. If there is a disability, they need to be able to learn to live with it so that it becomes less of a handicap. If these children do not learn to live with their condition, greater personal and social limitations are likely to arise. Families need to help these children recognize that they are worthwhile and that simply because they are different does not mean that they are undesirable.

Children with disabilities should be helped early to understand that they have nothing to make up for. They should be encouraged to engage or pursue those activities that they can do and that they find satisfying. To help them make the best choices is imperative.

For too long the notion has been promoted that those who belong to a minority group must compensate because they are automatically made to feel inferior. Their feelings of inferiority lead to the idea that in order not to be bad, they have to be especially good.

SECURITY

When one thinks of exceptionality, one thinks of a category of individuals with disabilities; when one thinks of the intellectually gifted, there is perhaps a different association. The disabled are "the poor things," the gifted, "the lucky things."

Maintenance of security, both physical and emotional, is essential when working with both groups of children. Exceptional children need to be protected from unnecessary physical and psychologic pain. They should not be exploited and/or deprived because of their exceptionality. It is painful to see how some exceptional children are subtly coerced and made to undergo undue pressures to force them into conformity before they are ready. Parents often build an image of their unborn child and what he will be like at birth. When the child comes and does not meet their expectations of physique, temperament, or ability, a pronounced bias may result.

These children must be free of exploitations by other adults also, particularly professionals such as the physician, the psychologist, the social worker, and the nurse who engage in the care of these children. Both psychologic and physical needs must be met. The human rights of these children must be respected just as they would be for any other individuals.

Those who work with exceptional children must understand that for many of them progress will be slow. The approach to these children should be one of patience, a recognition that they have some worth, and that they should be handled with dignity. Caring about how they feel, their assets and liabilities, and how to help them use their assets to make their world a more secure one for them is essential. It is important that their likes and dislikes are known, as well as their way of coping with situations. Security is a big umbrella under which much can be accomplished. Some exceptional children, because of the nature of their condition, will feel insecure. Our role is to find every means possible to make a secure environment for them. This can only be done if we assess each individual child and his family before determining how best to plan for him.

FREEDOM FROM GUILT AND FEAR

Excess guilt and fear are feelings that may afflict insecure children. These children need to feel that they belong to the family, and they need to be reassured that they are cared about and wanted. They should not feel that they are under constant threat. They need to receive affection and the warmth of human relationships. They need to confide in someone who understands and cares about them.

Guilt may arise out of humiliation. These children may be made to feel ashamed of how they look or behave. They should be respected and appreciated as they are and not made to feel that their disability is a punishment or that they are a burden.

FREEDOM TO DEVELOP INDIVIDUALLY

Exceptional children, like average children, should be allowed to develop and grow at their own rate. The norms that are set should not be used to judge them. They should have their own standards. It has been said that some people should not work too long with exceptional individuals because they start seeing them as the average. In some respects this is highly complimentary because these individual workers are judging the child by his own standard of growth, not by the fixed norms set down for chronological age.

> One teacher who taught a special education class for intermediate students had a 10-year-old boy who at the beginning of the semester would not react to other children, held his head down, and could not read or write. By the end of the first semester the boy was reading on a second-grade-level, was writing in cursive style, and was interacting well with the other children. The teacher was ecstatic over his progress and wanted to have the child retested. She made her request and was simply told that she should recognize that a child 10 years old, reading on a second-grade-level, was obviously not normal.

Surely, one can see that this is an individual case. Recognition that special help may be necessary to enhance the development of some exceptional children is essential. Comparisons with others, regardless of who they are, should be minimized. Even though the exceptional child may have greater limitations, it is important to help him see that he can succeed, no matter how long it takes.

HEALTH SERVICES

Community services that will aid the child's development can never be overlooked. Nurses can and do play a role in helping the community define the services it needs for its citizenry. Health planning councils and other groups are concerned about maintenance of health — not just crisis intervention. Nurses not only aid in planning services, but they help identify through case-finding those individuals in need of services.

REFERENCES

1. Barker, R. G. The social psychology of physical disability. J Soc Issues 4:28, 1948.
2. Cowen, E. L., Vortenberg, R. P., and Verillo, R. T. The development and testing attitudes to blindness scale. J Soc Psychol 48:291-304, 1958.
3. Gordon, N. The anatomy and physiology of body image in childhood. Dev Med Child Neurol 6:641, 1964.
4. Koppitz, E. M. Psychological Evaluation of Children's Human Figure Drawings. New York, Grune & Stratton, 1968.
5. Miller, N. E., and Dollard, J. Social Learning and Imitation. New Haven, Yale University, 1967.
6. Rusk, H. A., and Taylor, E. J. New Hope for the Handicapped. New York, Harper & Row, 1946.
7. Telford, C. W., and Sawrey, J. M. The Exceptional Individual. Engelwood Cliffs, N.J., Prentice-Hall, 1967.
8. Williams, J. F. Children with Specific Learning Disabilities. New York, Pergamon, 1970.
9. Wright, B. A. Physical Disability — A Psychological Approach. New York, Harper & Row, 1960.

2

FAMILY DYNAMICS AND EXCEPTIONAL CHILDREN

UNDERSTANDING FAMILY CRISIS

When a family has a less than perfect child, the stage is already set to elicit emotional stress from the moment that the disability is perceived. The child who is exceptional presents unusual problems to his family. The family's ability to cope with these problems will depend on how well it is equipped. The family cannot count on too much empathy from society because it more or less frowns on exceptional children, excluding the exceptionally bright who, incidentally, also have unique problems. The child with disabilities is accorded an inferior position in our society. Wright (1960) likens the position of persons with disabilities to that of the underprivileged ethnic and religious minority groups. They are restricted in many walks of life. The perception of the child's abnormality may propel a family that already has tendencies in that direction toward emotional instability. The family has the responsibility for, or function of, rearing the child, providing for him economically, protecting him, and socializing him. The nurse needs to understand some of the factors which may influence the family situation. Three broad classifications will be discussed: intrafamily relationships, family patterns, and external factors.

Before this discussion begins, however, some clarification of what we mean by the term "family" should be made. When we think of the nuclear family, we think of mother, father, and children. Extended families may include grandparents, aunts, uncles, and cousins. Irving (1971) has described what he calls the relevant family which includes the mother, father, children, and the parents-in-law. The literature includes information on fatherless families. Who makes up the family is not critical to how the nurse will work with them. It should not concern her whether or not a nuclear family exists. Her concern is to operate with those members who do make up the family and to help them carry out effectively the roles that they have chosen or that have been designated to them.

It is important that the family functions as a unit. As the family is a unity of interacting personalities, each member is dependent upon the others for satisfaction of his biologic, psychologic, social, and economic needs. A unique relationship exists between members of the family and each individual affects each of the others in some way. There is a one-to-one relationship operating among family members. It is of prime importance for those working with families of children who have disabilities to recognize this. It is not just a parent-child relationship but a family affair. The uniqueness of each paired relationship excludes a third person in that the response to each other is based on a set of cognitions, wants, attitudes, and interpersonal response traits that are unique.

INTRAFAMILY RELATIONS

Family relationships are usually affected when a child with a disability is introduced into the setting. The relationships are affected because an alteration in the roles of each family member results when the member with a disability is not able to fulfill his role as other members expect. Goode (1966) cites unwilled role failure — through mental, emotional, or physical pathologies such as mental retardation of the child, psychosis of the child, or chronic and incurable physical conditions — as one of the major forms of family disorganization.

One factor that seems to bring about cohesiveness in a family, or to enhance family integration, is the lack of role tension in the interpersonal relations between family members. Families perform the basic functions of extending physical and emotional support to its members. Parents take the responsibility for the socialization and enculturation of the children. The group is able to continue its structure by its division of labor and differentiation of roles. The children as well as the parents are expected to perform certain functions within the family group. The child with a disability may place the family role system in a tension state. Of course, this will depend on the nature of the disability, as role behavior is influenced by the individual's knowledge of the role, his motivation to perform the role, and his attitude towards himself and other persons in the interpersonal behavior event. The child with a disability may be unable to carry out his role as demanded by other members of the family. For the most part, the role one must play in the family is unlike roles demanded of one in other social groups. A child does not pick his family. He has no control over who his parents or siblings are. Since he has no choice in this at all, he cannot easily decide, as in some other social group, that he will not be a part and therefore not adhere to the role that is designated to him.

AFFECTIONAL RELATIONSHIPS

Affectional relationships can be placed on a continuum from excessive affection to out-and-out rejection. The possessive family, oversolicitous family, or overindulgent family are examples of excessive affection. The companionable family would be representative of normal affection. Discrimination of affection occurs in families in which there is impartiality or a child who is favored. The undependable family or the family that has constant altercations are examples of families that are likely to give inconsistent affection. The amount of affection the exceptional child receives is critical to his development. There are some studies done on attitudes of mothers toward children (Bayley, Schaefer, 1960; Schaefer, 1965). Some of the behavior characteristics of rejected children show them to be emotionally unstable, restless, overactive, given to attention-getting behavior, more resentful of authority, and more rebellious against society's rules and regulations. It is quite probable that the rejected exceptional child will develop similar personality and behavioral characteristics.

Rejection can take many forms; and, therefore, no two cases will present the same picture because no two children will encounter rejection in the same way. It is subtle but deadly. The family that has a new baby might displace affection. The nagging, neglectful, or cold and indifferent family might demonstrate lack of affection. The family of an unwanted child best represents frank rejection. If affectional relationships are unstable, role tension is likely to result.

The question of who controls the home can be considered under power relationships. The worker needs to know if the home is mother-dominated, father-dominated, child-centered; has several bosses; or is overly demanding or democratic.

The mother-controlled, father-dominated, or overly demanding home may tend to be repressive. A child-centered home may be viewed in two ways. The home may be one in which the child dictates, and results in anarchy, or it may be one in which the parents center their lives around the child's needs. An example of the latter type is the case of parents who feel they must take their children to any activities they attend. The home with too many bosses is likely to be confused.

The democratic home seems to be one which more nearly approaches balance in that it permits individuals to play a more definitive role. Individuals need to feel they each have something to contribute to the welfare of the family group. It is wise to caution against pigeonholing families. Classifications can serve as guides in our understanding, but they have their limitations.

Each member of the family must be conscious of and accept the role designated to him. Further, he must not only accept his role but he must recognize and accept the roles of other members of the family as well. Family life will be inadequate if role-functioning is minimized. The child learns during his formative years, both implicitly and explicitly, attitudes not only about himself but also about others. Each member must be capable of giving affection and emotional security to others in the group. The expectations vary for the child depending on his age, sex, and the number of children in the family.

FAMILY PATTERNS

SIZE AND POSITION

The number of children in the family can be an important factor in a chronic stress situation that often is brought about by having a child with a disability as a member. Kosa (1965) found that morbid episodes in a family generally correlate positively with the number of children in the family. The more children, the more problems. The larger the family, the less likely it is that the parents can provide attention and meet the needs of all the children. Some larger families rely upon older children to help meet the needs of the younger children. The older children do not always do a satisfactory job of meeting the younger children's needs because they too have unmet needs. In large families, relatives such as aunts, uncles, and grandparents may be very helpful in providing continuity of care and nurturance for other young children in the family, especially in those instances when there is an exceptional child. Position may be important in establishing role-functioning for the child. Certain expectations of the oldest, youngest, or the middle child are likely to emerge. Influence of the family cycle is important in assigning status to the child.

ORGANIZATION

In considering family organization, several organizational types could be discussed. Four family types will be presented based on their reactions to a crisis. It should again be emphasized that it is essential that these classifications be used as guides and not as absolutes. The nurse should be cognizant that what appears disorganized or in a state of confusion may indeed be a regular way of life for some families. It is necessary to establish what was the family's usual way of functioning and its present way of functioning to gain perspective.

Feldman and Scherz (1967) described four family types based on their reactions to stress or a crisis situation such as having an exceptional child. The *adequate* family is considered a reasonably mature one which is able to adapt to the varied experiences of life. An exceptional child may cause temporary regression and disorganization of the family. Much of this family's problem may be due to inadequate knowledge. Any of these families goes through a shock phase, at which time they tend to deny that there is a problem. They may "shop" by visiting different physicians all of whom may give the same diagnosis.

Then they experience immobilization. During this phase they appear disinterested. During the next stage — expectancy — the parents attempt to learn all they can about the condition. Intellectual obstacles which are frequently seen in families with exceptional children revolve around ignorance which causes a lack of understanding. It is not easy for parents to make inquiries about problems of which they do not comprehend the nature or the depth.

In some family groups fallacies about certain types of exceptionality take precedence over any concrete knowledge about the subject, and it is not until the expectancy stage that these fallacies can be corrected with some degree of success.

The parents are likely to go through two stages — mourning and, finally, adjustment. Adjustment is, of course, the most desirable stage because the parents are able to accept realistically the child's condition. The adequate family is able to learn about resources and take advantage of what is available for the exceptional member of the family group.

The *chaotic* family, according to Feldman and Scherz, has difficulties with trust, self-control, and other aspects of identity. This type of family has difficulty with role differentiation. Several things could happen to a family with an exceptional child introduced into it, such as marital separation, marital discord, sibling discord, refusal to assume responsibility for the exceptional child, denial that a problem exists, and the like. It might, with help, become an adequately functioning family. The exceptional child may not feel intensely his lack of role-functioning in this family since roles are not clearly defined. This may or may not work to his advantage.

The *neurotic* family, as described by Feldman and Scherz, may have difficulty in one area of functioning. This type of family may function well at one stage of family life and not at another. One cannot be sure what the result of introducing an exceptional child into a family of this type will precipitate. It depends on what other problems are already present in the family at the time of the crisis.

The *psychotic* family may operate in a bizarre manner. It may function satisfactorily with some life tasks and function psychotically with others. Guilt feelings and hostile feelings may emerge toward the exceptional child. These feelings may become so intense that psychotic behavior results.

Johnson (1970) has described how the nurse can work with these types of families. She maintains that the nurse can help the adequate family reorganize through helping them see the problem and utilize resources. She can help the chaotic family identify roles. She believes it will be frustrating to work with them because they will have to learn what most people learned at an earlier age. Johnson points out that the neurotic family will use defense patterns which have been well established to cope with unresolved residual conflicts of earlier years. She notes that the nurse will need to recognize this. The psychotic family will need the opportunity to express its feelings about the exceptional child and come to realistic ways of dealing with the problem. Most often the nurse will have to refer these families to a psychiatrist or psychiatric social worker because the family dynamics are beyond her ability to handle.

No two families will react alike to crisis situations. Each will have to move from the disorganized state, due to the crisis, to an organized state to maintain a desirable level of functioning in the society that will be acceptable to the family. What may be a desirable level of functioning for one family, need not be for another.

ACTIVITY

The activity of the family is one to consider when an exceptional child is introduced into the family. A family of very bright individuals may find it difficult to deal with an exceptional child who has limited intelligence.

> A wealthy physician, whose wife was college-educated and whose children were very bright, placed a daughter with an I.Q. of 70 in an institution that served other well-off clients. The girl, we were informed, enjoyed it better at the institution because she didn't have to embarrass her family. She loved her family and indicated she knew they loved her. She went home for visits but always returned to the institution.

The family that likes to be involved in many activities may find an exceptional child a bit of a burden unless they are able to adjust. The other extreme is a family whose activities are very limited. The nurse may want to encourage more activities for a family of this type. No assumptions on the part of the nurse, however, should be made. She should make plans based on what the family actually does and the goals the family has set for itself and not on what she believes or thinks. It is crucial that the nurse take note of the activity of the family and determine what it is that they like to do. If their style of life is to be altered, they will need the support of an individual like the nurse who can maintain objectivity.

VALUES AND GOALS

In assessing the family, it should be pointed out that values and goals are key considerations. Is the family one that likes to "keep up with the Joneses?" Is the family objective, conventional, very religious, materialistic, superstitious, or the like?"

> A mother gave birth to a mongoloid child. When she was told about the child's condition and his probable potential, she stated that "it was God's will."

In a counseling and guidance class at a university, several students were to interview parents of exceptional children. Ten parents out of 15 who were interviewed believed that God's will had been done. Some felt they were being punished, some felt that having an exceptional child would help purify them, and others simply said things such as "One can't question why God does what he does," and "Only God knows the reason."

Recognizing the attitudes of families may aid in developing more insight into the nature of some of the behavioral manifestations. Of course, the nurse will be primarily interested in helping families develop behavior patterns that will help them adequately function in a manner healthful to them.

Parent-child relationships, as well as mother-father relationships and sibling relationships, have an impact on the development of the exceptional child and the development of the family. The defenses the family takes to protect its values can be unwieldy and in some instances more to its detriment than to its good.

> A physician and his wife had two very bright children and one child that had been declared retarded. This family valued education in that they talked about how bright their older children were, the intelligent persons of the maternal and paternal side, and their own education and abilities. This family, however, was denying that anything was wrong with the child even though they had been told by three different competent evaluation centers that they believed the child to be retarded. The parents had resorted to arguments with agencies and constant arguments in the home. They started blaming each other and each other's family for the child's problem.

EXTERNAL FACTORS

SOCIO-ECONOMIC STATUS

Middle and lower socio-economic status individuals may react differently to their situations when an exceptional child is introduced into the family.

Some families of the lower socio-economic group may appear resigned and develop a fatalistic acceptance of the exceptional child. Many factors may be operating, two of which shall be discussed.

The exceptional child may be less of a threat to the family that does not have too much already. To have a dependent exceptional child may be simply expressing an ego need: This child is mine, and he will always be with me. Secondly, the low socio-economic family, who is already limited in financial resources, may not see how they can adequately do any more.

> A mother of four children, one of whom was a 3-year-old retarded child, claimed she was not able to take the child to a clinic for his immunizations because she didn't have the bus fare. This family was not able to get food stamps because the father did not have a stable income, but they were able to get surplus foods. The retarded child's diet was inadequate. His mother claimed she could not buy "baby foods," and the child refused all table foods even when mashed.

The mother cited other problems that were economically based, such as buying clothes for her other children in school, and not for this child who was home all the time. A casual observer may have concluded that this mother did not care about her retarded child. The facts, however, indicate that this mother had only so much money, and she tried to use it wisely. The nurse, in this situation, worked with this family for 1 year.

There is evidence to support the idea that families who are poor have more concern for the physical needs of the family than the psychologic needs. Jeffers (1970) notes that the adequate meeting of physical needs was a major aspect of good motherhood. Adequate physical care such as feeding, clothing, and providing shelter for the children was a feat in itself.

The lower class family may tend to be more restrictive in child-rearing practices than are middle-class families who tend to be more permissive. Middle-class families may still place more emphasis on early assumption of responsibility for self and on individual achievement. Fleming (1969) noted that mothers who were less well educated and whose husbands were employed in semiskilled or unskilled jobs tended to spank their children more than better educated mothers whose husbands had skilled or semiprofessional jobs. The latter mothers tended to talk with their children more.

It has been asserted that middle-class parents tend to follow presumably expert opinion and read more books on child rearing than working-class parents. Fleming found that the less well educated, semiskilled, and unskilled families had little or no reading material in their houses.

According to Davis and Havighurst (1946), middle-class parents were concerned about development and placed emphasis on early assumption of responsibility. They wanted their children to be orderly, conscientious, tame, and responsible. In addition, middle-class families attempted to curb those impulses of the child which would lead to poor health, waste of time, and bad moral habits as viewed by the middle class. Parents, perhaps, have changed over the years. We do, however, still have socio-economic groups and their differences.

The values of parents seem to be correlated to socio-economic level and have wide ramifications in regard to their relationship with their exceptional child. If the child deviates so greatly that the values held by the parents are threatened, problems are sure to arise.

Having an exceptional child can be an expensive proposition. Middle-class families are often affected by the drain that an exceptional child can have on the family budget.

> A young professional man and his wife and one child were doing very well financially. They had purchased a beautiful home and furnished it. An exceptional child was born in the family with a condition which characteristically accompanies mental retardation. This young couple had no insurance to speak of and had practically drained the family's financial resources in simply trying to get a satisfactory understanding of what their child's problem really was.

"Shopping" — that is, going from one medical source to another during the shock or initial phase of learning that one has an exceptional child — can be expensive.

Communities that have minimal services or whose services are not as desirable as other locations may cause the uprooting of the family to a community that meets more adequately the needs of the exceptional child. This can sometimes be disruptive to family life.

> A young third-year dental student and his wife had a deaf daughter. There was no facility for preschool education for the deaf child in the community in which they resided. The wife quit her teaching job against her husband's wishes and moved with her daughter to another community so that her daughter could have preschool education. She felt her husband was selfish, unreasonable, and did not care about his daughter. The husband felt the wife was hasty, had no foresight, and was trying to punish him.

There were several other problems involved in this family; having the exceptional child simply magnified them. This brings us to a final point under this heading of socio-economic status. It is doubtful that many will disagree that an exceptional child can add an additional financial burden to the family. In some cases this may be extreme. Nurses who work with families who have exeptional children should make it a point to know the resources in their communities that will provide services to families with exceptional children. In some communities there are unlimited services, many of which are free to the user and supported by benefactors who are concerned with exceptionality.

Communities are frequently adding or changing services. Nurses somehow need to keep up with these events. One of the nurse's biggest contributions to parents with exceptional children is to help them find services that they need. One of the biggest frustrations with parents, after they accept the fact that they have an exceptional child, is that they have little information about services available for the problems they encounter in rearing their exceptional children.

Many of our so-called poor or low socio-economic families are families without information. Nurses are in a position to provide them with information and to help them utilize this information in resourceful ways.

NEIGHBORHOOD

Where a family resides — whether it be in a rural area, a small town, or an urban area — can be a crucial factor when an exceptional child is involved. To illustrate:

> One mother of what one would describe as a hyperkinetic 5-year-old girl lived in a housing development that had no fenced yards but lovely homes. This mother fenced her yard so that her daughter could play outside. Soon the daughter climbed over the fence and ran around the neighborhood. Some parents claimed she frightened their children. The mother kept her daughter indoors to keep down confusion. She was unhappy about being different in putting up a fence and annoyed because she felt her daughter should be free to be outside.

> Another family had a hyperkinetic 8-year-old boy. They lived on a small farm. The boy was accepted by other boys in the community who came over to play with him sometimes, but he preferred to play alone. He was free to play anywhere on the farm. His mother was concerned that he did not seem interested in other children except a younger sibling.

> Parents of three children who resided in a middle income urban neighborhood explained that they wanted to place the youngest child, who was mentally retarded, in an institution because the older children were being penalized. Parents in the neighborhood did not want their children to associate with the children in this family.

Empirical studies of the effects of environmental conditions upon the retarded are numerous in literature. These studies are pimarily concerned with the effects of institutionalization. Few studies of the problems involving residing in a neighborhood with an exceptional child have been reported.

HEALTH

If the home has other ill persons besides the exceptional child, then this can create problems for the person charged with the responsibility of caring for them.

> A grandmother with a cardiac problem was caring for her invalid husband and her retarded grandson who was born to her "not-too-bright" daughter.

The family situation should be assessed by the nurse. Table 2.1 classifies the family situation. The nurse might find this a helpful guideline in working with families with exceptional children.

Parent-child relationships have already been mentioned, but since they are so pervasive, to discuss exceptional children without including such content would be naive.

The activities of parents in the care of children may be classified in two basic categories — nurturance and guidance. Meeting the physical and emotional needs, protecting the child, and regarding him as having personal worth would be classified as nurturance. Setting limits, rewarding desirable behavior and punishing undesirable behavior, stimulating social and intellectual growth, and serving as a model for the child are often associated with imperfections in the parent.

Parents who want children generally desire to have children that they can effectively nurture and guide. In other words, each parent wants what he or she considers the perfect child. Imperfections in the child are associated with imperfections in the parent.

Immediately after birth, mothers' reactions vary. The reactions may vary from elation to nonchalance. Most mothers are always interested in the sex, the weight of the newborn, and whether or not the infant is all right, but not necessarily in that order.

If the child has an obvious congenital condition that stigmatizes him as different from most babies, the chances of his parents reacting in one of the ways discussed below are highly probable. The impact of learning that the child, at any stage in his development, is less than what the average child is purported to be brings into play a variety of possible reactions such as shock, ambivalence, anger, avoidance, bewilderment, disappointment, disbelief, embarrassment, fear, frustration, worry, grief, helplessness, hopelessness, lethargy, puzzlement, regret, sorrow, mourning, depression, death wishes for child and self, guilt, blame, self-pity, rejection, anxiety, and the like.

TABLE 2.1. Classification of Family Situations[a]

Intrafamily Relationships

I. *Affectional relationships*
  A. excess of affection
  B. normal affection
  C. discrimination in affection
  D. inconsistency of affection
  E. displacement of affection
  F. lack of affection
  G. frank rejection

II. *Power relationships*
  A. repression
  B. anarchy
  C. confusion
  D. approaching balance

Family Patterns

  I. Size

  II. Organization

  III. Activity

  IV. Values and goals

External Factors

  I. Socio-economic status

  II. Neighborhood

  III. Health

[a] Adapted from Bossard and Boll. "Family Situations: An Introduction to the Study of Child Behavior," 1943.

Guilt is one of the reactions that has been discussed much in the literature. Anger and denial seem to be closely associated with guilt. No matter when the child's problem is discovered — at birth or during the later developmental stages — guilt on the part of the parents seems to be a universally described reaction to learning that the child is different from the average. How the guilt is handled seems to be a prime consideration rather than the guilt itself. Guilt may be a motivating force for action on the part of parents. The worker should help the parent move toward positive action in helping the child.

How one works with parents should be based on those things that they see as primary problems and concerns. It is up to the professional worker to determine what is the crucial problem as the parents see it. Contrary to what many believe, it is not simply a matter of having an exceptional child. Parents have expressed to me such reactions as: "Nobody would want to keep him if I got sick." "My husband is ashamed to take her out with us." "I can't do much with the other children and they need me, too." "It wouldn't be so bad if the other children didn't feel so badly about it." "My teenagers are ashamed to bring their friends home." "I accept him as my burden, but it's so unfair to the rest of the family." "He'll never be able to play and be accepted by other children." "I am afraid to let him go to school because children will make fun of him."

Depression, immobility, grief, helplessness, and mourning have been associated with what Stark and Solnit (1961) have described as "object-loss" when a defective child is born. The perception results in there being a loss of the expected healthy child. Olshansky (1962) has described a reaction he labels as "chronic sorrow" which has been attributed to parents who have a retarded child.

Professional workers should allow parents to talk about their concerns and feelings. Listening takes real practice. The care-by-parent unit at the University of Kentucky where parents are with their children is an excellent example of parents' seeming need to have someone listen to how they feel. Listening means concentrating on what the individual is telling you without introducing any thoughts or questions of your own. Nod slightly and wait; this gives the individual the feeling that you are with their conversation. Make casual remarks like "I see," "Is that so," "That's interesting," "Yes," "Uh huh." This gives the individual the feeling that you are sticking with him. Echo, repeat back the last few words the speaker said, and, finally, mirror; that is, relfect back to the speaker your understanding of what he has just said to you ("You feel that . . ."). Again the purpose of *listening* is to give the parents an opportunity to express their feelings to an interested, qualified person who can assist them in taking appropriate measures for handling their problems.

REFERENCES

1. Ackerman, N. W. The Psychodynamics of Family Life. New York, Basic Books, 1958.
2. Baumeister, A. A. Mental Retardation. Chicago, Aldine, 1967.
3. Bayley, N., and Schaefer, E. S. "Relationships between socio-economic variables and the behavior of mothers toward young children." Genet Psychol 96:61-77, March, 1960.
   Schaefer, E. S. "Children's reports of parental behavior: an inventory." Child Dev 36:413-24.
4. Bossard, J. H. S., and Boll, E. S. Family Situations: An Introduction to the Study of Child Behavior. Univ Penn Press, Phil., 1943.
5. Burgess, E. W. The family as a unit of interacting personalities. Family, 7:3, 1926.
6. Clausen, J. A. Family structure, socialization and personality. In Hoffman, L., and Hoffman, M. L., eds. Review of Child Development Research. New York, Russell Sage, 1966.
7. Committee on Child Health. American Public Health Association: Services for Handicapped Children. New York, The Association, 1961, p. 12.
8. Davis, A. and Havighurst, R. J. "Social class and color differences in child rearing." Am Sociol Rev 11:698-710, 1946.
9. Feldman, F. L., and Scherz, F. H. Family Social Welfare. Helping Troubled Families. New York, Atherton, 1967.

10. Fleming, Juanita W. The Interrelationship of Early Developmental Factors on the Academic Failure of Children. (Unpublished dissertation), Wash., D.C., Catholic University of America, School of Education, 1969.
11. Goode, W. J. Family disorganization. In Merton, R. K., and Nisbet, R. A. Contemporary Social Problems. New York, Harcourt, 1966, pp. 479-552.
12. Hoffman, L. W., and Hoffman, M. L., eds. Review of Child Development Research. New York, Russell Sage, 1966.
13. Irving, Howard H. "Relationships between married couples and their parents." Social Casework, 52:91-96, 1971.
14. Jeffers, C. Living poor: A participant observer study of priorities and choices. In Glasser, P. H., and Glasser, L. N., eds. Families in Crisis. New York, Harper & Row, 1970.
15. Johnson, D. The need for effective communication. In Fleming, J., Rudnick, B., and Denman, L., eds. Nursing Care of Handicapped Children. Lexington, University of Kentucky, College of Nursing, 1970.
16. Kessler, J. W. The impact of disability on the child. Phys Ther 46:153, 1966.
17. Kohut, S. A. The abnormal child: His impact on the family. Phys Ther 46(2):160, 1966.
18. Koos, E. L. The Sociology of the Patient. New York, McGraw-Hill, 1959.
19. Kosa, J., et al. Crisis and stress in family life: A re-examination of concepts. Wisconsin Sociol Summer, 1965, 11-19.
20. Krech, D., Crutchfield, R. S., and Ballachey, E. L. Individual in Society. New York, McGraw-Hill, 1962, 489-490.
21. Olshansky, S. Chronic sorrow: A response to having a mentally defective child. Soc Case Work 43:191-194, 1962.
22. Simmel, G. The Sociology of George Simmel. Wolff, K., ed. and trans. Chicago, Free Press, 1950.
23. Solnit, A. J., and Stark, Mary H. Mourning and the birth of a defective child. Psychoanal Study Child, 16:523-537, 1961.
24. Symonds, P. M. The Psychology of Parent-Child Relationships. New York, Appleton, 1939.
25. Wright, B. A. Physical Disability: A Psychological Approach. New York, Harper & Row, 1960.

3

CHANGING BEHAVIOR OF EXCEPTIONAL CHILDREN

JUANITA FLEMING,
BARBARA HAUS, and
SHARON THOMPSON

TYPES OF BEHAVIOR MODIFICATION

One strategy of working with children who have behaviors that are considered undesirable is the approach of rewards and reinforcements. This approach has been referred to by names such as operant conditioning, experimental analysis of behaviors, behavior modification, and others. The various approaches to behavior modification are as follows:

1. *Free operant conditioning.* This approach is one in which the individual is reinforced directly when desired behavior occurs in the right direction. This is a rewarding of behavior that approximates (shaping) the final behavior desired. In a stepwise, sequential fashion behavior is rewarded until the desired behavior emerges.
2. *Contingency management.* The desired behavior is announced in advance and rewards are offered in advance of the behavior to elicit from the individual the behavior desired.

3. *Associative learning.* Pleasurable events are paired with positive reactions, resulting in altering behavior.
4. *Social modeling.* Through imitation, role-playing simulation, or observation of real life situations, individuals are induced to change behavior.

The literature has shown that successful behavior modification through application of operant techniques can be done. Nurses can help parents carry out the techniques and expect success. The cases that follow are just a sampling to illustrate some of the problems for which the various techniques have been used.

Giles and Wolf (1966) used operant techniques in toilet training five severely retarded children through the use of negative and positive reinforcements. The subjects were conditioned to defecate in the toilet. As this behavior increased, the subjects also began urinating in the commode. Marshall (1966) used positive reinforcements — M&M's and salt — and in a few instances negative reinforcement and aversive control (slap on the buttocks) to toilet train an 8-year-old boy diagnosed as autistic. Masden (1965) used positive reinforcements of candy and praise to successfully toilet train a normal 19-month-old child in 12 days.

Williams (1967) gives an account of a procedure used by parents to eliminate tantrum behavior at bedtime of their 21-month-old son. The parents used negative reinforcement — unpleasant stimuli — such as ignoring the child and isolating him from others.

Hart and Allen (1965) showed how two preschool boys, with a high frequency of operant crying, were helped to develop more effective responses to mild frustrations after 1 week through reinforcement of adult attention for appropriate responses to mildly distressful situations and no attention to outcries, unless the child was actually hurt.

Holland (1969) reported how a behavior-modification program of positive reinforcement and the threat of punishment by loss carried out by the father of a 7-year-old boy proved effective in eliminating the latter's fire-setting habit which had persisted for 2 years in spite of various punishments used by the parents to control it.

Allen and Harris (1966) presented a case study of a 5-year-old child who scratched her head, nose, cheeks, chin, and one arm and leg so severely that large scabs and sores disfigured her body. The program of behavior modification set up was that of rewards for not scratching and her mother ignoring her when scratching — which was hard for the mother in that she and the child were in a constant state of friction, and the mother was excessively severe and critical with her. Thus it was hard for her to give social reinforcement. However, the treatment did prove successful. This is applicable for nurses in that they need to emphasize to the parents the importance of instituting new schedules of reinforcement and maintaining them in order to effectively produce a behavioral change.

Hellsman (1971) presented an interesting approach for establishing rapport with a child before assessing his development — by approaching him (literally) at his own level, whether it be on the floor or whatever.

Peterson and Barnard (1966) presented a nursing approach to the teaching of independent living skills, built on the principles of operant theory, through a case study in which principles of operant learning were applied to habilitate and recondition the feeding behavior of a retarded child.

Whitney (1966) discussed selected principles of operant learning and showed by examples how each was effective in instituting the desired behavioral change. The principles discussed were shaping, fading, imitation, and positive reinforcement. Techniques were presented to teach spoon-feeding, weaken inappropriate feeding behavior, reduce inappropriate behavior and strengthen appropriate behavior, strengthen independent dressing behavior and reduce inappropriate dressing responses, and strengthen play behavior and weaken inappropriate play behavior. This discussion showed that teaching retarded children to perform self-help skills is an area of nursing concern in that it relieves the parents of some of their burdens and, in the case of strengthening play behavior, it encourages the interest of retarded children in playing with their peers and play materials. The article also discussed how behavior may be strengthened in feminine hygiene during retarded girls' monthly menses, and stressed the importance of it being approached by nurses matter of factly, concentrating on the child's functional rather than chronological age. The need for breaking down the desired behavioral skills into simple components, reinforcing the step nearest the end of the chain, and progressing to reinforcing steps earlier in the chain was emphasized, such as in toilet training. The implications of the operant framework for nursing and, through the use of examples of positive results, the effectiveness of operant learning was illustrated. The article was helpful also in pointing out the importance of describing the behavior actually seen — that is, "John crawled into the chair and closed his eyes" — instead of making assumptions and inferences such as, "The child seemed tired." Also, it showed how a narrative account of behavior is transcribed into a three-column form of (1) antecedent events, (2) child behavior, and (3) consequent events in order to categorize and conceptualize those events that may be producing and maintaining behavior. A form such as this could be used by parents to record their child's behavior.

Coyne, Peterson, and Peterson (1968) used techniques derived from operant learning principles in a case study of Julie, age 3 years, who had been blind since birth but displayed no other physical impairments. She could not feed herself, dress herself, was not toilet trained, and, except for random sounds, exhibited no speech. The object of this study was to teach this child to feed herself. The study was divided into four parts: the baseline, first reinforcement periods, reversal, and second reinforcement periods.

During the baseline period the child's feeding behavior was assessed. Her mother was taught to observe and record the number of correct responses and the time involved. At times a second observer participated with the mother to establish the reliability of her observations. The reversal and second reinforcement periods included not reinforcing spoon-feeding which caused it to cease and to return during the period of second reinforcement.

Wooten, Wood, and Barnes (1970) presented another aspect of shaping techniques — utilizing it in play behavior. This study was undertaken in order to determine (1) if play behavior of preschool children who demonstrated delayed play activities could be shaped by "play nurses" to a level commensurate with their chronological age and (2) if these children involved in the shaping process would reach a significantly more mature rate of play behavior than delayed children not undergoing the shaping process in their play behavior. The reinforcement for the desired behavior was brief attention from the play nurse, and for the undesired behavior, unless dangerous, ignoring it.

Urry (1970) described how head-banging was eliminated, and eye contact and an interest in toys was developed in a 3-year-old autistic child, Billy. The study did not give much background about Billy, but discussed theories on autism, characteristics of autism, and gave a brief description of operant conditioning methods and reinforcements of behavior.

Gardner and Briskin (1969) dealt with the use of punishment procedures in managing behavioral difficulties in severely retarded children. They discussed several punishment procedures which were used successfully with the severely retarded and evaluated these in terms of effectiveness and efficiency. The study stated as part of its rationale for punishment techniques that the operant principles of extinction and behavior-shaping involved too much time to effect behavioral changes in these children. They felt that the child might hurt himself or someone else severely before the effects of extinction or behavior-shaping could eliminate the behavior in question. Their belief was that since this group has limited language skills, a rather primitive social motivation system and a restricted range of stimulus events which are reinforcing caused them to respond too little or too slowly to extinction and/or behavior-shaping techniques. They documented this with other sources. The study differentiated the types of punishment into two classes: (1) operations which present stimulus consequences following undesirable behavior, e.g., (a) primary aversive stimulation (electric shock), (b) physical restraint (strapping to a chair or bed), and (c) conditioned aversive stimulation — "No" conditioned through prior association with primary aversive stimuli, and (2) operations which remove certain stimulus conditions after the occurrence of the undesirable behavior, e.g., (a) time out from positive reinforcement (placement in an isolation room), and (b) time out used in combinations with response-cost (placement in isolation and, in addition, loss of certain tangible positive reinforcers which the subject previously had available to him). Studies utilizing each of these punishment procedures, except item 2b, were cited as examples of how punishment can be effective in suppressing and eliminating behavior of the severely retarded, as they were all consistent in reporting positive results.

In addition, they discussed the danger of using punishment techniques indiscriminately since effects among retardates vary, even with the same individual from one time to the next. They also cited studies which reported that the effects of punishment are not short-lived, that for the severely, profoundly retarded, a positive relationship does exist between intensity of punishment and behavior-suppression effects. Widespread behavioral improvement was supported, and punishment was effective with the unsocialized, profoundly retarded. They also cited nine criteria for punishment operations to produce the most rapid and long-lasting results and discussed how punishment could be justified in view of ethical and humanitarian issues. They emphasized the importance of deciding on treatment regimens that are deliberate, well formulated, and arrived at only after careful consideration of questions of effectiveness, efficiency, and positive side effects.

Turner (1970) showed how behavior-modification techniques were applied successfully on a 4½-year-old boy, Tommy, with a history of tantrums and language of unintelligible babbles or single words, and a 7-year-old girl, Wendy, with a history of animalistic characteristics, head-banging, swallowing small objects, and eupholia (her five-word vocabulary). Tommy, through the time-out method of behavior-therapy punishment as described in the preceding study, eventually gained an awareness of the consequences of his actions, and his tantrums and other undesirable behavior (which the article did not mention) ceased. Also, through positive reinforcement using food, he was taught a vocabulary and speech pattern of a nearly normal rate. Wendy, treated according to the primary aversive method of behavior-therapy punishment, learned to cease her aggressive behavior of banging her head on hard objects or biting herself until she was black and blue. She was also taught, given food for positive reinforcement, that interacting with other persons can be a pleasurable experience. Wendy could not be taught to speak, although her eupholia was eliminated and she was taught to communicate in physically symbolic ways (of which examples were given). The article was presented well and the methodology produced dependable data. A baseline of behavior occurrences was established, and according to the charts of the behavioral changes, after operant learning techniques were applied, the findings seemed accurate. It is interesting to note that Wendy's aggressive behavior increased when time-out procedures were employed. This has relevance for nurses in that it points out the importance of evaluating the effects of the programmed behavior change in order to assist parents in reaching the desired result. Also, it was found in this study that short time-out periods of not more than 5 minutes (preferably 1 or 2) were most effective in that the child did not forget the reason for them.

Barnard (1968) described how Stevie, a retarded child, was taught to spoon-feed himself. The nurse helped his parents break down the task into its component parts. Also, by assessing his growth and development level and capabilities, the nurse was able to help them form a starting point. After this was accomplished, Stevie was taught to spoon-feed himself through the fading procedure (a process used in which there is gradual elimination of an activity no longer needed in helping an individual learn, for example, a skill) of the operant theory of learning. It was first attempted to teach Stevie by shaping, but this proved ineffective. Fading was tried, and by the fifth-observed session Stevie was picking up the spoon, bringing it to the bowl, and rapidly bringing the spoon to his mouth, his mother supporting only his forearm.

In attempting to carry out modification of behavior, the following principles are essential:

1. The desired response must be potentially available. No one can be taught to do anything that is not already in his behavior.
2. Desirable behaviors should be reinforced and undesirable ones ignored. The nurse could use her presence and/or her approval to reinforce.
3. Reinforcement should be immediate. The response temporally closest to the reward gains most in strength. The response that is reinforced is the one that is learned.
4. In establishing behavior, the reinforcement should be administered on each occasion of the response. As learning progresses, reinforcement should be delivered on an intermittent basis.
5. The desired behavior should be "shaped" by rewarding successive improvements in the components that constitute the behavior. In shaping, one waits until a component of the response is omitted and then reinforces the subject.
6. The subject's environment should be held as constant as possible during the intitial stages of learning.

Four-year-old Johnny had never talked. One day his mother served dessert but forgot to give Johnny his. He said, "I'll have some of that." His mother was surprised and asked, "Why have you never spoken before?" He replied, "Up to now things have been all right."

This old story, though it may not be absolutely true, illustrates the point that people act when they feel they have to; and if they feel no need to act, they do not.

Socializing the exceptional child so that he can live effectively in his society is the aim of those who work with him. Part of the plan of management is that of enhancing or changing behavior. The acquisition of desirable behavior or the changing of undesirable behavior are the goals of behavior-modification programs in which nurses would involve themselves. To guard against changing behavior in children, because of error or bias, the three basic criteria for unacceptable behavior are:

1. The behavior must occur with frequency; that is, it must be countable.
2. The behavior must be one that will end up being hurtful to the child or his environment.

3. The behavior must impede subsequent adaption and healthy development.

Conversely, then, acceptable behavior has the following criteria:

1. The behavior should be countable.
2. The behavior should not be hurtful to the child or his environment.
3. The behavior should enhance subsequent adaption and healthy development.

For the most part, exceptional children with defects and limitations have a low degree of social acceptance. Good training in politeness, manners, general conduct in public, proper dress, health hygiene, cleanliness, and neatness may enhance his acceptance by society. An accepted child will undoubtedly improve his concept of himself. When working with exceptional children, the worker must remember that all behavior has consequences, and that if desirable behavior is to evolve it must be reinforced.

Behavior-changing is based on the following principles:

1. *Behavior has consequence.*
2. *The consequences of an act (behavior) influence the probability of that action occurring again when conditions are similar.* In other words, if positive consequences (reinforcers) follow quickly after the action occurs, it is probable that the act will tend to occur more frequently under similar conditions. If negative consequences (punishers) follow quickly after the action occurs, the act will probably tend to occur less frequently under similar conditions.
3. *The environment can be manipulated so that positive reinforcement quickly follows desirable acts and negative reinforcement quickly follows undesirable acts.* Positive reinforcement refers to the presentation of satisfying rewards or the withdrawal of aversive conditions — hence, strengthening the behavior displayed. Negative reinforcement refers to the presentation of aversive conditions or the withdrawal of satisfying conditions in the presence of undesirable behavior. It is self-evident that the positive or negative nature of the consequences must be determined from the perspective of the learner.
4. *Changing behavior is dependent upon motivation.* Motivation is the key to changing behavior, as it is the drive or stimulus to action. What will motivate one child will not motivate another. Hunger or thirst are considered primary drives. One means of reinforcing behavior is to use food and water. These are known as primary reinforcers. Secondary drives — affection, money, social acceptance, and verbal praise — may also reinforce behavior. Social rewards such as smiling, pleasant words, and pats are known as secondary reinforcers. Little or no learning will take place unless the individual is motivated. The nurse can help a

parent determine what it is that will motivate the child to certain actions.

STEPS IN BEHAVIOR MODIFICATION

To utilize the above principles, the worker would need to:

1. *Define the behavior.* Behavior to be modified should be either about to emerge developmentally or behavior that bothers the parent. Both the terminal behavior desired (what you want the child to learn) and his beginning behavior which will lead to the terminal behavior must be identified. Suppose the goal is to have the child put on his undershirt without assistance. We would define this as the terminal behavior. Suppose the child picks the shirt up when asked to do so. We would define this as his beginning behavior.
2. *Assess the child's behavior.* Once the terminal and beginning behaviors are identified, a clearer determination should be made of what the child is able to do and what his functional level of development is.
3. *Verify the significance of the behavior.* The parent should be helped to determine what environmental factors support the behavior and how the environment can be manipulated to alter the undesirable behavior. To do this, it is often necessary to determine how frequently certain types of behavior occur. Schedules should be kept for a few days to determine just how frequently the behavior occurs. The worker should try to elicit from the parent a description of the behavior so that it can be counted. Parents sometimes say things like, "my child is nervous or anxious," or "he rarely keeps still," and so forth. This does not tell us much. "He pulls his hair and sucks his finger" is more descriptive and countable than "he is nervous and anxious." "He gets out of his chair, runs into the house" is more descriptive and countable than "he rarely keeps still."

After deciding what behavior is to be changed:

   a. Keep a record of how often the behavior occurs.
   b. Determine what in the environment precipitates the behavior (antecedent event).
   c. Determine how the environment can be manipulated (reinforced).
   d. Determine what happens after the child is rewarded (consequent event).
4. *Decide on the approximations.* The worker will need to break the activity into its simplest form.
5. *Begin Reinforcement.* As the child accomplishes each step, a reward is given until he is able to carry out the terminal behavior. This is shaping behavior in the desired direction. The rate of

reinforcement is essential or basic to behavioral change. In order to reinforce those responses which acquire a relation to prior stimulation, the rate must be increased. The increased rate of the response is an indicator of the increased probability of the response.

It would probably be helpful if a nurse could work with someone skilled in behavior modification in order to perfect her skills in using the techniques. Psychologists with interests in this area are usually willing to help nurses who desire to utilize behavior-modification techniques.

Behavior modification with all its effectiveness has had two major negative criticisms directed at it. First, it is said to be impersonal and mechanical. Secondly, it is said to be simply bribery. Each child who received behavior-modification therapy has a program based specifically on his needs and problems. The child is very much involved in carrying out his own treatment. To say that behavior modification is bribery misses the point, as this criticism seems to be implying that there is an attempt to manipulate the individual by corrupting his behavior rather than attempting to help him function more effectively in his society.

REFERENCES

1. Allen, K. E., and Harris, F. R. Elimination of a child's excessive scratching by training the mother in reinforcement procedures. Behav Res Ther 4:79, 1966.
2. Azrin, N. H., and Foxx, R. M. A rapid method of toilet training the institutionalized retarded. Unpublished study from Southern Illinois University, conducted 1970.
3. Baldwin, A. Theories of Child Development. New York, Wiley, 1967.
4. Bandura, A. Principles of Behavior Modification. New York, Holt, 1969.
5. Bandura, A., and Walters, R. Social Learning and Personality Development. New York, Holt, 1963.
6. Barnard, K. Teaching the retarded child is a family affair. Am J Nurs 68:305, 1968.
7. Bijou, S. W. An empirical concept of reinforcement and a functional analysis of child behavior. Genet Psychol Monogr 104:212, 1964.
8. Carrier, J. K., Jr. A program of articulation therapy administered by mothers. Speech Hearing Dis 35:344, 1970.
9. Coyne, P. H., Peterson, L. W., and Peterson, R. F. The development of spoon-feeding behaviors in a blind child. Int Educ Blind December, 1968, 108-112.
10. Crossen, J. E. The functional analysis of behavior: A technology for special education practices. Ment Retard 7:15, 1969.
11. Dennison, D. Operant conditioning principles applied to health instruction. Sch Health 40:368, 1970.

12. Fowler, R., Fordyce, W., and Berni, R. Operant conditioning in chronic illness. Am J Nurs 49:1126, 1969.
13. Fianhenburg, W. K., Camp, B. W., and Van Natta, P. A. Validity of the Denver development screening test. Child Develop 42:475, 1971.
14. Gardner, J. M. Behavior modification in mental retardation: A review of research and analysis of trends. Paper presented in Advances in Behavior Therapy, Proceedings of the Third Conference of the Association of Advancement of Behavior Therapy. New York, Academic, 1971, pp. 37-59.
15. Gardner, J. M., and Briskin, A. S. Use of punishment procedure in management of behavioral difficulties of the severely retarded. Psychiatr Nurs 8:5, 1969.
16. Giles, D. K., and Wolf, M. M. Toilet training institutionalized severe retardates: An application of operant behavior-modification techniques. Am J Ment Defic 70:766, 1966.
17. Hall, E. The Use of Operant Conditioning Techniques to Establish Nurse Patient Relationships. American Nurses Association Clinical Sessions. New York, Appleton, 1968.
18. Hamilton, J. A., et al. Training mentally retarded females to use sanitary napkins. Ment Retard 7:40, 1969.
19. Harris, F. R., et al. Effects of positive reinforcement on regressed crawling of a nursing school child. In Ullman, L. P., and Krasner, L., eds. Case Studies in Behavior Modification. New York, Holt, 1965.
20. Hart, B. M., et al. Effects of social reinforcement on operant crying. In Ullman, L. P., and Krasner, L., eds. Case Studies in Behavior Modification. New York, Holt, 1965.
21. Heindziak, M., Maurer, R. A., and Watson, L. S., Jr. Operant conditioning in toilet training of severely mentally retarded boys. Am J Ment Defic 70:120, 1965-1966.
22. Heizog, T. Staff development of child management: Utilizing the principles of behavior shaping. J Psychiatr Nurs 9:12, 1971
23. Hellsman, G. M. How I became the retarded nurse who crawls on the floor. Am J Nurs 71:1961, 1971.
24. Holland, C. J. Elimination by the parents of fire-setting behavior in a seven-year-old boy. Behav Res Ther 7:135, 1969.
25. Jones, R., ed. Behavior Modification and Operant Techniques. New Directions in Special Education. Boston, Allyn, 1971, pp 199-304.
26. Lane, R. G., and Domrath, R. P. Behavior therapy: A case history. Hosp Community Psychiatr 21:150, 1970
27. Lovett, T. Behavior modification: The current scene. Exceptional Chil 37:85, 1970.
28. Loynd, J., and Barclay, A. A case study in developing ambulation in a profoundly retarded child. Behav Res Ther 8:207, 1970.
29. Marer, H. W. Three Theories of Child Development. New York, Harper & Row, 1965.
30. Marshall, G. R. Toilet training of an autistic eight-year-old through conditioning therapy: A case report. Behav Res Ther 4:242, 1966.
31. Masden, C. H., Jr. Positive reinforcement in the toilet training of a normal child: A case report. In Ullmann, L. P., and Krasner, L., eds. Case Studies in Behavior Modification. New York, Holt, 1965.
32. Mayerson, L., and Kerr, N. Behavior Modification in Rehabilitation. Child Dev, 1966, p. 214.
33. Miller, N. E., and Dollard, J. Social Learning and Imitation. New Haven, Yale, 1967.
34. Mira, M. Results of behavior modification program for parents and teachers. Behav Res Ther 8:309, 1970.

35. Pattullo, A. W., and Barnard, K. E. Teaching menstrual hygiene to the mentally retarded child. Am J Nurs 68:2572, 1968.
36. Peterson, L. W. Operant approach to observation and recording. Nurs Outlook 15:28, 1967.
37. Peterson, L. W., and Barnard, K. E. Implications of operant learning theory for nursing care of the retarded child. Ment Retard 4:26, 1966.
38. Peterson, R. F., and Peterson, L. The use of positive reinforcement in the control of self-destructive behavior in a retarded boy. J Exp Child Psychol 6:351, 1968.
39. Rachman, S. Introduction to behavior therapy. Behav Res Ther 6:3, 1963.
40. Rotter, J. B. Social Learn Learning and Clinical Psychology. Englewood Cliffs, N.J. Prentice-Hall, 1954.
41. Scott, P. M., Burton, R. V., and Yarrow, M. R. Social reinforcement under natural conditions. Child Dev 38:53, 1967.
42. Skinner, B. F. Science and Human Behavior. New York, MacMillan, 1953.
43. Skinner, B. F. Contingencies of Reinforcement. New York, Meredith, 1969.
44. Terdal, L., and Buell, J. Parent education in managing retarded children with behavior deficits and inappropriate behaviors. Ment Retard 7:10, 1969.
45. Turner, R. A. method of working with disturbed children. Am J Nurs 70:2146, 1970.
46. Urry, N. Behavior modification with an autistic child. Nurs Times 64:456, 1970.
47. Valett, R. E. Modifying Children's Behavior. Belmont, Calif., Fearon, 1969.
48. Walker, R. G., Windel, G. H., Peterson, R. F., and Morrison, D. C. Mothers as behavior therapists for their own children. Behav Res Ther 3:113, 1965.
49. Walker, R. G., and Erickson, M. Child behavior therapy: A community program in Appalachia. Behav Res Ther 7:71, 1969.
50. Watson, L. S. Application of operant conditioning techniques to institutionalized severely and profoundly retarded children. Ment Retard, 1967: 1-18.
51. Whitney, L. Operant learning theory: A framework deserving nursing investigation. Nurs Res 15:229, 1966.
52. Whitney, L. Behavioral approaches to the nursing of the mentally retarded. Nurs Clin N Am 1:641, 1966.
53. Williams, C. D. The elimination of tantrum behavior by extinction procedures. In Bijou, S. W., and Baer, D. M., eds. Child Development: Readings in Experimental Analysis. New York, Appleton, 1967, pp. 142-145.
54. Wolf, M., Brinbrauer, J. S., Williams, T., and Lawler, J. A note on apparent extinction of the vomiting behavior of a retarded child. In Ullmann, L. P., and Krasner, L., eds. New York, Holt, 1965.
55. Wolf, M., Risley, T., and Hayden, M. Application of operant conditioning procedures to the behavior problems of an autistic child. In Ullmann, L. P., and Krasner, L., eds. Case Studies in Behavior Modification. New York, Holt, 1965.
56. Wooten, M., Wood, S., and Barnes, K. Shaping pre-schoolers' play behavior in the child health conference waiting area. Can J Public Health 61:10, 1970.

4

CHILDREN WHO ARE
MENTALLY RETARDED

Children who are mentally retarded are thought of as individuals with significantly impaired ability to learn and to adapt to the demands of society. Management of these children has changed drastically over the last two and one-half decades. The programs that have come into being for identification, diagnosis, and treatment are numerous. More emphasis is being placed on helping these children develop to their maximum potential and, in many instances, become contributing members of society.

There are many definitions of mental retardation. Most of these definitions are identified with various professional disciplines. The definition adopted by the American Association on Mental Deficiency is the one that will be used in this chapter.

DEFINITION

> Mental retardation refers to subaverage general intellectual functioning which originates during the development period and is associated with impairment in adaptive behavior (*Heber, 1961*).

Subaverage intellectual functioning, as used in this definition, refers to performance on objective testing at least one standard deviation below that expected for a given chronological age. Adaptive behavior refers to maturation, learning, and social adjustment. Maturation is emphasized during the period from birth through the preschool years. During this period the child is attempting to master basic daily living skills which are sensory-motor in nature, such as eating, sitting, walking, talking, toileting, and dressing. Learning and social adjustment appear as primary concerns of the child during the school years. Learning is manifested in acquisition of academic skills such as reading, writing, spelling, and arithmetic. Social adjustment is reflected in the degree to which the child gets along with others (interpersonal relationships), the child's ability to conform to social mores (cultural conformity), and his ability to delay gratification of needs (responsiveness). The multiplicity of problems implicit in the above definition of mental retardation is complicated further by the range of deficit that may be encountered. The range of deficit may be from slightly below average to severe, requiring custodial care.

Because of the multiple factors and the potentially wide range of abilities, it has been suggested that no real basis for distinction exists in utilization of such a term as "mental retardation." The addition of modifying terms such as "significantly" subaverage intellectual functioning and "distinct" impairment in adaptive behavior have been suggested for further clarification. Such modifiers still fall short of identifying specific behavior with which the health worker is concerned although they may be useful labels for administrative purposes. The danger is that one may become so concerned with the labels that the actual behavior becomes of secondary concern. The diagnosis of mental retardation is not critical in itself, although parents may be anxious for some clarification. More critical to parents once the diagnosis is made is knowing how to manage the child.

GENERAL CHARACTERISTICS

One behavior characteristic of most mentally retarded individuals is difficulty in communication skills. Deficit, like that in other areas among the mentally retarded, runs the gamut and ranges from mild to severe. Because of a primary difficulty with communication skills, the so-called socially disadvantaged or culturally different child has made up a large portion of the mildly retarded group. Some argue that the socially disadvantaged child should not be labeled mentally retarded since no demonstrable brain damage is evident. Logically it follows, then, that every child that is truly retarded has brain damage. To include or not include this group of children with the retarded has been a point of argument. Those who think of retardation as irreversible believe these children should not be included with the retarded, while some others believe that retardation may be reversible and that individuals may be functioning behaviorally as retarded but with help can function at a normal level. This argument is aimed particularly at the mildly retarded group which is comprised primarily of the so-called disadvantaged.

Mental retardation is both a medical and social problem and is no respecter of race, social, economic, or educational position. More than 200 conditions have been described in which mental retardation represents a more or less important symptom. Genetic, disease, accident, and psycho-social factors have been identified as associated with the etiology of mental retardation.

NATURE OF MENTAL RETARDATION

It is well to keep in mind that the gravity of the problem of the mentally retarded child actually depends largely on the society in which he lives. The middle-class urban retarded child is likely to have different problems from those of the lower class rural retarded child. His problems of retardation will only be difficult to manage if his condition interferes with his ability to assume an expected role as a member of his social group. Culturally, when we speak of the mentally retarded, we must consider the social milieu in which he moves. Individual differences may, of necessity, be allowed; but when they deviate too much from the established mores to the extent that the digression causes others concern for the individual, then abnormality may be said to exist.

The child may find he has no difficulty relating in his family as they accept his role-functioning in the family. However, he may have trouble in school. The description of the so-called 6-hour retardate is particularly illustrative of this. It is when the child is in his school culture that he gets into difficulty. For 6 hours a day, 5 days a week, his functioning is not in keeping with what is normally expected.

Mentally retarded children can learn. What they learn, how much they learn, and the way they learn is dependent upon many factors.

Our understanding of intellectual development is limited even for the average child. We are able to only speculate about the process of learning. However, it goes without saying that ability is an important factor to consider in planning to help a retarded child develop skills. Having some retarded children overlearn is perhaps one way of assuring retention of information.

CAUSES

The causes of mental retardation are many and complex. There is no single cause. Etiologic factors can be placed into several different categories. A category relating to the time of the occurrence in explaining etiology is one way of identifying factors related to cause. Factors of the prenatal, perinatal, and postnatal periods will be discussed.

PRENATAL FACTORS

Five primary groups of factors operant within the prenatal period have been identified as associated with mental retardation:

1. Toxic agents resulting from maternal infections
2. Drugs
3. Radiation
4. Genetics
5. Metabolism

Prenatal factors have been associated with toxic agents which affect the fetus. These toxic agents may result from maternal infections. The virus that causes rubella, if contracted during the first trimester of pregnancy, may cause a mental defect in the child. Toxoplasmosis, a protozoan disease, if contracted by the mother early in pregnancy, may result in a mentally defected child. Cytomegalic inclusion disease, another viral infection, if contracted by the mother, has also been associated with mental retardation.

Certain drugs which enter the mother's system accidentally, such as lead or carbon monoxide, or taken intentionally, such as heroin or LSD, may affect the unborn child. Thalidomide is known to produce deformities. Steroids may cause deformities if given in the first 8 weeks of pregnancy. Quinine, used sometimes to induce abortions, is known to cause deafness. Anticoagulants may cause fetal hemorrhage. There is evidence that infants born of mothers who smoke are more likely to be premature, which puts the infants at greater risk than those born to non-smoking mothers. Maternal injestion of amphetamines may result in a more cyanotic infant. LSD has been associated with chromosomal aberration; the affect of heroin on the newborn with severe withdrawal symptoms and obvious central nervous system (CNS) involvement is still not certain.

Excess exposure to radiation is known to have a deleterious affect on the unborn child. Chronic conditions such as hypertension, renal disease, and diabetes also may be factors. Emotional stress and improper nutrition also are suspected factors. Blood incompatibilities associated with ABO factors and the Rh factor may also predispose the neonate to problems.

Some genetic and metabolic factors have also been implicated in causing mental retardation. Mongolism, galactosemia, and phenylketonuria are three of the more commonly known. Phenylketonuria is a metabolic disorder which is transmitted genetically. Galactosemia is a congenital disorder of carbohydrate metabolism that causes an accumulation of galactose in the bloodstream.

Much has been learned in the past few years about chromosomes and their relation to various abnormalities. There are several chromosomal aberrations associated with mental retardation. Three of the commonly seen conditions associated with chromosomal aberrations are Klinefelter's syndrome, Turner's syndrome, and mongolism (Figs. 4.1 to 4.3 and Tables 4.1 to 4.3). Mongolism, referred to also as Down's syndrome and trisomy, is due to abnormality of the twenty-first chromosome (Fig. 4.4 and Table 4.4).

Standard trisomy occurs in 1:600 births. The total chromosome count is 47 instead of the normal 46. This type is rarely familial; it usually occurs in children born to older women. There is a failure of the two chromosomes of pair 21 to separate during gamogenesis in the mother. Translocation type of Down's syndrome is rare and is familial. In translocation type of Down's syndrome, the chromosome count is 46 but there is extra 21 chromosomal material at pair 15, making one of the pair appear abnormally large. These children are usually born to younger parents, one of whom carries the 15/21 translocation. The mosaicism type of Down's syndrome is the coexistence in one individual of different chromosome counts. One of the cells of the developing embryo, through error, gets an extra chromosome 21 and passes it on to its descendants. Consequently, there are two cell lives with different chromosome numbers. This type is not familial.

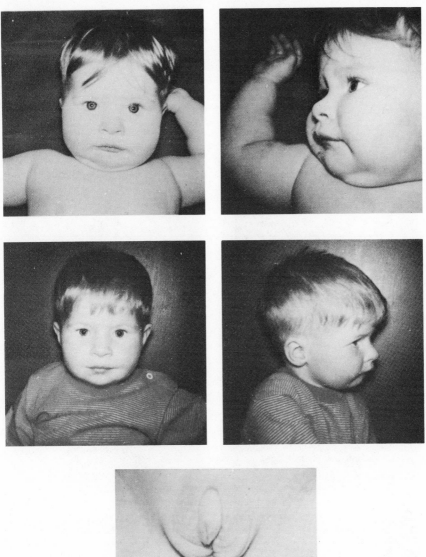

FIG. 1. Klinefelter's Syndrome (XXY, XXXY, XXXXY).

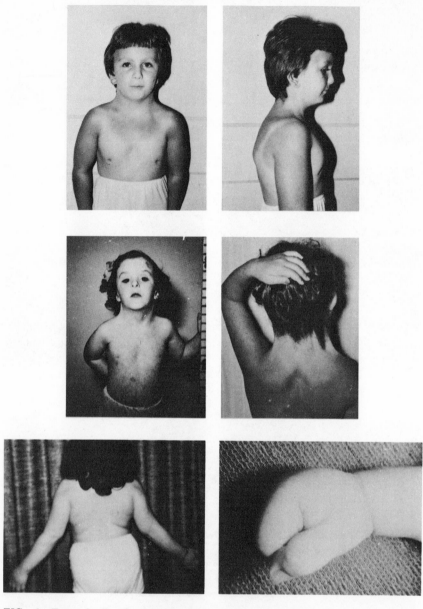

FIG. 2. Turner's Syndrome (Gonadal Dysgenesis, XO Syndrome, Bonnevie-Ulrich-Turner Syndrome). (Courtesy of Dr. Forrest Moyer.)

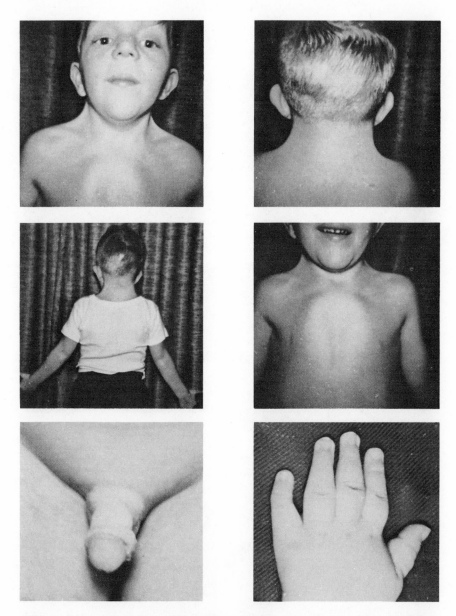

FIG. 3. Turner's Syndrome, Male (Turner's Phenotype in the Male, Noonan's Syndrome, Testicular Dysgenesis). (From Gellis and Feingold. Atlas of Mental Retardation Syndromes. *Courtesy of U.S. Department of Health, Education and Welfare.)*

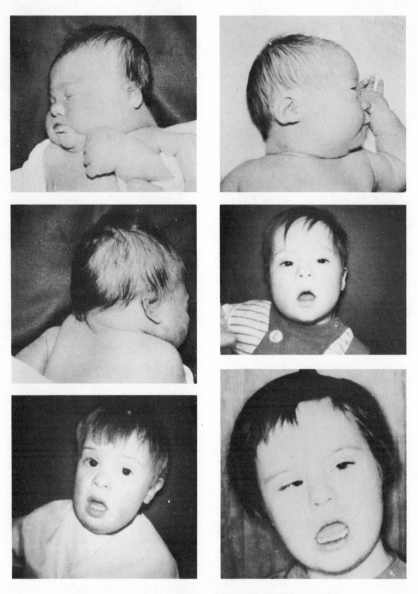

FIG. 4. Down's Syndrome (Mongolism, Trisomy 21).

TABLE 4.1. Klinefelter's Syndrome

Major Diagnostic Features

Tall stature and decreased secondary sexual characteristics

Mental Retardation

When present it is usually mild

Manifestations

General: Manifestations vary depending upon the number of Xs present. In classical XXY, few signs are present during childhood. Character or personality disorder are common

Head: Frontal hyperostosis

Eyes: Myopia and astigmatism

Mouth: Cleft palate; marked mandibular overgrowth in patients with XXXXY

G—U: Small, firm testes, varying degrees of eunuchoidism, azoospermia, progressive fibrosis, and hyalinization of the seminiferous tubules, decreased Leydig cell function; penis is normal in size although hypospadias is present in patients with XXXY or XXXXY; decreased secondary sexual characteristics; gynecomastia

Skin: Diminished facial and body hair

Skeletal: Tall and slender build although frequently patients are also obese; lower limbs may be larger than upper; radial ulnar synostosis; scoliosis; clinodactyly; chest deformities

Laboratory Findings: Increased urinary gonadotropin excretion and low or normal 17 ketosteroid levels

Genetics

Classical type reveals an XXY chromosomal pattern; variants include XXXY, XXXXY, and various forms of mosaicism.

Treatment

Hormonal therapy can promote increased secondary sexual characteristics. Personality disorders should be looked for and treated if possible.

From data of:

Klinefelter, H. F., Reifenstein, E. C., and Albright, F. Syndrome characterized by gynecomastia, aspermatogenesis without A-Leydigism, and increased excretion of follicle-stimulating hormone. J Clin Endocr 2:615, 1942.

Becker, K. L. et al. Klinefelter's syndrome: Clinical and laboratory findings in 50 patients. Arch Intern Med 118:314, 1966.

Stewart, J. S. S., and Ferguson-Smith, M. A. et al. Klinefelter's syndrome: Genetic studies. Lancet 2:117, 1958.

TABLE 4.2. Turner's Syndrome

Major Diagnostic Features

Short stature; webbing and/or shortening of the neck; absence of secondary sexual characteristics; typical facial appearance, including a broad bridge of the nose, epicanthal folds, and low set ears

Mental Retardation

Cognitive and hearing difficulties may cause learning problems

Manifestations

Neck:	Webbing and/or shortening; low posterior hairline; occasionally the hair of the lower neck will grow in an upward direction
Eyes:	Epicanthal folds, ptosis, strabismus, blue sclerae, and ocular abnormalities
Ears:	Protruding and/or low set; nerve deafness
Nose:	Broad bridge
Mouth:	High-arched palate and micrognathia
Cardiac:	Congenital heart disease with coarctation of the aorta and pulmonic stenosis most commonly found
G—U:	Variation in size of gonads from just a streak of gonadal tissue to normal size; absent or decreased secondary sexual characteristics varying with the type of chromosomal pattern. Renal abnormalities with horseshoe kidneys most frequently found
Skin:	Increased number of pigmented nevi and abnormal dermatoglyphics
Skeletal:	Lymphedema of the dorsum of the hands and feet present at birth and diminishing or disappearing with increasing age, broad shield-shaped crest with wide-spaced underdeveloped nipples, increased carrying angle at the elbows, hypoplastic nails, shortened phalanges, incurving and short second phalanx of the fifth fingers, fused cervical vertebrae, and osteoporosis

Genetics

The majority of these patients have only 45 chromosomes (XO) although various types of mosaicism may occur with the XX/XO being most frequent. Although other mechanisms cannot be ruled out, meiotic nondisjunction appears to be the cause of the loss of one of the sex chromosomes. The possibility of this recurring in the same family is unlikely. Buccal smears are usually chromatin negative.

Treatment

Hormonal therapy used at the proper time can increase secondary sexual maturation. Cardiac, renal, and ocular abnormalities should be corrected whenever possible. Growth hormone has shown no effect on the short stature. Because the cognitive and hearing difficulties may cause learning problems, special schooling may be of help.

From data of:
Engel, E., and Forbes, A. P. Cytogenetic and clinical findings in 48 patients with congenitally defective or absent ovaries. Medicine 44:135, 1965.
Lemli, L., and Smith, D. W. The XO syndrome: A study of the differentiated phenotype in 25 patients. J Pediat 63:577, 1963.
Greenblatt, R. B. et al. The spectrum of gonadal dysgenesis. Am J Obstet Gynec 98:151, 1967.

TABLE 4.3. Turner's Syndrome (Male)

Major Diagnostic Features

Short stature, webbing of the neck, ocular abnormalities, pulmonary stenosis, testicular dysgenesis, and decreased secondary sexual characteristics

Mental Retardation

Usually mild to moderate

Manifestations

General: Physical findings are similar to ovarian dysgenesis (Turner's syndrome) but the mental retardation and pulmonary stenosis are more common; short stature is usually striking

Head: Posterior hairline is low

Eyes: Ptosis, epicanthal folds, antimongoloid slant, hypertelorism, myopia, and strabismus

Ears: Low set, occasionally protruding, nerve deafness

Nose: Broad bridge

Mouth: High-arched palate and malocclusions

Neck: Webbed and/or short

Cardiac: Congenital heart disease with pulmonary stenosis most frequently found

G–U: Normal or small penis, cryptorchidism, small scrotum; decreased secondary sexual characteristics; usually no renal involvement

Skin: Hypoplastic and/or inverted nipples, hypoplastic nails, increased number of nevi, ectodermal defects of the scalp and keloid formation; decreased ridge count

Skeletal: Shortened phalanges, clinodactyly, cubitus valgus, pectus excavatum or carinatum and spina bifida; lymphedema of the dorsum of the hands and feet (present at birth and may or may not disappear)

Laboratory Findings: Increased urinary gonadotropins and normal or decreased 17-ketosteroid levels. Biopsy of the testicles may be normal or show anorchia or germinal aplasia or hypoplasia

Genetics

Is usually not an inherited disorder although there have been rare cases of two patients in the same family, one with gonadal and the other with testicular dysgenesis. The chromosomal count is almost always 46.

Treatment

The cardiac and ocular abnormalities should be corrected whenever possible. Hormonal therapy may be used to increase secondary sexual maturation. Growth hormone has shown no effect on the short stature.

From data of:
Heller, R. H. The Turner phenotype in the male. J. Pediat 66:48, 1965.
Meyerson, L., and Gwinup, G. Turner's syndrome in the male. Arch Intern Med 116:125, 1965.
Chaves-Carballo, E., and Hayles, A. B. Ullrich-Turner syndrome in the male: Review of the literature and report of a case with lymphocytic (Hashimoto's) thyroiditis. Proc Mayo Clin 41:843, 1966.

TABLE 4.4. Down's Syndrome

Major Diagnostic Features

Typical facial appearance (epicanthal folds, oblique palpebral fissures, broad bridge of the nose, protruding tongue, open mouth, square-shaped ears, and flattened facial profile), mental retardation, muscular hypotonia, and congenital heart disease.

Mental Retardation

Usually moderate but may range considerably

Manifestations

Head:	Brachycephaly with a flattened occiput
Neck:	Broad and short with excessive loose skin over the nape
Eyes:	Epicanthal folds, oblique palpebral fissures, Brushfield spots, strabismus, and nystagmus
Ears:	Malformed with an angular, overlapping helix and a prominent antihelix
Nose:	Small with a broad bridge
Mouth:	Held open, protruding tongue, small teeth, occasionally cleft lip and palate, high-arched palate, fissured lips, and a furrowed tongue
Cardiac:	Congenital heart disease is frequently found with atrio-ventricular communis and ventricular septal defects being most common
Skin:	Simian line, abnormal dermatoglyphics, and a single flexion crease of the fifth finger
Skeletal:	Hands are short and broad, the fifth finger may have clinodactyly and a dysplastic middle phalanx; there is increased space between the first and second toes plus a plantar furrow. Hyperextensibility and flexibility of the joints, dorsolumbar kyphosis, dislocated hips, funnel-shaped or pigeon-breasted chest, syndactyly, polydactyly, and clubbed feet may also be present.
X-ray Findings:	Dysplastic pelvis, lateral flare of the iliac wings, flattening of the lower edge of the ilium, and a decreased acetabular angle
CNS:	Mental/motor retardation and muscular hypotonia
Other Findings:	Diastasis recti, umbilical hernia, duodenal stenosis or atresia, agenesis of the pancreas, and renal abnormalities

Genetics

The majority of these patients are trisomic for chromosome number 21 due to nondisjunction. As the maternal age increases so does the risk of having a child with Down's syndrome. The translocation and mosaic types occur with less frequency but can be carried by a normal-appearing parent or sibling.

Treatment

Begins with the parents' understanding and adjusting to the diagnosis. Special schooling can help the patients realize their full potential. Correction of the congenital malformations should be considered as the need arises.

From data of:
Federman, D. D. Down's syndrome. Clin Pediat 4:331, 1965.
Hall, B. Mongolism in newborn infants. Clin Pediat 5:4, 1966.
Penrose, L. S., and Smith, G. F. Down's anomaly. Boston, Little, 1966.

Critical periods of brain development from an embryologic point of view perhaps cannot yet be accurately established. Investigators associate most of the problems to the first trimester even though the brain has not completed its development. The possibility of problems occurring any time during the pregnancy cannot be dismissed. It is an accepted fact that the largest percentage of factors associated with mental retardation occur prenatally.

PERINATAL FACTORS

There are two major factors associated with retardation:

1. Prematurity
2. Complications of labor and delivery

Prematurity has been considered a major contributing entity to mental retardation. The outcomes associated with premature births and "reproductive casualty" have been explained well by Pasamanick and Knobloch (1960). Reproductive casualty is a term used to explain the sequelae of harmful events during pregnancy and parturition resulting in damage to the fetus or newborn infant and primarily localized in the central nervous system. The term "reproductive casualty" is conceived as a continuum from death through varying degrees of disability.

The continuum of reproductive casualty is explained by Pasamanick and Knobloch (1960) as "a lethal component of cerebral damages which result in fetal neonatal deaths and a sublethal component which gives rise to a series of clinical neuro-psychiatric syndromes depending on the degree and location of the damage." Abnormalities ranged from more obvious difficulties such as mental deficiency, cerebral palsy, and behavior disorders of childhood, through more subtle disorders such as learning disabilities and minor behavior problems. The damage may be so minor that it is not detected by known instruments.

There are some problems during delivery which have been associated with mental retardation. Asphyxiation of the infant during delivery or anoxia may have an adverse affect on the perinate. Difficult labor and hemorrhage have also been cited as causative factors. Birth injury during the delivery process should also be cited. Any situations during the delivery that may result in central nervous system damage should be considered here.

Five major postnatal factors are discussed which are associated with mental retardation:

1. Acute illness
2. Trauma
3. Progressive disorders
4. Lead poisoning
5. Deprived environment

The postnatal causative factors may be classed generally as those associated with acute illness such as meningitis and measle encephalitis; traumatic events usually involve head injuries; and progressive disorders are associated with degenerative diseases of the central nervous system. Lead poisoning is a completely preventable condition; yet in a follow-up study of 425 children in Chicago, some 38 percent were found to be retarded as a result of lead poisoning. Children, ages one to three, who eat lead-based paint that flakes off of walls and woodwork of old houses are most affected. Children born into depriving environments have also been placed in this group.

More is known — or at least has been reported — about the biologic factors than the cultural factors. The socially disadvantaged or the cultural-familial retardates are those whose environments are intellectually nonstimulating or those with at least one parent who is retarded and incapable of providing stimulation for the child. The culturally deprived group can be discovered at an early age. The characteristics of this group are that they tend to come from the poor or low-income brackets and have rural backgrounds. Racially, they are blacks from the rural South, whites from the rural South and southern mountains who have migrated recently to northern industrial cities, Puerto Ricans who have migrated to a few cities, Mexicans with rural backgrounds who have migrated to the Midwest and West, and European immigrants who have rural backgrounds from Southern and Eastern Europe. A great many are from one-parent homes. Most, but not all, of the socially disadvantaged come from these groups. In areas where retardation is high, there is an unusually high incident of malnutrition, illness, unsanitary conditions, inadequate housing, accidents, and the prevailing apathy of poverty. The nurse, as a team member, can play an invaluable role in helping these families prevent retardation, not only in the postnatal period but prenatal as well.

Mental retardation can be identified in children at any time from birth through the school years. Communication is one of the basic problems we see in children who are retarded. In Table 4.5 we are able to see how children who are mentally retarded and children with other disorders compare with children who have normal characteristics in their reactions to sounds, reactions to gestures, sensory reactions, motor functions, and social responses.

More children are identified as retarded during the school years than at any other time. From the time the child is born until he reaches school age, an increasing awareness of slowed development becomes apparent. The school, because it does more comparing in that it evaluates all of its students in a specific age group, tends to focus specifically on the child if he does not measure up academically. School children must be ready to adhere to the rigorous standards of adaptive behavior. Earlier identification should be stressed primarily from the point of view that it can lead to early amelioration.

CLASSIFICATION OF RETARDATION

Levels of retardation have been established based on overall adequacy in meeting personal, social, academic, intellectual, and developmental or vocational requirements normally expected of individuals at various chronological ages. Those who manage the mentally retarded should be cognizant of the limitations of these strong demarcations and simply use them as guides instead of absolutes. The degree of mental retardation varies from individual to individual. Preciseness in defining the levels simply cannot be made. The levels have been simply classified as mild, moderate, severe, and profound. Each group will be discussed briefly.

MILDLY RETARDED

The mild group is also referred to as the educable group by professionals. This group is said to be capable of becoming self-supporting

TABLE 4.5. Clues as to Causes of Delayed Speech[a]

NORMAL	PERIPHERAL DEAFNESS	'CONGENITAL APHASIA'	'PSYCHIC DEAFNESS' (AUTISM)	MENTAL RETARDATION
Reactions to Sound				
Turns toward or startles	Only if loud	Inconsistent: frequently delayed	Inconsistent, delayed; responds to *absence* of sound	Normal; rarely delayed
Listens projectively	Only if loud	No	No	May: short attention span
Responds to imitation of own sounds	Yes (unless severe)	Yes	Is disturbed stops babbling	Yes
No echolalia	No echolalia	Variable	Frequent, especially to whisper	Sometimes
Reactions to Gestures				
Responds	Very much so	No usually	No	Yes
Uses gestures himself	Very much so	May or may not	Symbolises "internally" only, if at all	Yes
Reacts to movement	Excessively	Not usually	Insensitive	Yes
Watches faces and lips	Very much so	Less than deaf	Avoids faces	Only normally, or less
Sensory Reactions				
To visual cues, shadows	Excessively	May ignore or delay response	May avoid, or delay	Normal or diminished
To touch	Excessively	Relatively insensitive	Ignores (even pain at times)	Normal or diminished
To tapping or vibration	Excessively	Confused, erratic	Ignores	Often excessive
Vocalization				
Spontaneous babble at 6 to 8 months	Normal but soon lost	Variable; none or soon lost	Often none	Normal or delayed
Later babble for pleasure	None, but not mute	None, but not usually mute	None; may be totally mute	Usually
Vocalizes for attention	Yes	Often not	No	Yes
Normal intonation and inflexion	No	Variable	No	Normal or partially reduced
Jargon (appropriate for age only)	Abnormal; monotonous	Meaningless	No	Usually
Laughs and cries	Diminished; monotonous	Diminished; whines	Depressed to absent	Yes
Motor Function				
Coordination of hands	Normal	Usually clumsy	Abnormal mannerisms	Often clumsy

[a]From Paine and Oppe. Neurological Examination of Children, London, Heinemann, 1966.

Table 4.5 (cont.)

Gait	Shuffles feet (no auditory feedback) ataxic if vestibular damage	Often delayed	Not delayed; circling movements of body; walks on toes	Often clumsy; milestones often late, not always
Social Responses				
Normal maturity	Immature	Immature	Immature to none	Immature
Normal personality	Relatively normal	Indiscriminate; not shy; lacks depth; perseveration; distractibility; inhibition poor	Bizarre; lack of affect; fascination by spinning objects; prefers objects to persons; desire for ritual, routine, and 'sameness'	May be odd but less bizarre than in autism

in adulthood if trained. The mildly mentally retarded child is usually identified when he goes to school. Some have been referred to as the "6-hour retardates." Based on histories given by their parents, these children were undoubtedly slower in maturation than their more normal peers. Parents report that they did not sit, walk, or talk at the usual time. They did not notice objects or they were feeding problems — they did not eat or had difficulty retaining food. These are signs of trouble to come. These children usually have no physical stigmata. Their deviation is likely to be manifested in behavior related to the normal developmental milestones. Some of the deviations are picked up early but most are not identified until the child begins school.

The following characteristics that seem typical of the mildly mentally retarded child are important for the nurse to know so that she can help the family understand the child's behavior:

1. *Slower reactions.* It takes a longer time for him to adjust to a new idea. He performs best where there is a routine that follows consistently day after day.
2. *Short attention span.* He cannot attend to any one activity for a long period of time. Therefore, in order to maintain his attention, the activities must be geared to his short attention span. This will prevent him from distraction and will enhance his comprehension of materials presented.
3. *Language limitation.* A large number of the educable mentally retarded are considered to have familial retardation. Language deficits in this group are prime factors. Likenesses and differences must be pointed out repeatedly, and an oral vocabulary must be established. Both verbal and numerical symbols need to be used to aid in the development of knowledge so that comprehension of abstract meaning occurs. This is a tedious, long process but the

family can play a tremendous role in helping the child with language. Simple exercises such as determining the difference between bigger and smaller items; the differences between hard and soft by using concrete materials to teach such a concept; the differences between first, second, and last — again, using objects to teach the concept — are but a few ways to begin helping the child with his langauge limitations.

4. *Poor judgment.* They will need help in planning and determining which situations are important. Families could be encouraged to help the child in his planning. Such things as allowing the child to have a party may be one way of getting at this. With his parents he would decide on number of guests, time for the party, and type and amount of refreshments.

Often mildly retarded children are not able to determine what is essential and what is not. Nor are they able to distinguish between right and wrong because they have a limited ability to anticipate the consequences of an action.

Mildly mentally retarded individuals develop habits without too much difficulty. It is important that habit formation be to their best interest. The following are essential for the individual's social survival.

1. Health habits — physical fitness and cleanliness
2. Interpersonal habits — how to interact and get social acceptance from peers
3. Communication habits — ability to seek help from reliable sources

The mildly mentally retarded are generally able to achieve basic academic skills that will aid them in becoming economically efficient. They will achieve socially acceptable behavior and will be able, as adults, to become a part of society and function fairly well if they have adequate training.

In working with the family of the mildly and moderately retarded, the nurse's role, as a manager, would be to do what she could to help the family aid the child reach his fullest capacity. The primary goal for the mildly retarded would be to help the child develop independence as one would any other child so that he will eventually be able to function economically as an independent person in the community rather than as an economic liability to his family and community.

Preschool years. It is of importance that the nurse-manager be cognizant of the fact that in both the mildly and moderately retarded she is helping to gear and individual for as independent a life style as possible. Parents need support and understanding during the child's preschool years in assessing the effects of mental retardation and needs of the child, helping the child develop habits, recognizing stages of development, disciplining, becoming aware of community facilities available for recreation, care, etc., and gaining a realistic view of the child now and in the future.

Stimulating the child toward performance of these activities may aid him in overcoming part of his problem. Parents often become discouraged because the child is slow. Many have difficulty accepting the fact that the child is slow and try to give reasons for his slow development. They should, however, be encouraged to continue intensive stimulation. The nurse is or could be an invaluable support to families during this period. She has to interpret over and over the realistic facts as well as help the family see the progress of the child.

> The mother of a 2-year-old boy who had not yet talked or walked and was not toilet-trained was about to give up. "He just won't learn," she said. She had done all of the things suggested by the nurse and anyone else that she thought could help, yet the child, in her opinion, showed no real improvement. The nurse had noted that the child was progressing through the expected stages of development but was just very slow. During his third year of life, within a period of 10 months, the child sat without support, creeped, stood with support, and stood momentarily without support. He also said three words — mommy, daddy, and eat.
>
> Though his mother was concerned about the child's lack of skills, she was more concerned with his inability to walk, so much so that she paid little attention to his other accomplishments. She insisted that something must be wrong with the child's legs. "He looks like other children but isn't doing things like them." An appointment was made for him to see an orthopedist; his report showed no pathology. The mother still was not satisfied and kept insisting that something was wrong with the child's spine. He was seen twice by a neurologist. His report was simply that the child was slow but had made progress since the last visit.
>
> The nurse reassured the mother that the child would eventually walk. She helped the mother see the progress the child had made and tried to help her see that the child was simply slow. The child did walk the next month. His mother then declared that his hearing was impaired and insisted upon having his hearing checked again. She believed this was why he could not talk. The child did, however, show understanding of language in that he followed verbal directions well and, as has been mentioned, said a few words.

The above case points out further that the nurse should try to help parents with those things that bother them most. This mother had priority concerns. It simply does no good to try to work on areas in which the parent sees no problem.

> A man brought his child to the development clinic because he had the child in the park one day and realized that his 3-year-old wasn't as verbal as other 3-year-old children there. On physical examination the child was found to have a mild strabismus as well as some other minor problems. The father wanted only the speech therapist to work with the child. He refused to even consider the possibility of other problems.

As the child grows older the development of self-confidence is a must. The nurse can help parents by suggesting activities around the home that the child could engage in depending on his age, size, and abilities. Selection of toys, materials, etc., are of prime importance in helping the child develop concepts that will prove valuable during the school years.

School Years. During these years the child is moving out from the family and interacting more with others such as his peers and teachers.

The mentally retarded child is considered to be a socially marginal person. His incompetence is shown in relation to tasks that involve spatial, temporal, and numerical relationships. There is enough documentation pointing to the school as an environment which poses the most adjustment problems for the mildly mentally retarded. It is here that the retarded child's deficiencies become most noticeable. The omnipresence of the intellectual factors — space, time, and numbers — may become "social competence." The retarded child, unlike the normal child, is "not able to," and, because of these incompetencies, circumvents and moves about socially in an unobtrusive way. His behavior either gets him into difficulty or permits him some degree of adjustment. It seems that the more mild the retardation, the greater the potential adjustment, all other things being equal.

The nature of tasks suggested to increase social competency will depend on the child and his family. Such tasks as answering the telephone, participating in homemaking by suggesting foods that the family might buy, having some say regarding his clothes, helping with household chores, writing thank you notes for gifts given, participating in peer-group clubs, sharing experiences, caring for a pet, caring for his own room, and selecting his personal possessions are but a few general things that can be done.

The school-age child learns how to handle money. Some of the ways to help this development in children who are slow is to allow them to pay for lunch, give them an allowance to use as they see fit, and help them learn to count money.

MODERATELY RETARDED

Moderately retarded individuals have characteristics similar to those of the mildly retarded. Their deficits seem to be to a greater degree. In some of the mildly retarded, the characteristics are hardly noticeable, but in moderately retarded individuals they will be noticed. Moderately retarded individuals often have obvious physical stigmata. There are very noticeable delays in motor development, especially in speech. Moderately retarded individuals usually achieve their maximum potential if they learn the basics of self-care, a degree of social behavior, and some semblance of independence under structured supervision. They are generally viewed as semidependent.

The moderately retarded children who have apparent physical stigmata may have difficulty with self-esteem because of body-image difficulties. Body image is defined as that mental picture each individual has of his own appearance in space. It includes such things as facial appearance, height, weight, and body build. An individual is regarded as unattractive or attractive insofar as he conforms or deviates from the idealized anatomical measurements of his peer group.

> Martin, a 10-year-old, overweight, mongoloid boy, refused to play with boys his own age because he said "they make fun of me."

A child who has a physical stigma is likely to maintain a desirable self-image if he is instrinsically valued by his parents. The moderately retarded child is capable of developing a self-concept; thus it is important to help parents understand that their attitudes toward the child will affect how he may feel about himself.

Since many cases of mental retardation are diagnosed at school age, parental counseling is advisable. As has already been stated, parents may have ideas that the child is developing slowly; there is no suddenness of impact about the child's problem. The formal diagnosis actually confirms what the parents have already suspected. Consensual validation of mental retardation occurs at this time.

Much has been written about counseling parents of the retarded. Basic to working with families who have a child that is different from the average is how they feel about the child and the impact of the diagnosis upon them. One can assume that there is some feeling about the child being different. What that feeling is and how the parent reacts to it is individual. Since retardation is not an acute condition but a long-term one, the family is likely to have continued reactions and crises. The worker should keep in mind that the parents are always with the child and are often able to assess fairly well his abilities in many instances. Parents should be integral participants in realistic planning for the child. For without their cooperation, all planning that will necessitate their involvement is doomed.

> Johnny, a well-dressed, handsome, 12-year-old retarded child, had been socially promoted through the elementary school. His middle-class parents were faced with the fact that he was not ready for junior high school. He was taken to a developmental clinic primarily to aid in getting a school placement. The parents had never been told the boy was retarded, but they felt he was. The questions they asked were, "How slow is he?", "Will he be able to get a job eventually?" The parents were pleased to learn that he was brighter than they thought and that his potential for learning vocational skills was good. For 12 years this child had been overprotected by the parents who were afraid he would be traumatized. The "smothering" by both parents had practically sapped all the independence from the boy, who dared not rebel. The parents, with the help of the multidisciplinary team, decided how they could help the boy develop independence and recognized that some of their own actions had prevented this previously.

Our understanding of families, mental retardation, and the society in which we live is constantly changing. Much of what has been written about counseling parents of retarded children applies to only a small segment of those who have retarded children.

SEVERELY RETARDED

Severely mentally retarded children are affected by a variety of pathological factors. They are more apt to have a defective nervous system, causing motor responses to be somewhat awkward and uncoordinated. Their sensory acuity may cause them to react slowly to stimuli. Even when their sensory acuity is in the normal range, they are likely to have evident perceptual difficulties. Their physical makeup is likely to be weak, resulting in their being more prone to infection or lacking the normal resistance to infection. Health maintenance in these children is of prime importance. Other physical abnormalities may also be involved, such as epilepsy, loss of hearing, or loss of vision. Physical stigma are likely to be apparent in the severely retarded child. In some instances these children are likely to be multiply handicapped. Some may have cerebral involvement which may manifest itself in impaired speech, visual and/or auditory deficits, and one or a mixture of these movement abnormalities: rigid, spastic, ataxic incoordination. There is an increased number of such children surviving in the population. General improvement of health factors — that is, treatment of communicable and infectious diseases, better public health services, improved parental care and nutrition, better housing, increased education — have contributed to the higher number of these children.

Development. Normal 1-year-old children show finger dexterity and usually are able to hold a spoon, move it across the plate, and bring it to the mouth. They are able to hold a cup; and they can say a few words. By age 2, they are generally able to have bowel movements in the potty or toilet, assist with their clothing, chew their food more effectively, and hold a glass with one hand. Three-year-old children often graduate to a fork, remain dry during the day, can unbutton front buttons, put on their shoes (even though often on the wrong foot), and put on pullover shirts. By age 4 they show more independence; if we observe them, we notice that they are able to serve their own plate (with supervision), are able to cut with scissors, have completed their toilet training, and have acquired the beginning skills of giving themselves a bath. Five-year-old children can dress and undress themselves. They are learning to tie shoes and are about ready to enter a school situation. By age 8 they can cut their meat with a knife, have beginning skills of telling time, have a vocabulary of over 3,000 words, and are able to select clothing suitable for the weather.

Severely retarded children, though older when they learn each skill, are capable of functioning in this range of development throughout life. Consequently, severely retarded children, like very young children, are apt to feel insecure because they are not able to understand much about their environment and the people in it. Their activities need to be supervised, and they need help to maintain themselves in the community. They can learn, but the limitations are great. The activities they are capable of learning are very routine and repetitive.

In working with families who have severely retarded children, management should be based on what the individuals can do and seem to have the potential to do and not on what they cannot do. The emphasis should be on helping such individuals become as independent as possible. Severely retarded children usually can learn to care for themselves. Families often need to be helped in allowing their retarded children to do things for themselves. A set of general principles that could be communicated to families with severely retarded children are:

1. Judge the child not with others, but on the basis of what he can do. No two children are alike.
2. Try to associate each thing that is taught with pleasure. Find out what the child enjoys and associate the activity with something pleasant.
3. Teach skills one step at a time. The child has a simple mind and too many things coming at once are distracting, not helpful. The child can only attend to one thing at a time. Each skill should be broken down into its smallest steps.
4. Teach the easiest part first. Allow the child to have success.
5. *Consistency* is imperative.
6. Encourage and praise the child for each step he makes toward the desired goal.

Most communities have some facilities for severely retarded children, and many communities have programs in the public schools for them. The programs are designed for what the educators call the trainable child. These programs are set up to enhance the development of daily living skills.

Development of social skills that will help them function more adeptly in their world are also stressed. It seems that the problems the severely retarded present have to do primarily with lack of social skills. Consequently, they do not fit because of the way they behave socially. Teaching these children simple tasks, such as how to eat with proper implements, can be a mammoth undertaking, but it can be done.

> There were 20 severely retarded males aged 10 to 24 on a unit in a state institution for the mentally retarded. These males ate with their hands or lapped their food like lower animals. A nurse felt that she could help the boys learn to eat properly. With the help of a psychologist who designed a behavior-modification program that the nurse and her assistants followed, all of the males of this unit were eating with proper implements in 2 months. She reported that they showed no regression in this particular phase of the behavior-modification program.

Rarely does a parent have to work with 20 individuals, but working with one can be exasperating at times. Parents need to have the support of a person who cares and believes that the child can learn.

> A mother of a severely retarded child that was not toilet-trained, reported that if the public health nurse had not encouraged her she would

have given up trying to "train . . . to the pot. She [the public health nurse] wouldn't let me give up."

The nurse can be an invaluable source in helping parents with daily living skills, such as feeding, dressing, and toileting severely retarded children. Behavior modification as a technique for teaching desired behavior in children was discussed in another chapter. A general discussion of some of the daily living skills a child needs to be accepted socially will be discussed briefly.

Feeding. Feeding is one of the first activities in the parent-child relationship. It is through feeding that children get to know their parents. Feeding helps children learn about the world around them.

Most children are born with the reflexes of sucking and swallowing. Severely retarded children may have difficulty with these, and later on with chewing. Ample time for feeding children who have difficulty should be allowed. Feeding should be pleasurable for the child; and he should be praised for small successes.*

Utilization of sensation to elicit sucking and swallowing have been suggested also. Touching the lips, first above, then below, and stroking the cheek is an aid in sucking. Stroking the throat area lightly from the chin down will encourage swallowing. Bosely (1965) suggests utilization of temperature, taste, and odors as effective means to get infants to suck. Various types of nipples are available and should be used depending upon the child's sucking problem. As the child gets older and has learned to suck, more solid foods can be introduced. Licking exercises help in tongue control, which may be a factor in swallowing difficulty.

In eating, positioning is very important. Back support, in a more or less sitting position, will enhance the child's ability to successfully take in food. Nurses need to help parents improvise as necessary if their child has had head and body control problems.

Special utensils may be necessary for the child with deficient hand function who is ready to self-feed. Suction cups on the bottom of deep dishes with sides will aid in keeping the dishes on the table and the food in the dish.

Selection of food is important because the child may have difficulty chewing. Softer foods may be necessary until the child learns mouth coordination, essential for chewing.

*For some helpful hints on feeding children who have difficulty with sucking, swallowing, and chewing, write for *Feeding the Child with a Handicap*, Children's Bureau Publication No. 450, 1968. Dept. of Health, Education and Welfare, Washington, D.C.

Dressing. Recognizing cues which indicate the child's readiness to learn how to dress himself is important. The characteristic behavior of the average child is that he begins to cooperate in dressing by holding still, extending his arms or legs, and developing an interest in clothes — more in taking off than putting on.

A step-by-step process should be used in helping the child learn to dress himself. Give the child plenty of time for each step and praise him for all his successes, no matter how small they are. Inner to outer clothes should certainly follow. Help the child learn front from back in each piece of clothing (underpants, undershirt, dress, pants, etc.) either by pointing out the label as back (since most are placed in the back) or placing a small patch on the back so that the child becomes accustomed to this as symbolic of back. This helps him to begin learning the concept of front and back. Give the child assistance as he needs it, and decrease assistance as he masters each step until he masters the entire task. Socks should be rolled to the toe and given to the child to put over toes and then pulled up. Zippering, snapping, and buttoning may be harder to do. One may want to use pullover garments and garments with elastic waists until the child has mastered putting garments on; then steps to zippering, snapping, and buttoning can proceed. When teaching these, start the process for the child and let him complete it. Again, gradually withdraw what you do as the child masters the activity. This is referred to as fading.

Toileting. Toilet-training has been referred to as a battle of wills between the child and his mother. Normally by the end of the second half of the second year the child has learned to distinguish sensations in connection with the passing of urine and feces. Eliminating feces, from a social point of view, can be considered a healthy sign if done with regularity in its proper place. Control of elimination is a mark that the individual has reached a particular level of responsibility. Society demands that each of its members become toilet-trained or pay the social penalty.

Psychologically, toilet-training is said to be necessary to resolve anxiety and speed along the achievement of independence. Realistically, it is a pretty messy housekeeping chore — diaper pails, wet clothes, wet beds — and results in a hypervigilant, weary mother.

It is an individual matter as to how fast a child can be trained. Various methods have been suggested. Generally we can help mothers detect signs that may be indicative of a need to eliminate — irritability, holding, jumping, and the like. If no signs can be detected, the child should be placed on the commode at regular intervals — before and after meals and before bed. Liquids should be given in small amounts or withheld before bedtime.

The child should sit for 3 to 5 minutes. He should be rewarded for sitting. He should be positioned comfortably. Running water in the sink has been suggested as a means to encourage the child to urinate (psychologic suggestion).

PROFOUNDLY RETARDED

There are a few retarded individuals who have very minimal abilities. Many of this group are custodial cases and are often found in residential insitutions. Their behavioral manifestations are sometimes primitive and bizarre. Physical stigmata are almost always evident in these individuals, and many are not able to do anything for themselves. Many are confined to bed or a wheelchair. Some may learn to use the toilet, walk, feed themselves, and vocalize a greeting.

The nurse who works with these individuals recognizes their limitations but continues to try to help them function at a higher level. A nurse once told a group that it took her 1 year to teach a profoundly retarded child to say hello. Communicating with these children through mime (utilization of gross movements) may be effective. Levett (1969) sees value in mime as a method of communication for nonspeaking, severely retarded children. Mime requires not just hand movement but facial expression and movement of the whole body as well. Though great gains cannot be expected in these children, attempts to help them achieve small gains are desirable.

PREVENTION OF RETARDATION

Prior to pregnancy, teaching families to maintain healthful lives is of great importance. There is evidence to suggest that those women who have interferences which result in ill health are more likely to deliver unhealthy infants. Lane and Fleming (1971) found that a large number of the infants admitted to a high-risk nursery were products of mothers with ill health. Prospective parents should be educated to the importance of somatic and psychologic factors that might be supportive or detrimental to the normal development and growth of their children. Prevention of accidents and poisonings, proper immunizations, intermittent health reviews for young children in the family, information about proper diet, and early treatment of illness for these children is indicated. Prevention of seizures in young children during febrile or toxic episodes is also important.

Both physical and emotional preparation of women during childbearing age is important to assure ideal health for each stage of pregnancy. The pregnancy should be diagnosed as promptly as possible and continued prenatal care encouraged. During the pregnancy, mothers should become aware of those factors which may affect the fetus, such as unprescribed drugs. Mothers should be taught what to expect during the labor and delivery phase and how they can participate in the delivery. Mothers should be helped to develop healthy attitudes about the pregnancy, as their attitudes may affect their performance during labor. It is believed that perinatal stress contributes to subsequent behavioral and cognitive problems. The fetus should be monitored during labor.

The early learning abilities of infants has been documented (Peiper, 1963). The adverse perinatal stress that may result from respiratory distress, jaundice, and dysmaturity may distort the process of learning. The worker in the nursery may note behaviors that may be induced by such stress factors as excess startle reflex, hypersensitivity to sounds, poor sucking reflex, and tremors. The worker needs to start in the nursery to correct these symptoms because each day that the infant is stressed to the point of being in disequilibrium he falls behind his "normal" counterpart. The cognitive and behavioral problems seen later in children who have perinatal stress are thought to be remediable if a systematic approach to sensorimotor stimulation is started early.

STIMULATION

To achieve the goal of developmental stimulation and to prevent potential handicaps in infants and toddlers several concepts should be understood. In order for a child to mature the environment must be conducive to growth. It is assumed that no matter what the genetic endowment of a child is, his behavior is still greatly influenced by environmental interactions. At *critical periods*, which are genetically directed, specific developmental skills emerge. *Individual differences* as to when these skills emerge fit within a standard or norm. *Nurturance*, a means of encouraging and supporting, if applied during maturation, will reinforce maturation.

Any children deemed potential risks, such as those who are born premature, those whose mothers had stressful labor and/or delivery, and those born into poor families, are the ones for which the nurse member of the professional team is likely to introduce a program of stimulation. Early stimulation of infants and young children could be considered one way of preventing behavior characteristics of the mentally retarded, particularly since a large percentage of the mental retardation that is seen has been attributed to factors due to sensory deprivation.

Experimental stimulation programs during the preschool years have been shown to increase intellectual achievement. It is recognized that children may become test-wise, but not enough to score as high as they do. What happens after the intense stimulation period is over and the children remain in the same environment is still uncertain. However, what happens to these children during their early childhood is likely to affect how they behave as adults. Stimulation, beginning with infancy and following through progressively as the children grow and develop, not only attempts to help the children reach their maximum at each level of their development but aids in preparing them for later life.

When one thinks of stimulation, one automatically thinks of deprivation. The assumption is that stimulation will enhance development while deprivation may impede development. Carter (1965) wrote, "All sensory modalities have collateral connections with the reticular activity system. When stimulated, this system leads to arousal and facilitation of perception, attention, learning, and motor activity. An unchanging stimuli pattern and a reduced quantity of sensory input may minimize the functioning of this system and impair learning." There is wide area between stimulation and deprivation.

In planning a developmental stimulation program for the first 5 years of life, vital considerations in aiding the child are:

1. Effective communication
   a. talking

2. Effective social skills
   a. eating solid foods; self-feeding
   b. toilet-training
   c. walking

Obtaining the above milestones is critical for determining or measuring developmental progress. The goal of a developmental stimulation program is to help children who might not, because of deprivation of sensory input or stress factors which affected the child at a point of earlier development, accomplish the developmental tasks of the first 5 years of life which are basic to future functioning.

The question of *critical periods* (the best time for the child to learn a skill) for initiating stimulation is perhaps not completely answered, as most current research has been done on animals. The importance of environment in providing stimulation cannot be overly stressed. There is evidence that supports the importance of critical periods. Children who are bedridden during their early maturational years may have an abnormal gait when they learn to walk later. Perceptual orientation is different when lying down than when in an upright position. The space perception of an object thrown in a small, crowded room is different than it would be in a large, uncrowded room. The nurse could help families identify critical periods for learning skills. Her knowledge of growth and development is invaluable in performing this task.

The concept of *individual differences* is important in considering how one learns and progresses. Individual differences should not be minimized in working with young children. There is evidence to support the ideas of variability and individuality in children. These differences are recognizable as early as the first day of life. Nurses and parents have long been aware of this and have reported these findings, and too often have been ignored. Providing stimulation early for young children does not negate the concept of individual differences because there is a general overall standard pattern of emergence of skills. The evidence, though not conclusive, supports the idea that children learn earlier than we heretofore believed.

Nurturance — that is, those techniques of nourishment, encouragement, and support provided during maturation — helps to reinforce maturation. The nurse could work with parents and help them enhance the nurturing of the young children in their families. Parents need to recognize when they reinforce undesirable behavior and when they reinforce desirable behavior.

> Johnny, a 2½-year-old child, had never talked. His mother brought him to the well baby clinic for a checkup and indicated that he just would not talk. In talking with the mother, the nurse learned that the child understood what he wanted. He pointed to things, pulled on his parents or siblings (two older sisters ages 10 and 12), led them to things, and had temper tantrums if they did not understand. Each time he had a temper tantrum he was picked up, cuddled, and held. The mother could not think of any other time that he was cuddled. Johnny was being rewarded, it seemed, for not talking. His nonverbal communication got him what he wanted. He had not found it necessary to talk.

An analysis of the child's needs is the first step in planning any program of stimulation. The worker would first assess the child. The nurse could use such tools as the Denver Developmental Screening Test and the Washington Guide to Promoting Development in Young Children to help her understand at what level the child is currently functioning developmentally. The Vineland Social Maturity Scale or the American Association on Mental Deficiency Adaptive Behavior Scales might also be useful. The nurse may have other tools for assessing development that she wishes to utilize.

During assessment the nurse should be sure to carefully take note of what the mother says about the child. What the mother says should not be ignored even though it may not fit the pattern of expectation. Occasionally, a mother's information about her child is accurate and gives a fairly good description of his behavior. There are studies which report that a parent's assessment ability of her child comes very close to that of professionals. Secondly, a mother-child relationship assessment might be useful. Parental attitudes, particularly the mother's, since she is the primary caretaker, about the young child are critical for planning a home developmental guidance program. A mother has many notions about the care of her young child. An apparently healthy attitude on the part of the mother may be observed from the manner in which she handles the child and in what she says. A mother who is not adapting to her young child may see him as ugly and unattractive. She may see the natural dependent needs of the child as dangerous, and constantly demand reassurance that no defect or disease exists. She may talk to her child too much or too little, or at the wrong time. As the mother handles the child, she may hold the child away from her body or pick him up without warning him by touch or speech. She may be unable to find in her child any physical or psychologic attribute which she values in herself.

Recognition of the tasks in process of the young child and the mother will aid the nurse in determining deviations from acceptable behavior. Senn has identified both the tasks of the mother and the young child that might be a helpful guide to the nurse (Tables 4.6 and 4.7).

TABLE 4.6. The Newborn and Young Infant[a]

Tasks in Process

INFANT	MOTHER
To adjust physiologically to extrauterine life	To sustain baby and self physically and pleasurably
To develop appropriate psychologic response	To give and get emotional gratification from nurturing baby
To assimilate experientially, with increasing capacity to postpone and accept substitutes	To foster and integrate baby's development

Acceptable Behavioral Characteristics

INFANT	MOTHER
Copes with mechanics of life (eating, sleeping, etc.)	Provides favorable feeding and handling. Gets to "know" baby
Body needs urgent	Develops good working relationship with baby
Reflexes dominate	
Has biologic unity with mother	Has tolerance for baby
Establishes symbiotic relationship to mother	Promotes sense of trust
Sucking behavior prominent	Learns baby's cues
Cries when distressed	Applies learning to management of baby
Responds to mouth, skin, sense modalities	Encourages baby's development
Is unstable physiologically	Has reasonable expectations of baby
Functions egocentrically	
Is completely dependent	
Has low patience tolerance	
Is noncognitive; expresses needs instinctually	
Develops trust in ministering adult	
Begins to "expect"	

[a]From Senn, M., and Solvit, A. J. Problems in Child Behavior and Development. Philadelphia, Leo and Febigan, 1968.

TABLE 4.7. The Toddler and Preschool Age[a]

Tasks in Process

CHILD	MOTHER
To reach physiologic plateaus (motor action, toilet training)	To promote training, habits, and physiologic progression
To differentiate self and secure sense of autonomy	To aid in family and group socialization of child
To tolerate separations from mother	To encourage speech and other learning
To develop conceptual understandings and "ethical" values	To reinforce child's sense of autonomy and identity
To master instinctual psychologic impulses (oedipal, sexual, guilt, shame)	To set a model for "ethical" conduct
To assimilate and handle socialization and enculturation (aggression, relationships, activities, feelings)	To delineate male and female roles
To learn sex distinctions	

Acceptable Behavioral Characteristics

CHILD	MOTHER
Gratification from exercise of neuromotor skills	Is moderate and flexible in training
Investigative, imitative, imaginative play	Shows pleasure and praise for child's advances
Action somewhat modulated by thought; memory good; animistic and original thinking	Encourages and participates with child in learning and in play
Exercises autonomy with body (sphincter control, eating)	Sets reasonable standards and controls
Feelings of dependence on mother and separation fears	Paces herself to child's capacities at a given time
Behavior identification with parents, siblings, peers	Consistent in own behavior, conduct and ethics
Learns speech for communication	Provides emotional reassurance to child
Awareness of own motives; beginnings of conscience	Promotes peer play and guided group activity
Intense feelings of shame, guilt, joy, love, desire to please	Reinforces child's cognition of male and female roles
Internalized standards of "bad," "good"; beginning of reality testing	
Broader sex curiosity and differentiation	
Ambivalence towards dependence and independence	
Questions birth and death	

[a]From Senn, M., and Solvit, A. J. Problems in Child Behavior and Development, Philadelphia, Leo and Febigan, 1968.

The nature of a particular stimulation program will probably depend on the individual child. The most we can say relative to this is that:

1. It is important to recognize which of the sensory modalities seem to be weak and malfunctioning and which seem to be strong and functioning well.
2. If a child is going to be able to function cognitively later on it is imperative that communication skills emerge during the preschool years.
3. Experiences for the child begin early, and definitive long-range goals should be identified and sequential steps for attaining them worked out.

The following suggestions for stimulating a child are general.

The dependent infant receives his nurturance primarily from his mother. She holds, caresses, and feeds him. Mothers should be encouraged to hold the infant at times other than just during feeding. The infant seats that many mothers use have, in some instances, minimized physical contact between mother and baby. Tactile stimulation could be enhanced by providing different texture objects, toys, baths, cuddling, and stroking. The feeding period should be a satisfying one and not rushed. The infant should have ample time to suck and eat. As he grows, he needs to be provided different foods that will not only be healthy but will help him learn to discriminate. It is through his mouth that he learns much about this world.

Visual stimulation can be encouraged by providing mobiles on the crib, eye contact from the caring person, and a mirror for the child's use. But mothers should be cautioned against utilization of mobiles and other gadgets to entertain the baby while they absent themselves from him. The infant needs a satisfying human interaction. He needs mothering. This helps him develop a feeling of security.

Auditory stimulation can be given by the parent through vocalization. Singing to the infant and providing quiet music are other means of supplying the infant with auditory stimulation.

As the child grows, his motor skills, both fine and gross, should also be stimulated — objects to grasp and to play with, and help in rolling over, sitting, and standing.

Picture books, other visual objects, and occasionally television could be used to enhance visual stimulation as the child grows older. Naming objects as shown and naming parts of the body during the bath will help the child learn.

Helping parents select toys suitable for their child is valuable. Many toys have designated ages but sometimes such toys are not what the individual child needs.

The key to an effective program of stimulation is to provide a wide range of sensory experiences so that the child can learn. Secondly, the notion of prereadiness in developmental skills is inherent. When one can anticipate the emergence of a developmental set of behaviors, the set should be developed (without neglecting to maintain skills already achieved) until the skill is evident. The Washington Guide may be most effective in helping the nurse and parents plan activities at critical periods to enhance development.

Preventing mental retardation certainly is not limited to those measures discussed here. These are, however, activities in which the nurse can participate directly. Philips (1966) has discussed a number of ways to decrease the frequency of mental retardation.

SUPPORT OF THE MENTALLY RETARDED

The nurse can aid the parents of the mentally retarded child provide an acceptable emotional climate. The retarded child, like any other child, should grow in an environment that shows him affection, accepts him, and approves of him. Parental influences are pervasive and critical to the developing child. Ricci (1970) found that parents of retarded children demonstrated more rejecting attitudes than the parents of emotionally disturbed children. Rejection, overindulgence and overprotection seem to evolve from the ambivalent feelings of parents. The nurse, in collaborative efforts with other professionals who give service to the child and his parents, should recognize what contribution she can make and have enough confidence to make it. The nurse will do what she can to help the family solve realistic problems. Invariably the question as to how the retarded child will affect the other children in the family emerges. Parents need to understand that their feelings will generally be reflected in their own children.

Keeping the retarded child in the family is likely to be a source of chronic stress to the parents. Respite care services (Paige, 1971) are designed to relieve the family of the retarded individual's care in order to (1) meet planned or emergency needs, (2) restore or maintain physical and mental well-being, and (3) initiate training procedures in or out of the home. The program is set up so that the retarded person is temporarily separated from his family for short, specified periods of time on a regular or intermittent basis.

Mental retardation in children is not an individual but a family problem. No two situations are similar, so each must be evaluated carefully. As the child grows and develops, his needs change and the family has to approach the problem in different ways. The nurse may be one member of a professional group who offers services to the family. It is important that she aid in coordinating the services to the child and his family so that some stability is maintained and the child can reach his maximum potential. Those who work with the mentally retarded child and his family should constantly reassess their skill and knowledge in meeting human needs.

FAMILY AND THE MENTALLY RETARDED

Parents of retarded children represent every walk of life and have diverse ideas about retardation and parenthood. Neither mental retardation nor parenthood has the same meaning for all parents. Factors that affect the family and the ways in which parents view mental retardation and/or parenthood are many. The parents' childhood experiences, subculture in which they grew up, value system, income, community status, education, religious belief, family size, and degree of marriage stability, and the child's appearance and degree of disability are but a few of the factors which affect their viewpoint.

In working with the family of a retarded child, the nurse may want to help the parents mobilize their energies in constructive ways. Some of what the nurse does will be through counseling.

She should have competency in counseling. If any points could be made, there are six that seem particularly relevant:

1. Try to involve both parents if they are both in the home. This prevents confusion and distortion of the information.
2. Be honest. Avoid having parents set up rigid defenses by averting the truth.
3. Use terminology that parents understand. Be sure your explanations are clear and understood.
4. Try to use a positive approach.
5. If the nurse is to be the constant or main contact with the family, establish this as early as possible so that there will be continuity. It is important to the family to know that there is one individual that they may call for help. It is deplorable to have several members of the team giving test results and advice.
6. Give parents the opportunity to verbalize their feelings to you. When you have a contact, be prepared to give them time to communicate.

REFERENCES

1. Ambrose, J. A. The development of smiling response in early infancy. In Foss, B. M., ed. Determinants of Infant Behavior. New York, Wiley, 1961.
2. Ausubel, D. P., and Sullivan, E. V. Theory and Problems of Child Development. New York, Grune & Stratton, 1970.
3. Bare, C., Boettke, E., and Waggoner, N. Self Help Clothing for Handicapped Children. 1962. National Society for Crippled Children and Adults, Chicago, Ill.
4. Barsch, R. H. The Parent of the Handicapped Child. Springfield, Ill., Charles C. Thomas, 1968.
5. Blodgett, H. E. Mentally Retarded Children. Minneapolis, University of Minnesota, 1971.
6. Bosley, B. "Retreading Public Health Workers Through Training." II. Public Health Nutritionist. Am J Public Health. 55:246-51, February, 1965.
7. Bower, T. G. R. The object in the world of the infant. Sci Am 225(4):30, 1971.
8. Bowlby, J. The nature of the child's tie to his mother. Int J Psychoanal 39:1, 1958.
9. Bradley, B. H., Hundziak, M., and Patterson, R. M. Teaching Moderately and Severely Retarded Children. Springfield, Ill., Charles C. Thomas, 1971.
10. Brooks, M. R. A stimulation program for young children performed by a public health nurse as a part of well baby care. ANA Clinical Sessions, American Nurses' Association. New York, Appleton, 1971, pp. 128-139.
11. Capobianco, R. J., and Knox, S. I. Q. estimates and the index of marital integration. Am J Ment Defic 68:718, 1964.
12. Carter, C. H. Medical Aspects of Mental Retardation. Springfield, Ill., Charles C Thomas, 1965.
13. Dunn, L. M. Exceptional Children in the Schools. New York, Holt, 1963.
14. Dybwad, G. Who are the mentally retarded? Children 15:43, 1968.
15. Evert, J. C., and Green, M. W. Conditions associated with the mother's estimate of the ability of her retarded child. Am J Ment Defic 62:521, 1957.
16. Frantz, R. L. Pattern vision in young infants. Psychol Rev 8:43, 1958.
17. Frantz, R. L., and Nevis, S. Pattern preferences and perceptual cognitive development in early infancy. Merrill-Palmer Quart 13:77, 1967.
18. Frantz, R. L. The origin of form perception. Sci Am 204:66, 1961.
19. Frantz, R. L. Visual perception from birth as shown by pattern selectivity. In H. E. Whipple, ed. New issues in infant development. Ann NY Acad Sci 118:793, 1965.
20. Frantz, R. L. Pattern discrimination and selective attention as determinants of perceptual development from birth. In Kidd, A. H., and Rivoire, J. L., eds. Perceptual Development in Children. New York, International University, 1966. pp. 143-173.
21. Frey, M. P. ABC's for parents aids to management of the slow child at home. Rehabilitation Literature, Sept., 1965, pp. 270-272.
22. Garton, M. D. Teaching Educable Mentally Retarded. Springfield, Ill., Charles C Thomas, 1970.
23. Havighurst, R. J. Who are the disadvantaged? In Webster, S. W., ed. The

Disadvantaged Learner: Knowing, Understanding, Educating. San Francisco, Chandler, 1966.
24. Heber, R. A. A manual on terminology and classification in mental retardation. Am J Ment Defic 65:3,4,20-40,96, 1961.
25. Hess, E. H. Imprinting. Sci 130:133, 1959.
26. Irving, P. Prevention and Treatment of Mental Retardation. New York, Basic Books, 1966.
27. Keirn, W. C. Shopping parents: Patient problem or professional problem? Ment Retard 9:6, 1971.
28. Kopp, L. M. An exploratory study of the responses of mothers to support during the second stage of labor (Dissertation). New Haven, Connecticut, Yale University School of Nursing, June, 1967, p. 87.
29. Kurtz, R. A. Implications of recent sociological research in mental retardation. Am J Ment Defic 69:16, 1964.
30. Lane, Virginia, and Fleming, Juanita. "A Comparative Study of High Risk and Normal Mothers and Infants." (Unpublished) U.K. College of Nursing, 1971.
31. Levett, L. A method of communication for non-speaking severely subnormal children. Br J Disord Commun 4:64, 1969.
32. Levine, S. Infantile experience and resistance to psychological stress. Sci 126:405, 1957.
33. McDermott, B. "Using media to teach self-help skills." In The Role of the Nurse in Caring for Children with Multiple Handicaps. Fleming, J., Denman, L., and Rudnick, B., eds. Univ Ky College of Nursing, Lexington, Ky., 1969.
34. Paige, M. Respite care for the retarded: An interval of relief for families. Washington, D.C., U.S. Dept. HEW Social and Rehabilitation Service. Rehabilitation Services Administration Division of Mental Retardation, 1971.
35. Paine, R. S., and Oppe, T. E. Neurological Examination of Children. London, Heinemann, 1966.
36. Paponsek, H. A physiological view of early onotogenesis of so-called voluntary movements. In Sobatka, P., ed. Functional and Metabolic Development of the Central Nervous System. Prague, State Pedagogie, 1961.
37. Pasamanick, B., and Knobloch, H. Brain damage and reproductive casualty, Am J Orthopsychiatry 30:298, 1960.
38. Patterson, E. G., and Rowland, G. T. Forward a theory of mental retardation nursing an educational model. Am J Nurs 70:531, 1970.
39. Peiper, A. Cerebral function in infancy and childhood. Int Behav Sci Ser, NY Consultant's Bur 15-16:92, 1963.
40. Philips, I., ed. Prevention and Treatment of Mental Retardation. New York, Basic Books, 1966.
41. Rebelsky, F., and Dorman, L., eds. Child Development and Behavior. New York, Knopf, 1970.
42. Rheingold, H. L. Interpreting mental retardation to parents. J Consult Clin Psychol 9:142, 1945.
43. Rheingold, H. L. The modification of social responsiveness in institutional babies. Monogr Soc Res Child Dev 21:2, 1956.
44. Ricci, C. S. Analysis of child rearing attitudes of mothers of retarded, emotionally disturbed, and normal children, Am J Ment Defic 74:756, 1970.
45. Richmond, J. B., and Caldwell, B. M. Child Rearing Practices and Their Consequences (In press).
46. Sarason, S. B., and Doris, J. Psychological Problems in Mental Deficiency, 4th ed. New York, Harper & Row, 1969.
47. Senn, M., and Solvit, A. J. Problems in Child Behavior and Development. Philadelphia, Leo and Febigan, 1968.

48. Watson, J. B. Psychological Care of Infant and Child. London, Allen & Son, 1928.
49. Webster, S. W., ed. The Disadvantaged Learner: Knowing, Understanding, Education. San Francisco, Chandler, 1966.
50. Wolff, P. H. The Developmental Psychologies of Jean Piaget and Psychoanalysis. New York, International University, 1960.
51. Wright, B. Physical Disability: A Psychological Approach. New York, Harper & Row, 1960.
52. Yannet, Herman. The Evaluation and Treatment of the Mentally Retarded Child in Clinics. National Association for Retarded Children, Inc., New York, 1956.

5

CHILDREN WHO ARE GIFTED

Nurses sometimes get exasperated with children who seem to be curious and ask many questions. Nurses have said, "That child just wants to know everything," or "You can't go in there unless he is asking a million questions," or "Do you know that brat was telling me what to do?" In childlife programs in the hospital, often the child who thinks up something unique to do with the supplies that the worker gives him is thought of as creative. Nurses are often heard describing a child as "alert," "very smart," "a keen little fellow," having a "good memory for details," and so on.

A nurse told her colleagues about a child that she described as having "a vivid imagination." She later said, "You just can't imagine some of the fascinating things he said."

Nurses do not usually think of the children they care for in the home, school, or hospital as gifted. If we look, however, at the child from a holistic point of view, we are bound to encounter children who would be considered gifted.

Gifted children are those children who have superior intellectual ability when it comes to dealing with facts, ideas, and relationships. They may also have special aptitudes in specific areas such as art and music. Physically, these children, as a group, generally appear stronger and healthier than the average child. Stalnaker (1961) described them as not only being physically healthier, but also as having more interest in people and greater confidence. Gifted children may be small for their age, socially immature, and prone to other problems of childhood. These children, however, may learn to walk and talk earlier than the average child and be more sensory adept. They often display the following characteristics: ability to perceive and identify the significant; interest and pleasure in intellectual pursuits; strong ability to think logically; ability to develop systems; high level of retention; high vocabulary level; facility in verbal expression; intellectual curiosity; critical ability; persistent long-ranging interests; need for freedom and individuality in study; and high energy, intense application, power of concentration.

Gifted children with minimum exposure seem to learn early or have precocious behavior. Terman (1947) found that parents identified the following cues that first caused them to suspect that their children were gifted:

1. Grasp ideas or understand quickly
2. Desire to know
3. Excellent memory
4. Maturity of conversation
5. Rapid school learning
6. Mature interests
7. Amount of information child knows

Gilford (1960) has proposed a three-dimensional structure of intellect. One dimension describes five different groups in intellectual abilities.

1. Cognition — ability to recognize or discover
2. Memory — ability to retain what is cognized
3. Divergent production — ability to reorganize known facts into new and/or varied relationships
4. Convergent production — ability to arrive at expected or conventional conclusions
5. Evaluation — ability to reach decisions that add to the adequacy or correctness of what is known

Freehill (1961) reports that gifted children are moralists. He says they accept responsibility and sometimes guilt for group actions or failures.

Contrary to popular thinking about gifted children, most are able to make good adjustments. They may also have a broad range of interests and wholesome personalities. Nurses need to identify those children who exhibit behavior that suggests that they are above average in their thinking and help manage them by:

1. Setting limits for them as needed. Sometimes, because they are bright and seem mature for their ages, people expect more from them and allow them too much independence.
2. Providing special enrichment opportunities that will enhance their development without making them feel that they are a privileged group.
3. Helping them understand themselves and learning to accept their own individualities. Unusually gifted children may feel alone and may need reassurance that they are worthy even though they are different; they need to be built up.
4. Responding to their genuine questions by suggesting ways to get the answers rather than simply ignoring their questions or answering them simply. Their curiosity should be kept alive and their independence fostered.
5. Helping parents with long-range planning for the child.

A 12-year-old girl from an average family was identified as bright but her intellect was not being challenged in her public school classes. She had been coming to the cardiac clinic for several years because of a rheumatic heart. With the help of one of her teachers, the nurse, and the social worker, she was enrolled on scholarship funds in one of the best private schools in her city.

There is no clear-cut kind of giftedness that one can define. It may appear in many different patterns. A physically impaired individual may also be gifted. Gifted children may be outgoing and friendly, but occasionally gifted children may be socially inadequate or emotionally disturbed.

The environment in which the child grows may help or hinder his giftedness. Gifted children who come from homes that provide little stimulation and encouragement may have difficulty in realizing their potential. The child may have no encouragement to fulfill his aspirations. Since he is gifted, he will probably find outlets for his talents whether they are socially desirable or not.

It is important that the nurse does not get caught up in using I.Q.'s as a means for identifying the gifted, but that instead she be an astute observer of behavior. Intelligence tests may penalize groups in certain socio-economic levels or certain locations in the country because of the high verbal content.

The bright child in psychosocial difficulty is probably a child whose environmental milieu has not been conducive to healthy development. Many gifted children have been unchallenged, undetected, and uncultivated. They may come from any socio-economic, racial, or ethnic group. It is easier to identify gifted children who come from well-educated, middle-class families.

A 10-year-old child, having difficulty in school, was regarded as retarded because he had two sisters and a brother who were older and all retarded. A professor, doing a study in this child's school, included the child in a sample of bilingual children. On a performance test he was found to have an I.Q. of 150. The child was seen in a developmental clinic and evaluated by the team. The problem was primarily that the child lived in a bilingual deprived family.

Some of the behavior problems that are manifested in some school children may be indicative of a bright child. Some children go through extraordinarily clever ways to avoid conforming to activities of the school. Some of these children are in constant difficulty with authority figures, many of whom do not seem to recognize that the child may be bright. Some of the histories of some young reform school students are not those of dull individuals but rather of very bright individuals that used their talents in socially unacceptable ways. Bright underachievers may be making an attempt to adjust to mediocrity, which seems more acceptable than being very bright and having problems that are more difficult to cope with. If children who are bright are identified early and their talents channeled properly, perhaps some of the aberrant behavior that is considered anti-social would be avoided.

If nurses in the community can aid in early identification of such children — so that they will not end up bored with life, unchallenged, and simply wasted — society would profit greatly by these potential contributors.

REFERENCES

1. Freehill, M. F. Gifted Children. New York, Macmillan, 1961, p. 51.
2. Guilford, J. P. Morphological model for human intelligence. Science 131:1318, 1960.
3. Hebb, D. O. The Organization of Behavior. New York, Wiley, 1949.
4. Stalnaker, J. M. Ability more than I.Q. Sci Newsletter 79:198, 1961.
5. Terman, L. M. Mental and Physical Traits of One Thousand Gifted Children: Genetic Studies of Genius, (Vol. 1). Stanford, Calif., Stanford Univ. Press, 1947.

6

CHILDREN WHO ARE VISUALLY IMPAIRED

Visually impaired children with severe defects have been classified educationally in two major categories: the blind and the partially sighted. Blind children are those children who have no useful vision. Legally, the blind are defined as those who have central visual acuity of 20/200 or less in the better eye with the best possible correction or restriction in the visual field to an angle subtending an arc of no greater than 20 deg. Stated simply, an individual who has 20/200 vision is one who can recognize symbols at a distance of 20 feet that a person with normal vision can recognize at 200 feet. The individual with a restricted visual field can only see a very limited area at a time and consequently is not able to make much practical use of his vision. Blindness may mean one has no light perception, has light perception, can recognize hand movements, or can count fingers at a distance of 3 feet (Table 6.1).

TABLE 6.1. Visual Acuity Based on Snellen Chart Rating

Normal Vision					Partially Seeing			Blind
$\frac{20}{20}$	$\frac{20}{30}$	$\frac{20}{40}$	$\frac{20}{50}$	$\frac{20}{60}$	$\frac{20}{70}$	$\frac{20}{100}$	$\frac{20}{200}$	Finger counting (distance of 3 feet)
								Hand movements
								Light perception
								No light perception

The partially sighted are defined as those whose remaining visual acuity is between 20/200 and 20/70 in the better eye with the best possible correction.

Lowenfeld (1955) has classified visual handicaps in six groups:

1. Total blindness, congenital or acquired before the age of 5 years
2. Total blindness, acquired after 5 years of age
3. Partial blindness, congenital
4. Partial blindness, acquired
5. Partial sight, congenital
6. Partial sight, acquired

Lowenfeld believes that individuals who lose their sight before 5 years of age are not able to retain any useful vision imagery. This is an important consideration for anyone working with blind children. The child who becomes blind before age 5 is probably very like the congenitally blind child.

A child who has a visual defect may have impairment of functioning which would be considered organic. The impairment may be in perceptual integration due to absence of visual input. Emotional reaction to unfavorable reactions of others may lead to distortions in social relationships. Cohen (1966) has explained these three impairments of functioning as neuropsychologic effects of visual deprivation and has indicated that a child can have one or a combination of the three.

CAUSES OF VISUAL DEFECTS

The major causes of blindness have been noted primarily in seven broad categories:

1. Prenatal
   a. Undetermined
   b. Hereditary
2. Poisonings
3. Tumors
4. Infectious diseases
5. Accidents and Injuries
6. General diseases
7. Unspecified causes

The more common defects noted in the partially seeing are:

1. Refractive errors (e.g., myopia, hyperopia, astigmatism)
2. Developmental anomalies (e.g., cataracts)
3. Defects of muscle function (e.g., strabismus)
4. Disease or defects of the eye (due to infection, injury, and other causes)

REFRACTION ERRORS

Refraction errors constitute a large portion of all visual defects. In the normal eye (emmetropic) the refractive media (cornea, aqueous humor, lens, and vitreous body) are such that the image of an object focuses directly on the retina (Fig. 6.1). In *myopia*, or nearsightedness, the eyeball is so long that the light rays focus at a point in the vitreous humor before reaching the retina. The individual must bring objects close to the eyes in order to see. In *hyperopia*, or farsightedness, the eyeball is so short that the light focuses behind the retina. The individual with this condition can see objects better at a distance. *Astigmatism* is caused by an irregularity in curvature of the cornea or lens of the eye. As a result, vision is distorted and blurred. The eye attempts to accommodate so that it can clarify the image, but part of the image falls behind the retina and part in the front, causing blurring.

DEVELOPMENTAL ANOMALIES

The most common developmental anomaly seen in children is cataract. A cataract is opacity or cloudiness of the lens blocking the normal passage of light rays through the pupil to the retina and thus preventing normal visual acuity. Children are sometimes born with a cataract. Congenital cataracts in children have been associated with heredity factors, such as rubella of the mother during the first trimester of pregnancy.

DEFECTS OF MUSCLE FUNCTION

Strabismus is caused by a lack of coordination of eye muscles. The two eyes do not simultaneously focus on the same object. In monocular strabismus, one eye is used for fixation. In an alternating squint, first one eye fixes and then the other eye fixes; in other words, the eye turns alternately in and out. The squint can also be

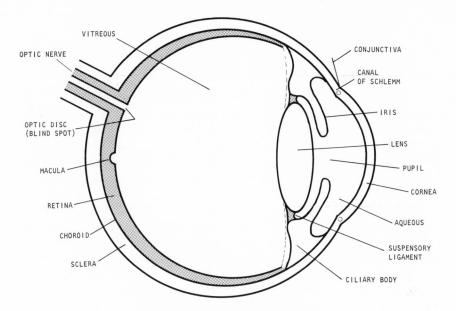

FIG. 1. Cross-section of the eye.

directional. When the deviating eye rotates inward, it is referred to as internal convergent squint or esotropia. When the deviating eye turns outward toward the temple, it is referred to as external strabismus, wall-eyedness, or exotropia. When the eye turns up or down, it is referred to as vertical strabismus, right or left hypertropia, or hypotropia.

There are other diseases and conditions than those already discussed that attack the child's eyeball, cornea, lens, vitreous humor, choroid, retina, optic nerve, or visual center of the brain and cause visual defects that either result in partial sightedness or blindness. Common among the diseases are diabetes, syphilis, keratitis, and retrolental fibroplasia. Less common conditions such as childhood glaucoma, retinoblastoma, and trachoma are others that may lead to blindness or severely impaired vision.

VISUAL DEVELOPMENT

Development of vision is a complex process and a major inseparable component of the central nervous system. Four of the cranial nerves

(II, III, IV, VI) are exclusively concerned with vision, and two (V, VII) are concerned to some extent with vision. The globes which appear early as outpouchings of the forebrain serve as functional extensions of the central nervous system throughout life in seeing individuals. As the embryo develops, the necessary visual components also develop. During the prenatal period, it seems likely that factors, known and unknown, could be precipitators of eye defects.

At birth the infant has some photophobia and the eyes are hyperopic. The pupils are miotic and the infant usually keeps the eyes closed. The tear glands begin to excrete about 2 to 4 weeks after birth. The infant is able to fixate on an object and is attracted by movement 1 to 2 weeks after birth. An infant will transiently follow 4-inch-long objects that are brought into the visual line.

By 8 weeks the infant is alert to moving objects, and by 12 weeks he will roughly follow an object through 180 degrees. Color preferences can be elicited between 3 and 6 months. Difficulties in hand-eye coordination are seen in infants as they attempt to grasp objects. By 7 months — and some authorities believe even earlier — discrimination of simple geometric forms can be demonstrated.

The 9-month-old infant has a visual acuity which exceeds 20/200. The child will attempt to pick up a small pellet or raisin using the pincer grasp. At 15 to 18 months the child can pick up a small pellet or raisin with precision, and will extend his head to gaze at objects. At 1 year visual acuity is near 20/100. If the child loses any ability to use both eyes together, amblyopia may result.

By 2 years acuity approaches 20/40, and the child is fascinated by small objects. The convergence-accommodation mechanisms which often lead to esotropia come into play. By age 3 convergence is smoother. The child will create designs on paper. Visual acuity seems well developed and may be about 20/30. Amblyopia may occur if acuity is not cultivated. By age 4 acuity is almost 20/20.

Color-naming is established by age 5, and visual acuity is susceptible to only a moderate reduction from disuse. By age 6 gross attention span has lengthened to almost 20 minutes and detail attention to about 2 minutes. Differentiation in shades of color can be made. Hyperopia, which is physiologically present during earlier life, begins to decrease, and emmetropic (normal or perfect) vision is established between the ages of 9 and 11 years. During the first 8 years of life the globe grows rapidly from about 16 to 24 mm.

The condition of the eyes of children is important. They not only give clues to systematic disorders but also to congenital disorders. Eliciting visual behavior from the child presents positive evidence of satisfactory nervous system functioning.

CHARACTERISTICS OF PARTIALLY SEEING AND BLIND CHILDREN

Partially seeing children are somewhat in limbo. They are neither blind nor fully seeing. They may have to live ambiguously, with some people expecting them to function like a fully seeing person and others treating them as if they were blind. Not a great deal of research has been done on partially seeing children, which may suggest that most workers do not see them as too different from their normally seeing peers. It is likely, however, that these children have more difficulty adjusting to their limitation because of problems arising from disturbed relationships with individuals who either expect more from them or do not expect enough. These children generally appear as other children but may tend to be somewhat more clumsy because they do not see well. They usually need special help in education.

Blind children are at a greater disadvantage because they are expected to function in a world that is geared to seeing people. They may be more vulnerable emotionally than other children because they are not able to pick up visual cues. They seem to be very sensitive to feeling tones of people around them. The attitudes of their parents toward them and their blindness are most important. Parents may react in any of the following ways: accept the child and his limitation; deny the effects of the limitation; or overtly reject the child. How the parents react to the child will determine, in large measure, how the child will adjust to his limitation and how he will mature socially. Extreme behavior in blind children, such as over-dependency, probably results from overprotecting parents. Restrictions on motor activities, because of the fear that the child will harm himself, have probably been enforced. The other extreme is the overly independent child.

Blind children will have difficulty with perceptual and cognitive tasks if they do not have a wide range and variety of experiences, opportunities to get about, and opportunities to experiment in their environment so that they can learn how to control themselves in relation to the environment.

Language development does not seem to be a problem for blind children even though they do not get visual cues — language is acquired primarily through auditory channels.

Children with visual defects come from all socio-economic groups and are no one set type. Those suspected of having impaired vision should be assessed individually. One of the major problems in screening or testing the vision of a young child is that he is often unable to tell the tester what he sees on the eye chart. Nurses may eventually be expected to use electronic means for detecting impairment in sight. By measuring the electric signals in the brain, determination of visual defects can be made. This is particularly true of amblyopia, one of the common eye problems seen in children. Electrodes are taped to the back of the head over the visual centers of the brain and signals are relayed much like an electroencephalogram.

The nurse can identify some signs of visual problems by using the checklist which follows. The symptoms have been categorized according to developmental stages, but it is obvious that they overlap. The signs listed in the checklist are important in that they may be valuable in helping the nurse detect visual problems that could lead to permanent visual impairment. One of the nurse's primary responsibilities is to do all she can to prevent visual impairment.

NURSE CHECK LIST

INFANTS

——Pupils do not react to light
——Appears comfortable when bright light is directed toward eyes
——Does not stare at surroundings
——Is unable to follow a moving object with eyes
——Has red-rimmed, encrusted, or swollen eyelids

TODDLERS AND PRESCHOOLERS

——Rubs eyes frequently
——Tries to brush away blur
——Has pain in and about the eyes
——Squints
——Frowns
——Is oversensitive to light
——Stumbles or trips over small objects
——Eyes are out of alignment (crossed eyes)

——Blinks
——Has repeated sties or watery, red eyes
——Holds playthings close to eyes

SCHOOL CHILDREN

——Holds book close to eyes while reading
——Tilts head forward when looking at objects
——Holds head to one side while reading
——Frowns when reading from a distance
——Closes one eye when looking at an object
——Skips words when reading aloud
——Confuses the letters *o* and *a* when reading
——Reads above or below the line
——Eyes do not work together
——Has double or blurred vision
——Experiences dizziness and/or headaches following close eye work.

MANAGING CHILDREN WITH VISUAL IMPAIRMENT

Partially sighted children should be managed much like normally sighted children, recognizing, however, the extent of their limitations. The environment should be made conducive for them to grow and develop with the limitation.

Some partially seeing children may wear glasses; however, glasses do not prevent or cure eye conditions. They will do only two things — relieve discomfort and/or improve vision if the basic cause is a refractive error in the eye.

> Myths such as, "residual vision is damaged by use," should be corrected to "residual vision is lost by disuse"; "wearing glasses will cure eye problems" should be corrected to "wearing glasses will change the character of the visual stimulus but not cure pathological conditions"; and "visually limited children are mentally retarded or emotionally disturbed" should be corrected to "mental retardation and emotional or social disturbances are not necessary correlates to vision problems."

Blind children have a deeper problem, and more input must be provided them so that they can function with minimum difficulty.

Affection, security, and consistency of care are important. Petting and cuddling the infant and talking to him in soft tones are essential since he is unable to have eye contact. He needs to hear plenty of conversation. Explanations are good, too, not because he necessarily understands, but because they provide more auditory input. The infant should be encouraged to be active, sit up, crawl, stand, and walk. Mobility training should start early. Unlike the seeing child, he will not have the visual incentive to motivate himself. Voice can be used to help him move.

The blind child should be fed as any other child. It is important to remember that the child misses facial cues about his responses to food. Toys that make noise, such as a rattle with bells, and water play are valuable.

TODDLER AND PRESCHOOLER

Food with bones, grapes with seeds, and so forth should be avoided. The child should feed himself. The environment can be arranged so that the child does things for himself with minimum difficulty. He should learn to dress and toilet himself. The blind child may be slower in his self-help skills because he does not have the benefit of imitating what he sees; but with help he should be able to accomplish the same tasks other children do. Consistency is especially important in the child's education.

He should be told about objects. When bathing, body parts should be named and touched. Various toys can teach him to discriminate — hard, soft, and so forth. He should be encouraged to use his muscles: climb, run, jump, dig.

SCHOOL

Developing manual dexterity, providing sense-training materials (shape, size, texture, volume), as well as beginning braille are important. The child should be helped to feel pride and self-respect for his skills and abilities. Proper stimulation will enhance social maturity. The child will undoubtedly have established a nonvisual communication system by school age and will also have developed mobility skills. Additional mobility training will, no doubt, be a part of his education. Social experiences are important; blind children are sometimes socially isolated because parents are afraid to allow them freedom.

The following are some suggestions from the Commonwealth of Massachusetts, Department of Education (1962), as to how to react to a blind child.

1. Be matter of fact. Treat him as you do any individual recognizing that he, like a sighted person, varies from others in his likes, dislikes, ability, talents, education, and family background.
2. Address him by name.
3. Make your presence known. Identify yourself if you are a stranger.
4. Let him hold your arm or hand; walk slightly ahead of him so that he can tell what direction you are going in without having to be told.
5. Give him opportunity to become thoroughly acquainted with a new place.
6. Find out how much he can do for himself.
7. Tell him what he is being served and the position of the foods. The clock method for identification of food placement is commonly used.
8. Give specific directions.
9. Leave things where he placed them.
10. Encourage independence.

The visually impaired child, like every child, needs to be accepted and loved. The blind child can tell by tone of voice, manner of touching, and extent to which his needs are met if he is loved and accepted. He needs to feel secure, so he must live in a consistent and fairly orderly family. His contributions as a member of the family must be acknowledged.

The world can be rather complicated without sight. Nurses should help parents adequately meet the needs of their blind child.

REFERENCES

1. Burian, H. M. Strabismus. Am J Nurs 60:653, 1960.
2. Cohen, J. The effects of blindness on children's development. Child, Jan/Feb 1966.
3. Fleming, J. Sensory losses in children. In Bergersen, B. S., Anderson, E. H., Duffey, M., Lohr, M., and Rose, M., eds. Current Concepts in Clinical Nursing. St. Louis, Mosby, 1967.

4. Foote, F., and Gibbons, H. The visually handicapped child. In Smith, H. M., ed. Management of the Handicapped Child. New York, Grune & Stratton, 1957, pp. 126-146.
5. Lowenfeld, B. Our Blind Children: Growing and Learning with them. Springfield, Ill. Charles C Thomas, 1956.
6. Moor, P. M. Suggestions from Training a Blind Child. American Foundation for the Blind, New York.
7. Moor, P. M. Blind children with developmental problems. Child, Jan/Feb 1961.
8. Norris, M. What affects blind children development. Child, July/Aug 1956.
9. Raskin, N. J. Visual disability. In Garrett, J. F., and Levine, E. S., eds. Psychological Practices with the Physically Disabled. New York, Columbia University Press, 1962.
10. Spencer, M. Blind Children in Family and Community. Minneapolis, Minnesota, 1960.
11. Steinzor, L. V. Visually handicapped children: Their attitudes toward blindness. New Outlook for the Blind, Dec. 1966 (reprint).

7

CHILDREN WITH SPEECH AND LANGUAGE DISORDERS

PEARL L. ROSSER,
SHIRLEY M. SCALES, and
CAROLYN H. STEWART

INTRODUCTION

Delayed speech and language development is by far the most common and complex communication disorder of the pediatric age group. At least 10 percent of the nation's children have significant speech, hearing, and language handicaps. One of the most frequent questions the pediatrician and nurse may encounter is "Why isn't Johnny talking?" or "Why doesn't Johnny talk plain [clearly]?" This question is soon followed by "What's wrong with him?" The child whose speech and language development is delayed deserves — and indeed it is imperative that he receive — a detailed pediatric neurophysiologic examination and a speech, language, and hearing evaluation if the various possible etiological factors are to be differentiated, the degree of delay ascertained, and a determination made of the extent to which the problem may be eliminated or measurably reduced. Giving parents some understanding of the developmental pattern of the acquisition of speech and language should be routine practice for all pediatricians and nurse practitioners.

Since early intervention and amelioration are so important, the need for early diagnosis cannot be overemphasized. The objective is to help the child to develop fluent and intelligible speech and to grow up as healthily as possible socially, intellectually, and emotionally. The nurse has a particularly significant role to fulfill in the early identification of children with speech, hearing, and language problems: of all the members of the health team, the child is more often under her sustained, direct observation.

PERSPECTIVE

Most of us tend to regard oral speech and language — with its communication of desires, of ideas, and emotions — as one of the automatic end products of a child's development into adulthood. Our oral repetition of the names of persons, places, and things, our expositions incorporating color, size, texture, sound, and taste, and our indications to children that certain words are symbolic of actions reveal an awareness that speech and language are something to be learned. However, neither the school, the medical clinic, nor our vestigial and fragmented folkways accord oral speech and language usage the primary place in the teaching-learning tasks of infancy and early childhood it deserves until and unless the child fails to talk or talks so unintelligibly that he cannot be understood.

In either of the above eventualities, we can measure the historical progression of our understanding of speech production by the names and treatment that, all too often, have been accorded those who do not speak or who speak with marked imperfection. From exclusion as possessed of devils to objects of repulsion, derision, or pity; from idiots, buffoons, and court fools to the subjects of latter-day comic routines and sticky, hastily applied labels, the nonspeaking and those whose speech is noticeably defective continue to bear the burden of our human failure to know or to act effectively upon what is known.

Perhaps the development of the written word and the making of books as a more durable means of sharing experiences, exchanging ideas, and retrieving and transmitting knowledge between individuals and groups and from one generation to another contributed to deemphasizing the importance of speech, just as the former exclusivity of education and a social and religious awe of the learned heightened the importance of reading and writing. In any case, we have come to overlook the overwhelming evidence that speech continues to be the most widely used, efficient, and convenient communication system developed by man, and to underestimate its importance as an individually acquired, complex, multidimensional behavioral process utilizing anatomical structures and neurophysiologic processes designed to serve other more basic bodily functions. For example, the lungs, whose primary purpose is provision of the body's oxygen supply, provide the breath stream for speech. Similarly the teeth and tongue, intended initially for chewing and swallowing food, articulate the sounds of speech.

Speech develops in a series of time- and growth-related stages dependent upon the original normality and health of these anatomic and neurophysiologic structures, their maturation, and their optimum integrative functioning. The individual human organism must be able to receive stimuli and to utilize them in a complex physical activity involving the coding, sorting, selecting, classifying, organizing, storing, retrieving, associating, integrating, and transmitting of an organized set of linguistic symbols. These symbols which comprise the language system must be taught and learned, directly or indirectly, if the nonmeaningful, reflexive sounds of infancy are to develop into oral sound-symbol associations and vocal productions closely related to our ability to think abstractly and useful as tools of purposeful communication.

Meanwhile, other behaviors and skills and other mental and physical processes must be learned by the developing child. These processes relate to and provide a basis for speech and language acquisition. The child must learn to *hear*, learn to *see*, and learn to use his musculature in developing patterns of movement demanding both gross and fine motor skills — crawling, standing, walking, smelling, tasting, feeling, reaching, touching, grasping, cooing, babbling, echoing, acquiring knowledge from and about the persons, places, and things, the interrelationships and the interactions that comprise his environment, and the human entity that is himself. Thus, speech can be seen as a skill developing in relation to and interdependent with many skills and other growth processes, rather than as an isolated phenomenon that at a given time or within a discreetly defined interval develops in and of itself. This growth and learning does not always proceed uniformly in the individual child, developing equally in all areas at the same time. Neither does this skill's development take place within the same time span for all children. Considerable variation may occur for the individual child in the acquisition of different skills and in achieving the different aspects of growth. Also, variation may even occur between children of the same age and sex. Yet each child may be developing normally.

The professional, whether pediatrician, nurse, or speech pathologist, is charged with the responsibility of considering the speech development of the individual child in relation to his total development: motor, sensory, social, intellectual, and emotional; of assisting parents in differentiating between a speech and language problem and the acquisition and use of an interrelated complex of skills that require additional time for *normal* maturation. These tasks involve not only knowledge of speech and language acquisition as related to progressive stages of child development but increased accuracy in the detection or recognition of speech and language problems needing professional diagnostic referral and/or treatment services.

ETIOLOGICAL FACTORS INVOLVED IN DELAYED SPEECH AND LANGUAGE DEVELOPMENT

Any condition which significantly impairs or disrupts the normal development of the child may disrupt the development of his speech and language skills. Table 7.1 outlines a very useful clinical classification of speech disorders in childhood.

It may be noted that "delayed speech" does not appear as a clinical term because it is not a diagnosis, but merely a broad classification indicating that the child has not acquired speech at an expected time or with the expected accuracy considered appropriate to his chronological age. Diagnosis is concerned with the detection of causes, if possible assessing the degree of severity or functional characteristics of the problem and determining the extent to which the problem may be alleviated or measurably reduced by therapeutic procedures.

Increasingly there is a tendency among those studying speech and language development in the child to define terms in functional or operational terms rather than to apply labels that have proliferated alarmingly, confused therapeutic habilitative or rehabilitative procedures, and, sometimes, drastically limited the possibility of effective management. At the Howard University Child Development Center, we are in substantial agreement with Bangs (1968) that the most useful labels permit the greatest homogeneity in grouping children: "hearing impairment, visual impairment, mental retardation, specific learning disabilities (including aphasia), emotionally

TABLE 7.1. Clinical Classification of Speech Disorders in Childhood[a]

1. **Disorders of Voicing (Dysphonia)**
2. **Disorders of Respiratory Coordination (Dysrhythmia)**
3. **Disorders of Speech Sound Production with Demonstrable Dysfunction or Structural Abnormality of Tongue, Lips, Teeth, or Palate (Dysarthria)**
   a. *Due to neurologic abnormalities*
       upper motor neuron lesions
       nuclear agenesis
       lower motor neuron lesions
       abnormal movement patterns
   b. *Due to local abnormalities*
       jaws and teeth
       tongue
       lips
       palate
       pharynx
       mixed
4. **Disorders of Speech Sound Production Not Attributable to Dysfunction or Structural Abnormalities of Tongue, Lips, Teeth, or Palate, but Associated with Other Disease or Adverse Environmental Factors (Secondary Speech Disorders)**
   a. *Associated with mental defect*
   b. *Associated with hearing defect*
   c. *Associated with true dysphasia*
   d. *Associated with psychiatric disorders*
   e. *Associated with adverse environmental factors*
   f. *Combinations of the above*
5. **Development Speech Disorder Syndrome (Specific Developmental Speech Disorders)**
6. **Mixed Speech Disorders, Comprising Two or More of the Above Categories**

[a]From Ingram. Speech Disorders in children. Pediatr Clin N Amer 15(3), 1968.

disturbed, multiply handicapped, normal, and gifted" for purposes of education, habilitation, or rehabilitation.

The following discussion does not attempt to include all the known or suspected causes of speech delay or deficiency. Only the major ones are briefly considered.

1. *Mental retardation* is by far the most frequently suspected factor in the delayed development of speech and language. However, mentally retarded children usually are slow in developing other skills as well. It is vital to be sure that mental retardation is the cause of the delay, and not the other way around.
2. *Prematurity*, which occurs in significantly higher incidence in lower socio-economic groups, and its associated complications (including minimal organic insults) may affect normal speech and language development. The prematurely born infant of normal mentality, and without organic injury, generally begins to attain normal speech and language function by about age 2 years.

3. *Prolonged hospitalization,* extensive treatment procedures, and serious illness or injury, especially during the first year of life, may delay or distort speech growth.
4. *Neurologic dysfunction,* whether gross or minimal, overt or subtle, congenital or acquired, may be associated with delayed speech and language development. When these skills do develop, they may be quite deficient.
5. *Hearing impairment* usually causes communication disorders. Hearing impairment of even a mild or moderate nature, which is often unrecognized, frequently results in distortions of both receptive and expressive communicative skills.
6. The *tongue* is rarely responsible, though commonly blamed, for speech distortions unless there is some actual structural damage or paralysis. Only in rare instances where the tongue is bound down by an extremely tight frenulum, is surgery ("tongue-clipping") indicated.
7. Some *dental and facial abnormalities* may cause articulatory problems. "Tongue-thrust" is a condition that occurs when the tip of the tongue is forced strongly between the teeth or against the upper incisors during speaking and swallowing. Since swallowing occurs about once every 2 minutes during the waking hours, particularly in the infant and young child, the common oral habit of thrusting the tongue forward during swallowing produces almost continuous lingual pressure on the teeth. This produces forward displacement of the upper incisors causing interference with sibilant sounds, especially *s* and *z*. This condition is usually reversible if detected before the age of 8 years.
8. Hyponasal voice quality may be caused by *excessive adenoid tissue.* However, this rarely interferes with the development of intelligible speech and vocabulary. Removal of the adenoid tissue rarely improves voice quality, and may in some cases produce the opposite problem of hypernasality.
9. *Social, psychologic,* and *environmental conditions* are known to influence all speech and language development be it normal or abnormal. If severe, these conditions most assuredly interfere with speech and language development.
10. Children with cerebral palsy *(abnormalities of neuromuscular function)* are frequently delayed in speech and language development during the first 2 to 3 years, even in the presence of normal mentality. Hypernasality, inadequate voice, and faulty articulation are frequently associated problems.
11. *Structural anomalies of the external speech apparatus* such as cleft lip and cleft palate may interfere with normal voice and speech and language development. Since the immediate visibility of these abnormalities in the newborn frequently creates such anxiety in parents, perhaps a brief discussion concerning them is indicated at this point.

The incidence of developmental abnormalities in speech and language is stated to be anywhere from one in 600 to one in 1250 births (Berry and Eisenson, 1956). Genetic factors are of more importance in cleft lip with or without cleft palate than in cleft palate alone. The incidence of cleft lip with or without cleft palate is about one in 1000 births; of cleft palate alone it is about one in 1500 births. Cleft lip (harelip) with or without cleft palate is more frequent in males, while cleft palate alone is more frequent in females.

The immediate problems of the infant with a cleft lip or palate are feeding and the prevention of aspiration. Surgical repair for cleft lip is usually made at 1 or 2 months of age, after the infant is gaining weight satisfactorily. Since clefts of the palate vary considerably in size, shape, and degree of defect, the timing for surgical repair must be individualized.

The optimal time for palatal surgery varies from 6 months to 5 years of age depending on the need to take advantage of the palatal changes which occur with growth. The goals of surgical repair are (1) union of the cleft parts, (2) intelligible and pleasant speech, and (3) avoidance of injury to the growing maxilla.

INTELLIGENCE AND MINIMAL NEUROPHYSIOLOGIC DYSFUNCTION AS RELATED TO SPEECH AND LANGUAGE DEVELOPMENT

Less than 20 years ago many psychologists and educators believed intelligence to be a fixed entity, and the ability of the child to learn was regarded as determined by this irreversible and immovable limitation. Unfortunately there are still people whose ideas and activities affect society profoundly who continue to cling to the outmoded ideas and educational methodologies to which this concept gave rise. They do so in utter disregard of overwhelming evidence that the tests devised are more valid measures of the limitations of scientific knowledge and the biases of examiners than of that aspect of the structure and functioning of the human nervous system and the brain that has been called "intelligence."

This does not mean that considerable knowledge has not been achieved. A great deal is known about the anatomy of the nervous system and much has been learned about the neuron, or nerve cell, its basic building block. Neuroanatomy, biochemistry, and the relatively new field of neurophysiology continue to add to this store of information and to open exciting and promising avenues of exploration that, in time, may provide answers to today's endless and innumerable questions. At present, we may view our knowledge, our patients, and our pupils with greater humility if we remember that "the complete story of how any single function of the nervous system is carried out remains a mystery." Thus, we are prepared to understand the applicability of the statement by Tina Bangs that "Unfortunately, there is no single, universally accepted meaning for intelligence, and no one universally accepted means for measuring it."

Dr. Bangs likens the numerical intelligence quotient score in its functional relationship to educational management of the child to the numerical thermometer reading in deciding specific treatment for an undertermined illness. In so doing she indicates the importance of functional approaches to education and habilitation of the child based upon such knowledge as is available, such indications as present measures of specific avenues of learning provide, and continuing observation of the individual being taught. New knowledge added to learning theory, new discoveries in brain function, new insights into the effects of environment on learning, and further objective studies of genetic and hereditary influences will continue to challenge those who work in the behavioral sciences, whether as physicians, nurses, psychologists, teachers, or social workers, to continuous incorporation of data and to functional applications of theory and methodology to meet the needs of individuals in a rapidly changing society. Adaptivity and flexibility, operative across a wide range of interrelated disciplines whose findings, points of view, and methods of observation and investigation are synthesized in a holistic developmental approach to the evaluation, habilitation, and rehabilitation of individual dysfunction, will continue to be the hallmarks of reality-oriented, need-fulfilling therapeutic and educational practices.

As intellectual potential was thought to be fixed, brain damage was thought to be irreversible. Eric Denhoff* notes that long-term observation and treatment based on the developmental approach have made it evident that this premise is not borne out by his experiences (Denhoff and Robinault, 1960). Certain characteristics of organic dysfunction disappear with maturation, others are ameliorated or compensations made by surgery, therapy, and training. It is interesting to note that he describes the therapy as "enlightened" and indicates that not only is it predicated upon "the potentialities latent in the child" but upon the "growing resources of the therapist."

This approach and point of view are of particular importance in

---

*Medical Director of the Meeting Street School (a clinic employing the developmental approach for children with syndromes of cerebral dysfunction), Providence, R.I.

the consideration of the speech and language disorders of the so-called "minimally brain injured," "aphasic or aphasoid," or "learning disabled" child in whom the assumption of reversibility is implied; for with this frame of reference, assessment is directed toward determining what can be done to alleviate the problem or to improve the child's overall communicative functioning.

Differential diagnosis requires the combined input of a variety of specialists. In the absence of specific signs of neurologic impairment, the determination of central nervous system dysfunction may depend heavily upon observation of behavioral clues. The symptoms of aphasia, mental retardation, emotional disturbance, and deafness may bear a confusing resemblance, not the least of which is a failure to acquire speech and/or a marked delay in the development of language, including speech.

Aphasia in children refers to the child's inability, or seriously deficient ability, to use symbols for communication. The aphasic child is usually classified as having a problem involving greater or lesser deficiency in any one of three types of language or a combination of these. He may have deficient *expressive* language (the language used to communicate with others in speaking and writing), *receptive* language (the language used to understand what others say — listening and reading, and/or *integrative* language (the language used internally for thinking, reflecting, associating, organizing, selecting). Partial impairment in any one or combination of these is frequently referred to as dysphasia. Rarely does a child have a problem that involves only expressive language. Usually the child with aphasia has reduced ability to understand, store, and/or retrieve language symbols and limited expressive language. However, the primary significance of differentiation of aphasia from other diagnostic classifications relates to the particularity of the child's educational needs.

Many specialists have come to regard the behavioral approach to the language problems of children more fruitful in stimulating educational and remedial procedures than approaches concerned with the pathologic or etiologic aspects of diagnostic differentiation. At the Central Institute for the Deaf in St. Louis, the classification of a child as aphasic is based not only upon consideration of the child's ability in language as compared to his ability in hearing, but also upon observations of his intelligence (the process by which he solves problems, as much as the solutions he achieves) and his response to the social and physical environment. The most important source of information about the child is based on the child's *response to teach-*

ing. Basic to the C.I.D. diagnostic-teaching approach is a completely structured and organized set of procedures for teaching language known as "The McGinnis Method."*

Wood (1964), while advocating attention to behavioral clues for purposes of differentiation, indicates that she is concerned primarily with the way in which the different pathologies of the language-disordered child affect his needs and with educational approaches addressed specifically to alleviation of those revealed needs. Bangs (1968) indicates a like concern for the diagnostic evaluation of those avenues of learning that may or may not be used profitably in remedial or educational procedures, or that require specific procedures for remediation or development.

A long standing concern expressed by specialists who work with and are themselves members of nonwhite racial and ethnic groups is the extent to which unscientific and discriminatory concepts or biases taint the observations and testing instruments used to classify "in" or exclude "out" the children and adults of these groups. Erroneous assessment of so-called nonstandard language systems has resulted in the treatment of "difference" as a pathological condition requiring therapy and the "labeling" of those with racial and ethnic differences as everything from nonverbal to mentally retarded and/or emotionally disturbed. Academic deficiencies resulting from informational lags and limited learning experiences imposed by segregated and discriminatory educational institutions and poverty have all too often found examiners more than willing to diagnose children so disadvantaged as intellectually deficient.

The past 10 years have made some legal and psychosocial changes affecting this "attitudinal set"; however, the habitual responses of individuals often persist long after the concepts from which they were derived have been invalidated and the conditions surrounding them have changed. Thus, specialists should not be surprised to find suspicion and resistance to programs addressed to the special needs of speech- and language-disordered children in these racial and ethnic groups; nor should they relax their vigilance in preventing skewed diagnostic assessments and educational procedures from inflicting further psychosocial and/or speech and language damage on these children.

In this context, the Child Development Center staff has noted the frequency with which black children referred to the Center are pre-

*Named for Mildred McGinnis who pioneered this methodology at the Central Institute for the Deaf, St. Louis, Mo.

diagnosed or labeled as "mentally retarded," whereas our studies and observations reveal specific learning disabilities. Often we find these related to delayed maturation and/or minimal neurophysiologic dysfunctioning. In many such cases, the "labeling" is more often revealing of the unrealistic expectations of parents and teachers, of anxieties, ignorance of growth and development patterns, or of racial and ethnic biases than of observations based on the behavioral functioning of the child. It has not surprised us, therefore, to find that the "learning disabled" child was usually thought to be white and from the socio-economic groups in that population that have been termed "middle-class". We were not surprised to encounter the initial rejection by educated and knowledgeable members of a variety of racial and ethnic groups to the classification and grouping of children in whom gross organic abnormalities or very obvious neurologic signs were often absent. Both attitudes add an extra dimension of challenge to the responsibilities of those concerned with the growth and development of the child with speech and language disorders. It is a challenge that we cannot ignore or fail to meet.

HEARING IMPAIRMENT

Myklebust (1954) has broadened former definitions of hearing deficiency that were limited to a total or partial loss of the ability to hear sounds at varying intensities to include the perceptive and interpretative abilities of the individual in oral communication as well. Normal hearing from this point of view must be predicated not only on gross sound reception by the neuro-anatomic mechanism but upon the total auditory behavior of the individual. This concept has been developed further by Berry and Eisenson (1956) who suggest that to be meaningful in a functional diagnostic sense, hearing must be evaluated in relation to language development, to the maturation of other faculties, to patterns of general growth, and to the powers of reception, interpretation, and integration employed by the individual in processing the sounds used in speech. Differentiation must be made between impaired hearing acuity and central auditory dysfunction (processing).

Continuing study and clinical experience have supported this point of view and directed increased attention to those early developmental stages during which loss of acuity alone may profoundly alter or diminish the ability of the child's neuro-anatomic mechanism to develop those perceptive, interpretative, and integrative processes necessary not only to his speech and language growth but to other aspects of his physiologic and psycho-social functioning. That children of normal intellligence who suffer losses of acuity continue to be referred to specialists as being mentally deficient or as having behavioral problems without having had any significant study made of audition is indicative of the continuing lag between this knowledge and its effective use in preventative intervention.

MEASUREMENT OF HEARING ACUITY

The measurement of hearing acuity is concerned with (1) the intensity level at which sound is perceived, and (2) the ability of the child to discriminate complex sounds, especially those of speech (phonetic discrimination).

If a child perceives sound at hearing levels of 0 to 20 dB at all the frequencies commonly tested in the human speech range (500 to 4000 Hdz), hearing acuity is considered normal. Perception of sound is measured by delivery of puretones at specific frequencies to the auditory apparatus from a standardized audiometer. To measure air conduction, the tone is delivered to the external ear, and for bone conduction it is delivered to the mastoid tip. The intensity of the tone is designated in terms of decibels.

Children found to have losses of 20 dB or more should be referred for further otologic and audiologic evaluation.

TYPES OF HEARING DEFECTS

Hearing defects may be classified as follows:

1. *Conductive defects.* These defects result most commonly from pathologic changes in the middle ear, whether congenital or acquired, such as fluid, adhesions, or other materials in the middle ear. Conductive defects are the most common causes of impairment in hearing acuity in children.
2. *Sensorineural defects.* These result from abnormalities of the inner ear or the auditory nerve.
3. *Central auditory defects.* This type of defect is extremely complex; the cause and pathogenesis are poorly understood. The peripheral auditory apparatus is frequently intact, but the child is unable to interpret or utilize properly the stimulus that is conveyed to him, and exhibits complex problems in communication.

4. *Psychogenic loss of hearing.* This is not uncommon and is often difficult to differentiate from loss due to organic cause. Appropriate specialized audiologic techniques combined with careful clinical appraisal can usually make differentiation possible.

ETIOLOGY OF DEFECTS IN HEARING ACUITY

Hearing defects may be either congenital or acquired.

1. *Congenital.* These include the inherited defects (genetically transmitted), as well as those produced by prenatal and perinatal factors such as maternal infections (rubella), kernicterus, and complications resulting from prematurity.
2. *Acquired.* Most conductive defects are acquired, most commonly from the accumulation of fluid in the middle ear. Sensorineural defects may be acquired also, particularly following meningitis and certain viral infections (mumps, in particular). Certain drugs have specific ototoxic effects, some tending to be age-of-child related.

SCREENING TECHNIQUES

Pure-tone audiometry can be used by trained personnel for gross screening with relative reliability in children from about age 3 years. Procedures for screening younger infants and children have been developed. Some utilize tones delivered at various frequences and intensities; others use such sound generators as tissue paper for high tones and other appropriate noise makers for lower tones. Most such screenings are gross measures and indicators except when administered by a skilled audiologist. Definitive audiologic tests and procedures required referral to a skilled audiologist, particularly when such services as electrogalvanic skin testing procedures and the auditory evoked response techniques of electroencephalography are required, as in the newborn, young infants, and children unable to attend.

EARLY DETECTION AND PARENT COUNSELING

To the extent that increasing numbers of infants and preschool-aged children are seen routinely by nurses and pediatricians who provide continuing health supervision and maintain parental contact, responsibility for early detection, parent counseling, and follow-up must rest with them. In the overall assessment of the child and his family, many factors must be considered: (1) level of stimulation, (2) expectations of the family, (3) health history, and (4) evidence of neuromotor dysfunction (clumsiness, spasticity, rigidity, and the like).

The medical history should inquire into (1) hearing loss in members of the family, complications of pregnancy, delivery, prematurity, and neonatal disease known or even likely to affect auditory development, (2) repeated chronic or acute infections involving the respiratory system (middle ear) and/or the peripheral auditory mechanism in any way, (3) major or minor trauma to the peripheral auditory mechanism (and/or the central nervous system), and (4) ingestions of drugs or chemicals suspected or known to have adverse affects on audition. Children whose histories reveal these conditions should be considered vulnerable and given close and continuing scrutiny and follow-up, including periodic hearing tests.

The developmental assessment is a very useful procedure and should be done routinely. If there is a significant lag in all areas of development this should be noted and the child should be referred for diagnostic evaluation of overall performance. If there is a question in only his ability to hear or speak, this should be spelled out specifically when referral is made to his physician, the audiologist, or the speech pathologist.

Whenever parents report that the infant fails to react to environmental sounds or loud noises, or responds in deviant and unusual ways in situations demanding attentiveness, the pediatrician and nurse should be alerted to the possibility of hearing loss.

Nurses in the community health services and medical personnel in prenatal and well baby clinics may provide prospective and new parents information about normal auditory development. The nurse may detect hearing deficiencies in the infant and young child by employing simple developmental screening techniques.

DEVELOPMENTAL SCREENING TECHNIQUES

Immediately after birth the infant normally responds to sound. Noise will induce a flutter of the eyelid (palpebral reflex). In the very young infant there will be a response to sudden or loud noises: a clapping of the hands, a radio turned up loudly. As early as 4 weeks, attempts to locate the source of sound by turning the head are evidenced. Up to 2 months of age, sudden, moderately loud noises may evoke the startle response (Moro reflex) which includes inhibition of muscular activity, pronation of the hands, eye-blinking, etc.

Repeated testing with knowledge of other behavioral responses may permit a judgment of the newborn's responses to sound. However, a failure to respond may bear little relationship to the infant's ability to hear. A screening audiometer may also be used.

At 2 to 3 months the infant begins to relate vision to hearing and will respond to sound by turning his eyes in the direction of the sound. Sudden loud noises may evoke explosive crying, holding of the breath, a sudden cessation of movement, or any combination of these. Cooing emerges at this age.

From 4 to 6 months sounds do not have to be loud but do have to be within the child's immediate environment at a distance of not more than 3 feet away. Toys such as a bell or rattle or repetition of the baby's name may be used as sound stimuli. The head and upper torso turn toward interesting sounds. The child may smile, frown, or make vocal sounds. Visual cues as to identifying the sounds should be avoided. Toward the end of the fourth month the infant will chuckle and laugh aloud.

If the infant is not observed directly by the nurse in a situation where cooing and chuckling can be elicited, then during the parent interview the mother should be asked how he responds to loud noises, mother's singing, cooing, talking, and the like.

Between 6 months and 1 year the infant not only recognizes sound but traces it to its source. He usually awakens when his mother talks to him and becomes quiet at the sound of her voice.

A variety of sounds can be used — soft rustling noises, quiet rattling sounds, or speech at a very quiet level. Movements or shadows which give visual clues should be eliminated. However, the attention should not be so firmly engaged that he disregards an acoustic stimulus when it is presented.

Testing may be done by one or two persons (infant on mother's lap). The response should be prompt. Delayed reaction may indicate a possible hearing impairment or delayed mental or motor development. Persistent turning of the head to the same side, regardless of where sound is located, also suggests a hearing problem.

Between 1 and 2 years the child responds to quiet, familiar speaking voices and begins to differentiate environmental sounds and the different voices of those who are part of that environment. He may indicate a preference for one over another of his sound-producing toys. Now he understands an increasing number of words and has begun to say some of them. From 3 years onward, given a verbally rich, emotionally supportive, and stimulating environment, the child with normal hearing and healthy, intact neurophysiologic processes will have developed the auditory self-monitoring and listening skills necessary to adequate and continuous development of speech and language.

Testing of the preschool child requires a different technique. Although some children develop the ability to verbalize, the nurse must be aware of the ability to communicate effectively. Can he follow simple directions? Ask the child to point to a familiar object. Does he understand? Can he show that he understands the meaning of simple words and the names of things. For example: "Put the car on the floor." "Put your shoes on." "Bring me the hat."

By the time the child enters school his communication skills should be sophisticated to the degree that he understands and is understood by his parents, peers, and familiar adults.

Parents and professionals may suspect hearing loss when the infant or child:

1. Fails to react to loud, sudden, or strange sounds
2. Makes no attempt to locate the source of sound
3. Seems more aware of movement than of sound
4. Remains at the babbling stage or gradually ceases babbling altogether
5. Becomes attentive and responsive to spoken sounds only when the speaker's face, especially the lips, are visible
6. Is inattentive to things of interest to other children of his age
7. Is only, and sometimes excessively, attentive to loud sound-producing mechanisms whose vibrations are capable of being apprehended tactually or kinesthetically
8. Appears more dependent upon one ear than the other, turning his head or positioning his body so this ear is toward the source of sound
9. Appears to follow directions requiring bodily demonstration by the parent (e.g. pointing to an object) or siblings, particularly family-type rituals engaged in by other members of the household, better than voiced instructions in which there are few, if any, visual clues
10. Reveals strain, puzzlement, confusion, irritability, or unusual fatigue in situations demanding quiet listening
11. Becomes withdrawn or unusually aggressive and/or excessively active in situations requiring that he listen or follow directions for an extended period if he is to know what is expected of him
12. Reacts in catastrophic or "bizarre" ways in unfamiliar situations with strangers, situations which provide even normal-hearing children of his age few ritual "cultural" cues
13. Shows a "pattern" of unresponsive or unusual behavior whenever visual cues are minimal or absent and auditory cues are paramount
14. Replaces babbling with jargonlike speech and unusual vocal patterns, but communicative speech fails to develop

15. Evidences other physical responses and his body becomes a "language" system indicating intelligent and purposeful ways of expressing his wishes and otherwise relating persons, things, and familiar environmental situations

The *otologist, otolaryngologist,* and the *audiologist* enter the picture when an evaluation of the child's organic auditory and speech mechanism is to be made to determine:

1. The ability of these organs to function normally
2. The presence or absence of disease, obstruction, or physical limitation affecting normal function
3. Whether or not there is a hearing loss of developmental significance.

Because hearing is one of our most important senses, a hearing impairment usually produces psychologic problems in almost direct proportion to the severity and nature of the loss and the difficulties the child has in communicating with others and in adjusting to the demands of his environment. In few children is the auditory mechanism so damaged that no hearing remains. The usefulness of this residual hearing determines whether the child's sense of hearing is functional for the ordinary purposes of life.

If a child is born with defective hearing or suffers hearing impairment in the first year or year and a half of his life he will need to be taught to recognize speech on a word-by-word basis through increased reliance on visual and/or tactual clues with minimal auditory assistance. Without early detection and skilled intervention he may never acquire enough speech or language to achieve adequate social functioning.

Case-finding by public health nurses, pediatricians, other physicians, psychologists, psychiatrists, paramedical specialists, and teachers should be continuous and directed not only to locating children who suffer hearing loss, but toward identifying the child who may become hearing-impaired and acting to prevent this. Certain diseases, drugs whose auditory side effects are known or relatively unknown, rising environmental noise levels, and the increasing number of home and automobile accidents represent potential hazards to normal audition that require constant alertness to their implications for the individual child.

Referral may be made to the private specialist, otologist, or otolaryngologist if a comprehensive diagnostic assessment is indicated. Where there is reason to suspect a disease process or serious organic involvement, especially one having a progressively degenerative effect on the auditory or peripheral speech mechanism, such referral is of the utmost importance. Where loss is suspected in a medically stabilized case, the experienced audiologist may determine the extent of the loss and give some indication of its significance to speech and language acquisition.

In most urban areas, location of these specialists does not pose as serious a problem of referral as that faced by persons in rural, sparsely populated places. Although some source of economic assistance and the motivation and encouragement of the parent to seek diagnostic help for the child may present some difficulty in the former situation, the absence of enough trained personnel may be the greatest problem faced in the rural area. However, there is in most states some fairly large hospital complex, a medical association, or educational institution with which contact can be made and from which information can be obtained. Most state universities have speech and hearing departments and many hospitals employ speech and hearing personnel in addition to ear, nose, and throat specialists with whom arrangements may be made, if the referring individual, nurse, physician, or teacher is conscientious in assisting the parents.

Continued efforts to get local, state, and federal agencies to help in making such diagnostic and comprehensive treatment services available to aid citizens is no less important than extraordinary efforts to follow through in making referrals. Here, also, the trained and knowledgeable individual has a duty to perform in raising the level of community awareness to a perceived need and in seeking to bring about those conditions which permit each child, whatever his race or ethnic derivation, to achieve maximum personal and social functioning.

In those communities in which the nurse, pediatrician, or speech pathologist must perform auditory screening, it is imperative that there be more than a superficial orientation in the mechanical manipulation of an audiometer or other gross auditory screening device. Particularly with the preschool child, behavioral observation audiometry, the use of tuning forks, and other noisemakers provide, at best, only very gross indications of the child's auditory capacity and function. In rural areas and among black, Indian, Puerto Rican, and Mexican American populations where measures to eliminate or reduce the causal factors which contribute to conductive loss (perceptive or central) lag considerably, thorough preparation and training in audiological assessment and in knowledge of cultural differences are essential if these populations are not to be as damaged by incompetence as they have been by neglect and discrimination.

It is well not to lose sight of the purpose of all such audiological assessment:

1. To identify and remediate to the greatest extent possible any pathological process affecting audition, language development, and voice and speech production
2. To verify and measure the extent of hearing loss
3. To make a determination as to the nature of the loss and to utilize all such data to provide for the child's health and his educational and psychosocial development.

SPEECH AND LANGUAGE DEVELOPMENT

A knowledge of the patterns of normal child development is the basis of any method of assessment. Any type of disorder is simply a deviation from normal behavior. An understanding of the development of speech and language in relation to other patterns of growth is essential.

Before we consider the normal developmental stages of speech learning, and language acquisition in the mythical average child, a definition of terms is important. Although the terms "speech" and "language" are often used as if they were synonymous, they are nevertheless significantly different parts of the whole process of communication.

Language is an organized system in which symbols catalogue or stand for persons, places, things, ideas, feelings, sensations, events, and all the processes of human interaction with self, other humans, and the environment. Language has developed over a period of many centuries into this system of fixed and changing symbols and the particular rules for combining them into sequences (words, phrases, sentences, etc.) that express our thoughts, emotions, intentions, and experiences. It encompasses what we speak, what we read, and what we write, and is the broader term for an acquired (learned) process of which oral expression is a primary and significant part.

For functional analysis, language may be categorized broadly as being of three types: *expressive* (speaking and writing), *receptive* (listening and reading), and *integrative* (storing, retrieving, associating, organizing, selecting, reflecting, thinking). Dysfunctions, deviations, or deficiencies may appear in any one, several, or all of these categories from birth through adulthood in the life of the individual.

Disorders of language are concerned with the child's inability to perceive linguistic symbols, to combine them meaningfully in words, to understand their meanings in single words and combinations of these, to store them, to retrieve them on demand, and/or to integrate and transmit them purposefully in speaking, reading, and writing.

Speech is the oral production of units of sound combined into words, phrases, and sentences for transmission or communication between individuals and groups. Although the act of speech sound production appears to involve the jaw, tongue, teeth, and lips most obviously, it is a total bodily process utilizing anatomical structures and the systems of the human body in a complex of interdependent and interrelated neurophysiologic and psychosocial interactions. We marvel at the physical coordination and skill of the concert pianist. The oral production of meaningful words and sentences to express an idea or emotion requires a coordinated and integrated complex of mental and physical activity by the most uncelebrated human being that is no less phenomenal.

Reading and writing concern the child's ability to perceive, comprehend, store, and reproduce a complex and structured system of visual or tactual (in the case of the blind) graphic signs (symbols) used to represent oral language — in other words, his ability to understand and to produce abstract symbols of abstract symbols, or symbols to the second power.

Although some languages, French for instance, have developed over the centuries a language to be read and written that is called "literary" and increasingly unrelated to the speech of its citizens, this in no way invalidates the oral language system as the initial referrant for its read and written counterparts or changes the order of the process by which today's child, like his ancestors in earlier times, acquires the spoken, written, and read components of language.

PATTERNS OF SPEECH AND LANGUAGE DEVELOPMENT

In order to perform her role well, the nurse must be familiar with normal growth and development. In the following discussion of the communicative process, age-related and sequential patterns will be given particular attention:

1. *Birth to 3 months:* This is the prelinguistic stage in which the infant makes nonmeaningful, reflexive sounds related to physiologic changes.
2. *3 to 6 months:* This is the period in which infant begins verbal play and responds in a process of autonomic self-stimulation to his own babblings. Most sounds are vowel in character.

3. *6 to 9 months:* This is the period in which environmental speech and language stimulation begins to exert a major influence in accelerating the rate of speech development. During the final stage of this period the infant begins to produce paired syllables incorporating recognizable consonant formations: example: "Da-da", "Mama." These repetitive sounds are not considered "true" speech because they do not refer to and the infant does not associate them with specific persons; however, they are a significant step in the developmental speech process.

4. *18 months to 2 years:* During this period the child begins to associate words with their referrants — to understand that specific words "stand for" or name a variety of persons, places, and things. He acquires a 10-to-20-word vocabulary and begins to utilize these words in phrases. By the time he is two years of age, these become functional sentences. At this time twins may develop an exclusive jargon language system called *idioglossia,* which may require referral to the speech pathologist. This is the stage of confusion, erroneously described as "negativism," in which the child tests meanings by most often responding in opposites: come=go, go=come, yes=no, and no=yes.

5. *2 to 3 years:* Sentences have begun to appear in the child's speech, many of which are structurally complete and indicative of a developing language system incorporating some basic grammatical rules. He has begun to use this speech and language learning purposefully in the management of his environment. However, he continues to "echo" some words without understanding their meanings as he adds to his acquisitions of speech and language. During this phase the question becomes his preferred mode of communication; the labials *p, b,* and *m* are learned as he becomes more perseverative, rigid, and demanding.

6. *3½ to 4 years:* The dental gutteral sounds *t, d, n, k, g,* and *ng* are used with fewer substitutions, omissions, or distortions. At 4 years the child reaches a stage in which much of what he has learned appears to fall apart as if his initially organized developmental structure had come "unglued" to make room for later stages of growth. Physical coordination may be disrupted; hesitations, repetitions, and perseverations plague his speech, and situations mastered previously induce uncertainty. In some learnings he may appear to have reached a standstill or a plateau, and in others to have regressed. Awareness and understanding are essential at this point if anxiety and emotional trauma are to be avoided.

7. *5 years:* The labio-dentals, *f* and *v,* are produced with increasing accuracy.

8. *6 years:* The difficult lip-tongue sounds *l, r, zh,* and *ch* become part of the child's developing mastery of the individual sound components of the words he uses.

9. *7 years:* The more complex lip-tongue sounds *s, z, sh,* and the blends *st, sl,* and *pl* are acquired. By now many children have mastered the difficult three sound blends such as *str* (street), *spr* (spring), *skr* (scrub), and the two *th* sounds.

It is important to note that many adults make the error of expecting the child to produce all speech sounds correctly. However, it has been demonstrated that the speech sounds develop sequentially from the simple sounds to the more complex blends of sounds. For example the *p*, *b*, and *d* are among the first sounds to develop. The *s* and *r* sounds develop later. A blend such as *str* may not develop before the child is 7 years old.

We agree with Sayre (1966): "Pronunciation errors are sometimes confused with speech problems. If a child produces a sound correctly in most words but occasionally omits, substitutes, or adds the sound in a few words, he is probably making a pronunciation error. . . ."

There is a sexual difference in the development of sound. For reasons not yet clearly defined, boys normally develop speech sound more slowly than girls, are more subject to error, and appear to be more prone to speech defects.

PARENT COUNSELING

Parents should be advised that attempts to hasten the developmental process by insisting on the perfect articulation of individual speech sounds, fastidious pronunciation of multisyllabic words, and the production of structurally complete sentences delivered without hesitations and/or repetitions often cause psychologic disturbances which may result in stuttering or in a refusal to talk. Although they may be skilled and experienced speakers, few adults ever achieve such perfection. The expectation that the rapidly changing, unstable, uneven, normally developing anatomic structures and neurophysiologic processes of the child shall do so is *unrealistic.*

Speech and language stimulation by parents, older siblings, or parent surrogates does contribute significantly, however, to the child's development of vocabulary, his sense of language structure, and from ages 6 to 9 months onward to an accelerated rate of speech production. This speech and language stimulation begins when those who handle the infant talk to him — "Now Mama's going to change your diaper." . . . "You're hungry, aren't you?" . . . "There now, isn't that good!" — provide a running commentary on the day's activity; name things to and for the child; describe colors — "the *blue* suit", "your *white* shoes," "your *yellow* socks" — and identify sensations — "My, it's *cold* today. We'd better have some *warm* cereal." "Isn't that a pretty, *soft* blanket."

At the Howard University Child Development Center, speech and language examinations have revealed just such relatively simple descriptive language as indicated above to be most deficient in the speech of children from poor, multiproblem families. Yet this kind of descriptive language is usually part of the parents' known vocabulary. Ethnic language is often rich in the words of imagery, and poverty and limited school attendance do not necessarily rob individuals of this heritage though they may affect the academic or literary formality of the language structure.

Black language is notable for its historic and often poetic incorporation of such descriptive, abstract symbolism in speech production. The language of the Spanish-speaking peoples is no less replete with such terminology. A realm of research could be directed toward identifying the extent to which so-called "standard" English has incorporated into its spoken and written forms words, phrases and sentences derived from black, Puerto Rican, and American Indian Language. An interesting statistical analysis might be made, also, of the number of black Americans who speak these two languages as a matter of course, moving so easily from one to the other or so blending the usages as to be unconscious of the fact. Thus what is or so often seems constricted, and excessively concrete or indicative of limited abstract concepts and vocabularies in poor racial or ethnic group children, may be related to erroneous value judgments by examiners of non-Anglicized, nonacademic speech and grammar, and/or to the failure of parents to appreciate the value and importance of their own language in their person-to-person, hour-to-hour, day-to-day communication with the child from infancy. Here the nurse and pediatrician may play an invaluable role in helping the parent realize that talking to a baby who cannot talk back in one's own language system is teaching and comforting the child and is no less important to healthy growth than his immunizations!

For the older child, picture-alphabet story books, story records, word games, word-card games, etc. provide important additions to the conversation of parent and child. Story records and stories read or told by the parent at a special time each day help to emphasize the importance of listening to a child's speech and language development. While potentially of value, television with its speed of presentation and its inability to repeat often or to explain fully, may result in speech and language confusions and a too-heavily visual dependence before either the sight or hearing of the child have developed sufficiently to utilize these adequately in processing the televised speech and language presented. Thus, the nurse may be called upon to demonstrate to parents or surrogates the uses of these other materials and the important part close observation and imitation of the parents, movements of jaw, tongue and lips and the "slowed-down" listening to models that may be repeated or asked to tell what something means play in speech and language stimulation.

Repeated criticism and correction of the child's pronunciation, articulation, or of his rate of speech production are best avoided altogether. The first goal is *enough words to tell* what the child sees, feels, smells, thinks, tastes, touches, hears; the second goal is *the desire to tell* these things to someone else; the third is enough confidence in himself and the listener *to make telling possible;* and the fourth is the act of *telling as much as he can as often as he can to someone who really listens.* In this fourth step, correction should not interrupt the flow of speech or be directed toward *how* the child says what he says. Rather, the listener should exert himself to understand *what* is being said and to encourage the child to keep on saying. Admonitions to "slow down," "take your time," or "shut up" are likely to be more destructive of the child's speech and language development and self-esteem than any error he could make in pronunciation or articulation.

Twins sometimes present a special problem that is often a matter of legitimate concern to parents and professionals. In some cases, during the 18-to-24-months stage of development, as has already been stated, twins create a communication system, a jargonlike language of their own. This special language, while understood with apparent ease by the two children involved, may be utterly incomprehensible to everyone else and exclusive of parents and other persons.

Twinning seems to have a generally disadvantageous influence upon the speech and language development of the children. They begin to speak later than single children, and until the age of 6 are more retarded in their ability to produce sounds accurately. Their speech is marked by substitutions, omissions, and distortions of sounds for a longer period than that of single siblings. Berry and Eisenson (1956) have speculated that their ability to understand each other reduces their need to communicate with persons around them, a kind of built-in social isolation. Studies of multiple births reveal an excessive incidence of prematurity, low birth weight, and birth traumas, increasing the likelihood that inconspicuous impairments of a neurophysiologic nature and maturational retardation may also account for the later and more difficult acquisition of speech in twins.

Idioglossia requires indirect intervention by the parents of a kind that does not threaten the relationship the twins have, but that permits increased socialization with the parents, siblings, and other persons. Prevention is easier than cure, of course. Thus, activities directed toward individuation and differential relatedness to persons around them with appropriate speech stimulation reduces their mutual "social isolation" as it increases the number and kinds of individual socializing contacts each has with others. Insofar as they develop speech that is used to communicate with parent, siblings, and other persons, their "special" language does not require direct intervention.

REFERRAL AND ASSESSMENT

The criteria for referral of a child for language and speech problems are not as readily standardized as those for hearing problems. For hearing the criteria can be established on the basis of the afore-mentioned observable behavior indicating a failure to respond to general sound phenomena and to specified intensities of sound at specified audio frequencies.

The criteria for referral of a child for a language and speech diagnostic evaluation cannot be established so precisely. The communicative abilities expected of a 4-year-old are not expected of a 2-year-old. The examiner must know the developmental pattern for language acquisition, speech fluency, and articulation so that he can judge whether the discrepancy between the observed speech and language proficiency and the expected proficiency is sufficiently significant to warrant referral to the next step in the case finding program. A rule of thumb for the nurse observer may be "when in doubt, refer" — preferably to a qualified professional.

While procedures for testing the child's communicative abilities are not difficult, the interpretation of results may be, especially if the child has multiple handicaps and is not able to respond in the usual manner. Because some children do not develop the ability to verbalize freely on demand, the nurse must have a repertory of other ways to determine the child's understanding of what is said to him and, if possible, to stimulate some vocal response from him. For example, can the child point to familiar objects on request? Does he repeat the names of things or make sounds in imitation of the nurse? Can he follow simple directions such as "Put the car on the floor." or "Close your eyes."? Out of a carefully prepared "bag of tricks" and with sufficient time to establish familiarity, the nurse may be able to encourage the child to reveal his abilities and limitations in specific situations and to specific stimuli.

By the time the child enters school his communication skills should be sophisticated enough for him to be understood by his parents, peers, and familiar adults within the limits indicated previously.

The importance of the home and family in the growth of speech and language cannot be overstated. Speech defects are usually evident before a child reaches school. Of all the factors that affect language development in children, the home is the most significant, for it is reflected in the personalities of the parents and in their relationships with their children. In this jet age in which we live, there is a tendency for adults to impose stricter demands on young children for earlier and more accurate speech development than ever before. Many parents view effective speech as a status symbol. Not only are children expected to learn to communicate earlier but on a much more complex level.

Parents have a significant role in helping their children develop good speech and communication skills. There are basic procedures which can be of help to both the parents and the child. The parent should understand that speech is not a spontaneous skill that is automatically acquired by the child but the result of a series of learned behavior. Further, the rate of development in children is widely varied within the normal range.

Failure of the child to speak at the usual age causes much more anxiety in the parents than delays in other areas. There is the belief that the child who is slow to talk is not bright. Although it is true that the most common single cause of delayed speech is low mentality, it is dangerous to assume that a child is mentally retarded merely because he does not talk at the age other children do.

Since so much of speech readiness grows out of the child's relations with people around him, it is expected that parents can either help or hamper his progress. Parents should learn as much as they can about how speech develops and what they can do to provide early and rich opportunities for the child to grow.

The home should be a pleasant place in which to live. If the home is hectic and upset, full of tension and conflict, then speech or other development may be hindered. Opportunities should be provided for the child to learn. Language in the home should be a valuable tool for enjoying life — in conversation, through books and play. The child's early attempts to speak should be rewarded but his lapses into gesture should not be rebuffed.

Any physical condition that can affect speech must be corrected. Earaches are danger signals and should not be ignored. Early dental care is important. Parents of children with a speech handicap should learn as much as possible about the defect. They should make every attempt to learn exactly how it affects the child and what can be done to minimize the effects.

Pennington and James (1965) consider the 3-year-old who does not speak well enough to communicate with his parents as a speech-handicapped child and suggest that the parents look objectively at the home in which the child has been expected to learn to talk, questioning their own attitudes toward the child. They list several things that the parents can do that will be helpful to the child. Some of these are discussed below.

1. *Find ways to strengthen your communication with the child.* Do not refuse to understand simply because the child is not using words. This can be damaging to his self-esteem and will not make him speak. Make the child physically sure of your continued presence and love. Encourage meaningful gestures and sounds. Most children without speech, with the exception of the receptive aphasics, can comprehend language and understand what is wanted. Play games that require movement.

2. *Make sure that the child who does not talk is getting enough meaningful and pleasant language experience.* Talk to him using stories, games, and rhymes. When the child is old enough to realize that speech is expected he will often try to speak if he is not forced.

3. *Give the child opportunities for social learning.* The child needs lots of family contact. He should be included in family conversation. Encourage him to play with children of his own age who have his interests.

4. *Reward speech but do not punish the lack of it.*

5. *Add vocalization to gesture.* It need not be speech. Imitate the sound of the animals and of the cars, trains, and planes in the course of the game. During storytime ask the child to make the sound of the animal or machine whenever it appears in the story. Hand puppets may be used in teaching gesture and sound.

6. *Use whatever sound can be made and associate it with some object or action.* The sound need not be a word or name. It will come to have meaning by association, and that is the desired end. Do not try to teach more than one such response at one time. Use a toy which the child manipulates to indicate a word or idea — a stop-and-go signal is excellent.

7. *For the child who communicates by gesture or pointing only, select one particular thing for which a sound must be used as well.*

8. *Make use of the names of other children.* The names of children are often more easily learned than other words. Let the child without speech pass out things to other family members and call the person's name as this is done.

9. *Sometimes it may be valuable to limit the stimuli around the child.* Many children learn better when there are few distractions.

10. *Use all the intelligible speech the child has and build on it.* Give the child who has had little practice in speaking things to say.
11. *Make sure that emotional conflict is not a primary cause.*

PREVENTION

The nurse should be involved in programs of prevention at all stages of the child's life: prenatal, birth, neonatal, infancy, and early childhood. A few preventative measures are discussed below.

GOOD MATERNITY CARE

In order to reduce the incidence of complications and their sequelae, good prenatal care is essential. Of particular importance are the avoidance of infections in the mother during the first trimester of pregnancy, especially syphilis and rubella; early recognition of fetal-maternal blood factor incompatibility; the prevention of conditions causing or predisposing to premature birth; and the avoidance of ototoxic drugs during pregnancy.

The nurse should help the pregnant woman understand the need for early and continued medical supervision and for good nutrition. Counseling should include information on the symptoms of rubella, particularly since the symptoms of this infection can be so mild as to be overlooked if the mother is not alerted. Careful interview is necessary to determine other areas indicative of complications not necessarily disclosed by routine examination and to determine if there are genetic factors to be considered. Further, the nurse should review the patient's record to determine the possible existence of other significant problems. For example, the recognition of fetal-maternal blood factor incompatibilities mentioned previously. The nurse should be aware that in black babies the incidence of ABO incompatibilities may be more frequent than Rh incompatibility.

GOOD MEDICAL AND NURSING ATTENTION
DURING LABOR, AT THE TIME OF DELIVERY,
AND DURING THE NEONATAL PERIOD

The newborn child should be observed carefully prior to leaving the delivery room. The Apgar score is a good indicator of the infant's condition shortly after birth. In the nursery, the newborn should be carefully observed for the early symptoms of hemolytic processes. Early diagnosis will reduce the chance of serious neurologic involvement. The physician should be notified of any jaundice or signs of other illness noted in the infant.

The newborn's ear should be inspected for the presence of any deformity, asymmetry, placement, skin tags, or other anomalies. A malformed ear may be associated with other congenital defects.

Ideally the infant should be observed in the home within the first 4 to 6 weeks. The sometimes nervous parents may be overwhelmed by the care of the child, and firm supportive help from a representative of the health team (the nurse) may make the difference between a child with a healthy personality or a child with an unhealthy personality because of a poor mother-child relationship. A developmental approach should be incorporated into the general observation techniques of the nurse.

HEALTH SERVICE PROGRAMS FOR CHILDREN

Comprehensive programs of health services for children are needed throughout infancy, the preschool, and school-age periods to detect, diagnose, and treat those diseases and conditions which could lead to hearing, language, and learning disabilities.

During the preschool and school-age period the child should be evaluated periodically to determine whether he is progressing within the normal range of development. Immunizations against infectious diseases should be encouraged. The parent should be advised to seek a physician's advice anytime infections or pain in the ear are present. Any abnormal ear conditions should be evaluated by a physician. Infections of this type may lead to deafness, mastoiditis, or meningitis.

WHERE TO TURN

Help may be found for children with communication disorders in college and university speech and hearing clinics, in community speech and hearing facilities, through private certified speech pathologists and audiologists, in departments of special education of public schools, child development programs, rehabilitation centers, medical schools and hospitals, and child guidance centers.

To assure that the speech and hearing specialist is a qualified one, he should be certified (Certificate of Clinical Competence) by the American Speech and Hearing Association.

REFERENCES

1. Bangs, T. E. Language and Learning Disorders. New York, Appleton, 1968.
2. Berry, M. V., and Eisenson, J. Speech Disorders. New York, Appleton, 1956.
3. Denhoff, E., and Robinault, I. P. Cerebral Palsy and Related Disorders. New York, McGraw-Hill, 1960.
4. Myklebust, H. Auditory Disorders of Children. New York, Grune & Stratton, 1954.
5. Nelson, W. E., Vaughan, V. C., and McKay, R. J. Textbook of Pediatrics, 9th ed. Philadelphia, Saunders, 1969.
6. Pennington, R. C., and James, E. For the Parents of a Child Whose Speech is Delayed. Ill. Interstate, 1965.
7. Danville, Sayre, J. M. Helping the Child to Listen and Talk: Suggestions for Parents and Teachers. Danville, Ill., 1966.
8. Wood, N. E. Delayed Speech and Language Development. Engelwood Cliffs, N.J., Prentice-Hall, 1964.

CHILDREN WHO ARE ORTHOPEDICALLY OR NEUROLOGICALLY IMPAIRED

THEORY

Children who are neurologically impaired are best described by their behaviors. These behaviors exist because of supposed organic damage to the brain. However, some of the behavior may be the result of patterns developed in relation to the interpersonal, objective, and social features of the environment. There is a growing concern about the child who has minimal brain damage. The damage is seen as causing behavioral manifestations that keep the child in difficulty with his parents and others. Further, children with cerebral dysfunction often have learning disabilities. Since learning is one of the central tasks of childhood, these children have stimulated much interest in the past few years. Many of them do not have other frank disability or obvious physical stigmata.

Penfield and Rasmussen's (1950) discovery of the "reticular brain stem formation" has led to revision of earlier theories regarding brain functioning. This system or formation is regarded as a type of "feedback" system whereby information coming in can be sent to the cortex and then returned to the midbrain, along with relevant information from the memory and associative areas, so that the midbrain can make the final evaluation and decision as to what action the organism should take.

The second major function of this system is that of an "arousal" mechanism for the cortex. Sensory messages arrive directly to specific parts of the cortex via the projection fibers and also arrive through the tangle thickets of the reticular system to wide cortical areas. This arousal of extensive parts of the cortex seems necessary for the incoming messages to be received in their full association and meaning by the individual.

Hebb (1949) declares that without the arousal system the sensory impulses by direct route reach the sensory cortex but go no further; the rest of the cortex is unaffected and the learned stimulus-response relations are lost.

The reticular activating system has been compared to the volume on a radio. If the control is placed too high or too low the listener's opportunity to learn new information from the radio or to integrate it with established knowledge is tremendously reduced.

Hebb believes that groups of cortical cells, activated at the same time by certain sensory stimuli, can become associated upon constant repetition of that stimuli into functional units called cell assemblies. A large number of these cell assemblies would need to be stimulated for any one perception to occur. Simple perception of a house, cat, or chair would involve large numbers of cell assemblies.

The cell assemblies may in turn become interlaced into more complex functional units which make up a set of closed pathways. If a series of these pathways is stimulated in close temporal association, this stimulation produces a larger functional unit referred to as a phase sequence. Hebb further hypothesizes that the neural activity involved in complex perceptions and conceptions occurs through a superordinate structure formed by recurrent multiple cell-assembly action which he labels as a phase cycle. The phase cycles can integrate stimuli from a variety of sensory avenues which can then produce the phenomenon of a single experience.

The importance of this theoretical notion is that intellect develops through experiences (in addition to maturation) and that changes which can affect the reticular brain stem formation can cause imbalance in the attentional state of that person.

The brain-injured individual usually has perceptual problems. These may be mild or severe depending on the injury. Piaget (1952) reasons that the structure of the organism itself places limits and necessary directions on the types of perception and conceptualization that will be or can be experienced. This certainly supports the view that man orders his environment in certain ways because he is structurally unable to order it differently.

Gibson (1966) classifies sensitivity along functional lines. He describes perceptual systems at length in his work. These systems include the auditory, haptic, taste-smell, and the visual. These classifications are made in terms of modes of attention and not specific energies of the nerves.

A definite pattern of consistency seems to be indicated in brain-injured and non-brain-injured children as far as perceptual discrimination is concerned. Brain-injured children show a strong deficiency in perceiving apparent motion while performing acceptably on tasks demanding perception of motion.

The factors contributing to orthopedic and neurologic problems in young children are generally the same as those in mental retardation. In obtaining historical data the nurse would need information about:

> *Prenatal period.* Any infections or problems the mother may have had such as spotting, and/or hemorrhage, accidents, blood incompatibilities, and vitamin deficiencies
>
> *Perinatal period.* Type of labor (long, precipitate, difficult, and how soon); any complications (toxemia, pelvic malformation, hemorrhage, and so forth); birth of infant — forceps, Caesarean section, anesthesia, cord around neck, breech or difficult presentation, lack of oxygen, prematurity
>
> *Postnatal period.* Severe illness (respiratory infections, encephalitis, meningitis, and so on); traumatic head injuries; convulsions.

In addition to the above, the nurse would also need to obtain information relative to the child's development from birth to the present. Developmental milestone history is a valuable way to evaluate brain development. Family history is also important. In a family where one child has neurologic problems, there are often other children who have similar, milder, or more severe problems. Nutritional information is important if the child appears to be thriving poorly.

Present behavioral functioning is essential to determine, and it is also the parents' chief concern.

It is therefore important that physical factors such as poor nutrition and physical defects, environmental factors such as sensory deprivation and family pressure and psychologic factors must be part of the data the nurse obtains. It should be pointed out here that perceptually impaired children (with learning disabilities) are being discussed as if they do have neurologic damage. The damage may be mild or severe and may be due to lack of complete development or injury. Injury is thought of in the broadest sense as that which may result from environment, physical trauma, or psychologic trauma.

DIAGNOSIS

The orthopedically and neurologically impaired may be faced with learning problems. Therefore laboratory tests concerned with the study of the nervous system are frequently performed. These are necessary to make an adequate diagnosis so that management can be planned. The nurse should help parents understand the various tests that might be done.

X-rays. Skull x-rays and x-rays of the wrist may be done. A skull x-ray may reveal unusual thinness or thickness of the bone. It shows whether the fontanels are the proper size and are in the usual position. X-ray can detect abnormal deposits of calcium which might be indicative of a calcified blood clot or a tumor with calcification in it. Wrist x-rays can tell if normal development is occurring. Bone age is important in determining retarded physical development which may be associated with other conditions. X-rays are one means of detecting conditions but they do not penetrate bone readily and therefore limit the diagnosis of conditions of the nervous system.

Pneumonencephalogram. This test carries the study of x-ray a step farther. In children it is done under anesthesia. Air is injected into the ventricles. The amount of air injected usually depends on the amount of fluid withdrawn and the size of the child. X-rays are then made of the skull and the air shows up the size of the ventricles and any thinning of the brain or lopsidedness of the ventricles.

Arteriogram. This test gives information about the blood vessels or arteries of the brain. Sometimes a child with a large red birthmark on the face or scalp may have abnormal neurologic findings. An arteriogram is then valuable in determining whether or not there is an abnormality of the blood vessels or the circulation of the brain.

Electroencephalogram. The electroencephalogram (EEG) is not as valuable a test as many think because it cannot give very detailed information about an organ so complicated as the brain. It is of value, however, in detecting some types of convulsive disorders. The important thing to tell the parents is that a normal EEG does not mean there is not a problem. There still may be neurologic problems even though the brain wave is normal. An abnormal brain wave may simply represent immaturity or delay in development and does not necessarily mean serious pathology.

Chromosome count. This test is used in suspected or uncertain cases and sometimes to detect carriers. It is not done often because many conditions due to abnormal chromosomal count can be recognized without the test.

Chemical tests. These tests are made to rule out or diagnose certain conditions. Calcium and phosphorous levels may be particularly indicative in orthopedic handicapping conditions.

Thyroid test. This test is done to assure that the child has an adequate amount of thyroid secretion.

Pathologic studies. Muscle and bone biopsies are another means for making diagnosis of the orthopedically impaired.

Electrodiagnostic methods. These are used to detect denervation, to observe reinnervation, to assess the progress of a lesion, and to localize the lesion.

Physical examination. This includes inspection, palpation, passive and active motion of part examined, muscle power, measurement of length of limb, auscultation, and neurologic examination, which consists of sensory and motor components.

Observation. This cannot be overstressed particularly for a child with what appears to be neurologic involvement.

Behavior may be variable depending on where the damage has been done. These children may fall into two broad categories:

Type I may not be identified until the child begins to have learning disabilities. These children are usually identified in the early school years — kindergarten, first, second, or third grade. The background information is usually that of a slow developing child; that is, slow to creep, crawl, walk, and talk. He might have been described as a small or large baby for his age. This type of brain-damaged child is often described as atypical because he appears average except for the slow development of milestones.

Type II is considered a more typical type. These children have motor involvement and are sometimes described as cerebral palsied. These children may have muscular rigidity, spasms, tremors, involuntary movements, abnormal muscle tones, and other physical signs.

PERCEPTUALLY IMPAIRED

The neurologically impaired child with learning disabilities may be referred to as the "perceptually handicapped." Terms such as "minimal brain damage" and "minimal cerebral dysfunction" are also used to describe children with neurologic problems. Parents have described these children in many ways. Listed below are some of the descriptions they have expressed.

"He's stubborn."
"He's moody."
"He will not follow instructions."
"He will not do what is asked."
"He acts like he understands but just won't do what you tell him."
"He does not pay attention."
"He's so active it's hard to keep up with him."
"He's so clumsy."
"He can't keep his mind on anything for a minute."
"He just gets into everything."
"He talks all the time."
"He's constantly bothering things."

Outstanding characteristics of these children are that they:

1. May be below average, average, or above average intellectually
2. Have perceptual-motor deficits
3. Have coordination problems
4. Are hyperkinetic
5. Are impulsive
6. Have emotional lability
7. Have short attention spans

A discussion of each of these characteristics will follow.

INTELLECTUAL ABILITY

These children are usually of average intelligence; many are considered above average or bright. Comments such as, "He's very bright but just doesn't pay attention," are commonly heard.

Some of the school-age children have great difficulty in reading. Reading disorders are a major cause of school failures. Approximately 15 per cent of those who begin school will be slow readers. Causes are variable; one, however, is due to a specific learning disorder labeled *dyslexia*. These children are unable to read or spell at a grade level commensurate with their chronological age. It is important for the nurse to know this because families suspect that the child may have visual problems and are eager to take the child to an ophthalmologist to correct the suspected visual problems.

Difficulty in arithmetic may be slight to great. There may be difficulty in determining left from right. The ability to reproduce designs from memory may be markedly poor. Chances are that comprehension and vocabulary are good even though spelling is poor.

The essential point to make about intellectual abilities is that these children, for the most part, are capable of learning. Because they have problems related to input, integration, mediation, and output, techniques have to be used to help them learn effectively.

Because these children are average to above average intellectually, things are complicated for them because they are misunderstood. Parents and teachers are often exasperated by their behavior which seems to interfere with their performance.

Intellectual manifestations of problems may be as follows:

Receptive Problems. There is difficulty in receiving the impulses of the sensory modalities. This may be shown as (1) hyperactivity, (2) visual perception difficulties, (3) auditory perception difficulties, and (4) body movement problems — directionality problems: reversal of arm movements when imitating; inability to skip with both sides of body.

Inner Problems. There is difficulty integrating information from sensory modalities with previous information to remember, make relationships, categorize, and form concepts. This may be shown by (1) *memory impairments* — has difficulty in remembering words and parts of words out of sequence; difficulty following directions; (2) *language disorders* — lacks words to express experiences; has difficulty putting ideas together to form concepts; seems unable to understand categories; gets things mixed up (symbols and so on); (3) *integration problems* — cannot seem to put together what is seen or heard; cannot coordinate body response with visual or auditory stimuli; seems awkward and clumsy; (4) *expressive problems* — has an inability to give back what has been taken in.

Problems in these areas may indicate difficulty in the cerebral cortex. Having the child make simple geometric forms may be helpful. An 18-month-old child should be able to copy a vertical mark; a 21-month-old, a horizontal mark; a 2-year-old child should be able to replicate a circle; a 3-year-old, a cross; a 4-year-old, a triangle; and by age 5 years, a square.

PERCEPTUAL MOTOR DEFICITS

Figure-Ground. These children may have difficulty perceiving important parts of a picture from the rest of the page. They may pick out minute details but not the whole object itself. There may be confusion and inability to distinguish between figures and background. They seem to be attracted by bright objects and background cues and have difficulty in discriminating whole-part relationships. Some display a strong interest in black-white designs and are often able to copy such designs.

Perseveration. This refers to the notion, behavior, written or spoken, which is continuously repeated. Like a phonograph needle stuck in a groove, the child repeats over and over until he is able to move on to another idea. The child seems to have little control over this type of behavior. Often the child will react to nonessential stimuli rather than to essential stimuli. Actually this behavior is an impediment to adequate functioning. In severe cases of perseveration and echolalia (meaningless repeating back what someone says) emotional disturbances are likely to result.

Laterality. Disturbance in positional relationships may be apparent. The child may be confused as to his left and right. A school-age child should be able to tell the right from the left. Simple ways of testing these are to have the child touch his right eye with his left hand, jump on his left foot, and so on. Note any errors and check these with additional requests.

Disorientation of right and left may be accompanied by finger agnosia. This is best tested by having the child place one hand flat on a sheet of paper. The nurse can draw around it and number the nails one to five on the outline of the hand. Hold the child's hand out of sight, touch one finger, and ask the child to tell what finger from the numbers on the outline was touched. Note errors — particularly hesitations — in children over 8 years old.

Dominance of either the left or right side is essential for reading and smooth motor coordination. Some children with neurologic impairment may have mixed dominance. Observation of the child is the best detector. Note hand and foot preferences while reaching for objects, holding objects, kicking or catching a ball, stepping down, and drawing. The nurse should be cautioned in data-gathering that mixed dominance may simply be a reflection of immaturity. Cranial nerve functioning should be considered when assessing a child suspected of having perceptual-motor difficulties. The nurse may explain through demonstration some of the tests the neurologist will probably perform.

COORDINATION PROBLEMS

These children are often referred to as clumsy and awkward. Special help for the clumsy child is important to prevent secondary emotional problems. The nurse may screen balance and coordination by having the child stand erect with feet together; have child close his eyes and note movement to keep balance; with eyes open and then closed, have child touch his finger to his nose and eye. Problems in coordination and balance would indicate difficulty in the cerebellum.

Distorted concept of self may also be a concern not only because of incoordination but also because of other subtle disturbances and the lack of successes the child may have experienced. These disturbances probably cause the child to feel insecure and anxious about himself and others. His feelings may precipitate him to act in ways that result in negative reactions from others. Having a child draw a person may help the astute nurse in assessing. Note the drawings of children with disturbed body image problems and brain damage. The nurse must be careful not to jump to conclusions based on drawings alone.

Disturbances in sensation may be screened in a number of ways by the nurse. Since a number of these children seem to have mild, tactile disturbances, mention of two tests for tactile sensation will be made. The nurse could have the child close his eyes and on the palm of his hand trace a letter, A, B, C, and so on. Have the child identify a letter that was traced; have the child close his eyes and discriminate various textures — hard, soft, rough, and so forth. Disturbance in sensation would be indicative of problems in the cortical modalities with involvement in the parietal lobe.

The Babinski reflex is perhaps one of the best indicators of neuropathology. In pyramidal tract damage a positive Babinski results. One of the primary roles of the nurse is to help the child and his parents understand what the neurologist will do when he examines the child. The data the nurse gathers during he assessment might also be valuable to share with the neurologist.

Seizures. Seizures or epilepsy may also be a problem that may be placed under perceptual motor problems sometimes seen in brain-damaged children. A seizure, according to Barnett (1968), is an episode of cerebral dysfunction produced by abnormal, excessive neuronal discharges occurring in the brain. Seizures may result from a number of causes, one of which may be brain damage. Seizures are considered a symptom and not a disease. Electroencephalograms are likely to be used to aid in diagnosing location of seizure activity. The nurse should explain to parents the procedure used. Many parents are appalled at what is done, and it can easily be explained. It is helpful to show parents the machine and the paste that will be used to place the electrodes. The seizure may be so mild that it is not perceptible to the casual observer, or it may be severe and intense. It may last from a few seconds to 10 minutes or longer.

The simplest type of seizure is referred to as petit mal. This type is characterized by episodes of momentary loss of consciousness and cessation of voluntary activities for 5 to 15 seconds. The symptoms come on abruptly and leave abruptly. Observation of children with petit mal seizures reveals that they may stare into space and have a blank expression on their face.

A common type of seizure seen in childhood is the psychomotor seizure. The incidence of this type is highest between the ages of 3 and 6 years. The seizure is believed to be in the temporal lobe which may have been damaged during birth. An aura, sensation or experience preceding a seizure is usually associated with the attack. Expression of fear, pain, or alarm may be on the child's face. The seizure may last from a few seconds to several minutes. Jerky movements may be noted and the child may sleep following the attack.

The most common type of seizure seen in childhood is referred to as generalized convulsions. This type of seizure is thought to originate in the centroencephalic structures and to spread rapidly to both hemispheres with immediate loss of consciousness. Both tonic spasms and clonic jerking are seen. The child may cry out sharply and fall to the ground. The muscle contractions are violent; there may be involuntary bowel and bladder evacuation and the tongue may be bitten.

Infantile spasms are usually myoclonic type seizures. Seizures may range from a few a day to several hundred; the onset is 5 to 6 months of age. The cause is sometimes associated with phenylketonuria, pyridoxine deficiency, structural abnormalities, degenerative nervous system disorders, or perinatal brain damage. Steroids and ACTH are the best treatment. Many need other drugs such as those used for grand mal seizures. In cases where pyridoxine deficiency is suspected as the cause, pyridoxine is given. The seizures may subside between the ages of 2 and 5 years. The brain damage is irreversible, and severe mental retardation is usually present.

Self-induced seizures are not common but do occasionally occur in some children. Severe breath-holding in children may result in seizure activity. Children between the ages of 6 months and 2 years may have seizures as a result of breath-holding. The child may have a crying spell, then hold his breath, have apnea with associated cyanosis and loss of consciousness. The EEG is almost always normal. Medication is not the choice of treatment. The condition is associated with behavioral disturbances and the choice of treatment is parental guidance. The child should not be rewarded for this behavior. By the age of 6 the episodes of breath-holding have ceased. There are rare cases where children induce their own seizures when seizures can be precipitated by sensory stimulation such as flashing lights. Family therapy has been reported as an effective means of treatment.

Drugs are given to control the seizure. Undesirable side effects may result, so careful observation of the child receiving drugs is essential. Parents should be told what the side effects are, the importance of giving the drug at the prescribed time as the medication must be adequately spaced to give the maximum effect desired, and not to abruptly discontinue drugs without notifying the physician. Abrupt discontinuation may cause status epilepticus which is the recurrence of convulsions without recovering consciousness between episodes. Approximately 15 percent of the time, death occurs either because of the status epilepticus or the negative effects of sedatives upon the depressed medullary centers.

The nurse should help the parents cope with seizures by suggesting to them that they:

1. Prevent the child from harming himself.
   a. Keep the area around the child clear of hard, sharp, or other objects that may hurt him.
   b. Do not force his mouth open but place a soft object rolled up and placed between the teeth if he opens his mouth.
   c. Put the child on his stomach to prevent choking on saliva or his own tongue.
   d. Place an infant or very young child across the lap with head tilted downward. Gravity will help keep the tongue forward.
   e. Do not allow the child to swim alone, climb trees, or to ride bicycle in heavy traffic areas.
2. Treat the child as they would any child; that is, permit him to be involved in activities similar to those as any other child if he has no other limiting problems.
3. Prevent high fever. There is a high incidence of febrile convulsions in children with seizure disorders. In some instances the first manifestation of epilepsy is a febrile convulsion. At the first sign of an infection the child should be taken to the physician, who might prescribe aspirin, sponging, and phenobarbital for the purpose of reducing the temperature and sedating. Other therapy may be prescribed also.
4. Give drugs as prescribed. The nurse should help parents understand the general principles of anticonvulsant therapy. Drugs commonly used in treatment of seizures are phenobarbital, Dilantin, and Mysoline. Phenobarbital may cause a young child to be irritable and hyperactive but may cause sluggishness in an older child. Overdoses of Dilantin in infants may be indicated by vomiting and irritability; gum hypertrophy may also be seen in children on Dilantin as the drug is excreted via the salivary glands. This should be explained to parents as not an unfavorable sign but one that simply occurs with the drug. Mysoline may cause anorexia as well as irritability. Diazepam (Valium) has been used with a variety of seizure types in children with good to excellent results in suppressing seizures. The

drug seems to be useful in treating petit mal seizures. Drowsiness is the major side effect. These drugs are generally well tolerated by most children once the doses are regulated.

HYPERKINETIC

These children are often described as children who act as if they have "ants in their pants." They are fidgety, constantly in motion, moving from one activity to another. Not all children who have brain damage are hyperactive. Some may be on the other extreme. They may be very slow in moving, talking, and thinking. Either extreme seems frustrating to cope with for the average parent.

In addition to the above, it is important that the nurse assess, with the parents, the duration of the seizure, the pattern of the attack, the frequency of occurrence, the time of day the seizure occurs, precipitating factors and any related events.

IMPULSIVITY

Most of the antisocial acts that are seen in these children result from their impulsiveness. They do not seem to be able to control themselves and seem to be overstimulated by the environment. Very young children appear to have more than the normal child's share of temper tantrums.

EMOTIONAL LABILITY

One mother stated, "One minute he is happy and playing and suddenly for no apparent reason he is crying and upset." There are often quick changes in the emotional behavior of these children. Their reactions seem to be excessive in that they respond too quickly or in an explosive manner. These children may exhibit irritability, insecurity, and be excitable; their reactions may also be unpredictable and inconsistent. They appear to get very upset by things that would not upset other children.

SHORT ATTENTION SPAN

These children seem to be easily distracted and have difficulty concentrating on any one thing. They have difficulty limiting themselves to what they should be seeing, hearing, or doing; they have difficulty distinguishing between what is important at the time and what is not. Not one thing is more demanding of attention than the other. This has been described as *hyperirritability of attention.* Poor judgment seems to also be characteristic of these children.

The hyperactive, emotionally labile, and the child with a short attention span may need pharmacologic help. Drugs are useful in treating many of these children. The notion is that if the child can be calmed down enough, he will be less emotionally labile, will attend more; and if he is in school, will be able to learn better. These drugs, in many instances, have the opposite affect on brain-damaged children than they would on a normal individual. There are controversies about the use of drugs but it is perhaps generally accepted that they do effect change. Side effects of the drugs should be reported immediately to the physician and it should be stressed to parents that the drugs be used exactly as the physician has ordered. Drugs that can alter behavior as these do should be used with utmost caution.

Ritalin is one of the drugs that seems to be commonly used. The drug is a stimulant but calms down hyperactive and inattentive children. Benzedrine and Dexedrine have been used with a great deal of effectiveness in helping the hyperactive, jittery, impulsive, and easily frustrated child. Atarax, Vistaril, and Librium have proven to be of excellent value with children who are jittery and easily upset. There are other drugs that are being used also, but those mentioned are the more commonly used and the ones that present the least side effects.

The nurse should help the parents work with the child in other ways also. Behavior modification may be a means of working with the child, particularly if things in his environment are precipitating much of his behavior. Concrete rather than abstract reasoning should be used with the child.

Extraneous sounds and objects should initially be moved out of the environment of children who are hyperactive or have difficulty maintaining attention. The child should be helped in selecting those things to which he can attend. Gradually an increase in stimulating objects can be reintroduced into the child's world as he will have to learn to live in a world filled with stimulating sights, sounds, and so forth. The child with an impairment that results in his inability to recognize forms, to learn by visual movement or imitation, and who appears awkward and unable to identify left from right may be helped by providing tactile stimulation of forms. (Have the child feel shapes of different objects. Have child learn movements through limb manipulation and auditory cues.)

The nurse can help the family with the child who perserverates or has echolalia by suggesting that a less verbal environment operate in the family. Language should be used in connection with other meaningful stimuli. In other words the child can grasp the meaning of the language when he can see, touch or do something associated with the words. All speech should be accompanied with an activity. Consistency in the use of words must be employed. Language must be associated with visual cues. Some parents have difficulty dealing with a "child that talks all the time" but doesn't say anything meaningful. If the nurse can help the family by using some of the suggested methods above she may prevent parental frustration and perhaps psychotic reactions in the child.

The nurse needs to help parents look for positive skills of the perceptually impaired child. Some of them have highly developed skills in some areas. For example, some children who seem to have figure-ground difficulty and who attend to background details seem to have an unusual ability to find their way out of complicated places. Some seem to enjoy just wandering away on their own. The average child would get lost, but not these children. The ability to manipulate mechanical apparatus seems to be highly developed in some of these children.

There are no clear-cut answers as to how one manages a child with perceptual impairment. There are multiple factors operating within the child and how the child is viewed and handled depends much upon the perception and background of the observer.

Increased knowledge of brain dysfunction and its manifestations makes it possible for these children to have a more sophisticated neurologic examination. Awareness of the relationship between brain dysfunction and perinatal problems, such as hypoxia, nutritional disturbances, and unfavorable social environment, has contributed to greater understanding of the problems. The nurse has great opportunity to contribute to the knowledge in this field. Her emphasis should be toward prevention and management.

The chart on the following page shows some of the causative factors associated with learning disabilities and their preventive corollaries.

The nurse who is involved in helping parents manage these children is likely to be involved in working with other professionals, one of whom will be the educator. Sharing her understanding of the family's home situation might be useful.

> An eight year old boy's teacher referred him to a developmental clinic. The child was doing poorly in school, was constantly taking things from other children and described as "mean and grouchy." The child was discussed in a team conference. The nurse reported the child usually had no breakfast before he left for school. The meals he did have consisted primarily of starchy foods offered at irregular times. The child was put on a breakfast and lunch plan at school. Though the child was diagnosed as having a learning disability he stopped taking things

from other children and was not as "mean and grouchy." The conclusion was that part of his problem was that he was simply hungry.

Learning Disability*

Causative Factors	Preventive Corollaries
Cultural deprivation	Cultural enrichment
Developmental abnormalities	Genetic counselling: prevention of fetal insults. Developmental assessment for early recognition.
Nutritional deprivation	Provision of an adequate diet. Economic improvement.
Physical problems	Preventive health care and early remediation of defects.
Emotional deprivation	Provision of comfortable and stimulating psychologic environment.
Psychiatric disturbance	Favorable environment; preventive child guidance.
Specific educational problems	Early identification; special education and psychologic services.

Start the child off by helping him attend to those things in which he has shown interest; however, try not to provoke the child. Stress his good points and minimize his bad ones. Being positive is important in dealing with the child who is brain damaged. Provide structure for the child. Consistency should be emphasized so that a predictable pattern can emerge for the child. If the parents are inconsistent additional problems are likely to arise. Encourage the parents to have balance in how they treat the child — not overprotecting or rejecting. It is not always easy to work with parents of these children, as often the children seem normal in every way but excessive in their behavioral manifestations. The nurse should support the parents in their attempts to understand and provide structure for these children so that they can grow and develop in the best possible way.

CEREBRAL PALSY

Cerebral palsy is another designation of brain damage in which those affected may behave in quite different ways depending on the location of the damage. Motor disabilities as well as some physical dis-

*Modified from *Learning Disorders in Children.* Report of the Sixty-first Ross Conference on Pediatric Research. Columbus, Ohio, Ross Laboratories, 1971.

ability are evident, as there is a weakness or lack of control of muscles due to a defect in the brain. Paralysis, weakness, overactivity, and incoordination are some of the characteristics that may be seen in children with cerebral palsy. The condition is usually not a result of heredity, but rather most often due to a lack of oxygen to the brain either before birth, during birth, or immediately afterward. Any condition that would alter proper nutrients to the brain of the fetus or infant could result in damage. Cerebral palsied children may or may not have perceptual impairment.

Cerebral palsy has five basic subtypes which aid in describing its reactions.

1. *Spastic.* Usually has stiffness of the muscles. Movement of the extremities is made slowly and with great effort. When attempts are made to bend the various joints, the opposing muscles contract. The motor cortex and pyramidal tracts seem to be the location of the lesion.
2. *Athetoid.* Usually has constant motion of the extremities. The movements of muscles are involuntary and the involuntary movement results in marked incoordination. The basal ganglia and extrapyramidal tracts seem to be the location of the lesion.
3. *Ataxia.* Movements are incoordinated. There is disturbed equilibrium and muscle flaccidity as well as poor muscle tone. The lesion in ataxia is probably subcortical and in the cerebellum.
4. *Rigid.* Muscles of these children are tight, thus diminishing very much motion. Muscle tension is widespread. The damage in this type is probably diffuse.
5. *Tremor.* Rhythmic pattern of constant involuntary movements is evident. The basal ganglia are probably affected.

The child with cerebral palsy, like most exceptional children, will probably be managed by a professional team. The child is likely, however, to have more involvement with a physical therapist than any other professional once diagnosed. The child may receive special exercises, supplemented when necessary by braces or other orthopedic measures such as surgery. Many parents are taught by the physical therapist to carry out exercises in the home, particularly where intensive exercises are required.

The nurse's role in working with families that have cerebral palsied children whose care is being managed primarily by the physical therapist is that of support and health maintenance. The nurse can assist in evaluative the child's problem so that proper aides can be provided. Habilitation is a great part of this child's management. Feeding seems to be one of the more exasperating problems of mothers with young cerebral palsied children.

Positioning is most important in teaching a child with disabilities to eat. The position should be such that it breaks the motor pattern of total hyperextension or hyperflexion of the body and makes it possible for isolated movements of arms, head, jaws, tongue, and lips. The child should be seated comfortably in an upright position or held in an upright position on the mother's lap. To get a child to eat solid food, place a small amount of thick food on the tip of a shallow spoon. Have the child use the lips to remove the food from the spoon. Do not allow the spoon to scrape the upper teeth. In teaching the child to chew, show the child by moving his jaws up and down; then show the child how it is done. The nurse or mother should keep a hand free to aid the child in jaw control. Encourage the child to keep his mouth closed and to use the tongue to move the food around. When teaching the child to swallow, have him move his jaws as little as possible. A child with a severe suckling and swallowing problem should be placed in a prone position for feeding. This brings the mandible, lips, and tongue to a more normal position and better coordination of the organs will result. A banana-shaped bottle may be necessary for feeding in the prone position.

When drinking, the cerebral palsied child may have difficulty adjusting his lips to seal the sides and prevent leaking. He often cannot close the jaws and coordinate the tongue for proper swallowing.

Some cerebral palsy children have intellectual deficits, hearing and speech problems, visual problems, and a large number of them have difficulty with seizures. Management of their problems would naturally depend on what they are. Caring for children with multiple difficulties can be trying. The earlier the intervention the better it is for the child.

ORTHOPEDICALLY IMPAIRED

The so-called orthopedically impaired, in most reference sources, considers a wide range of behaviors and conditions. Physical disabilities resulting from impairment of the bones, joints, or muscles to such an extent that special arrangements or consideration must be made for the child to adequately function are included. Congenital anomalies such as dislocated hip, spinal bifida, scoliosis, congenital amputation, club feet, and so on are examples of the conditions that would be considered orthopedic impairments. Conditions which may have resulted from injury or accidents such as amputations would also be included. Orthopedic conditions which resulted from infectious or degenerative processes such as poliomyelitis, muscular dystrophy, and rheumatoid arthritis are others. These conditions may be aggravated by neglect, disease, or ignorance. The term orthopedically impaired is often broadened to include children with physical impairments such as diabetes, cystic fibrosis, and cardiac problems. This stems from the association of the word cripple with these conditions.

Intellectually, the child with orthopedic impairment abilities may range from superior to inferior. These physically impaired children may have learning disabilities. The disabilities when evident are usually related to cognitive, perceptual, motoric, or environmental factors which complicate or prevent development of skills in spoken or written language, reading, arithmetic, and other academic areas. Though intellectual deficits often accompany physical impairment, the nurse should be aware that many children with severe physical handicaps are quite able intellectually.

Each child must be considered individually. Some have been misdiagnosed as retarded because of motor and/or communication problems which interfere with test performance. Test performance may be below the norm because of time lost from school, limited exposure to the environment, and lower expectations from the child because of his physical disability.

If these children are hospitalized or confined to their homes, arrangements should be made to have the teacher come in to teach them. The hospitalized child's scheduled activities would need to be arranged so that he could participate in a school program. The nurse plays an important role in planning and organizing the child's activities so that he cannot only have time to spend with the teacher but have periods when he can study either with a group of other children or alone. Empathy for the child should not be so extreme that excuses are made and expectations lowered. Exposure to the environment in as many ways as possible is important to the child's development.

Emotionally, many physically disabled children make good adjustments both to their disability and environment. In order to adjust adequately to the disability, the child must not only perceive himself as a worthwhile person but must also believe that others perceive him that way. The nurse will need to explore not only how the child feels about himself but how he thinks others feel about him. The child who is able to accept himself as a worthwhile person with something of value to offer, regardless of the type of disability, will, because of his own self-acceptance and determination, have a better relation with others.

Socially, children with orthopedic disabilities are seen as being less socially mature than physically normal children. Again, however, this seems to be related to the child's acceptance of himself. The well-adjusted, physically disabled child recognizes his limitations and the assistance needed from others. In other words, the child accepts his handicap and reacts positively toward his dependency needs rather than suppressing them.

The nurse should remember that the physically disabled child has the same needs as other children but has limited means for meeting them. Frustration and tolerance may precipitate negative behavior. The frustrated child may respond in one of the following ways: become aggressive either physically or verbally; blame his failure on others; repress his desires and not seek other means of adjustment; abandon an original goal when he cannot achieve it and declare it as unworthy but degrade others who achieve it; withdraw from the task and others; regress and have less mature behavior; and compensate for his disability by finding another interest.

Realistic acceptance of a child with a physical disability constitutes an integral part of the comprehensive management. Parental counseling may help parents better understand and cope with their feelings. The psychologic mechanisms underlying the pathology of parental outlook on the child with a disability may range from overt denial of the disability, through parental impotence in face of it, intellectualized glossing it over, a sense of stigma driving it underground, or parental overprotection compensating for it, to angry ambivalance or guilt-ridden self-blame.

The nurse can help by listening to the parents and discussing misconceptions and fallacies that cause them anxiety and fear. Allowing parents to ventilate their feelings to an individual who has knowledge of the condition may be one of the most beneficial aspects of managing the child with a physical disability. The nurse should be prepared to make subsequent explanations and to interpret and reinterpret to parents to help them achieve realistic acceptance.

MUSCULAR DYSTROPHY

This condition is characterized by symmetrical weakness and atrophy of the muscles and slowly progressive deformity and disability. Most patients are male, and a family history of the disease is common. There are three basic classifications.

1. *Progressive muscular dystrophy (Mendelian recessive).* This is the most common type. The onset is between 3 and 6 years of age. The first symptoms are in the lower extremities with difficulty in walking and a waddling gait. Later, trunk muscle weakness occurs and there is marked lordosis in the upright position.

2. *Juvenile form.* The onset is in late childhood or shortly after adolescence. The muscles of the shoulders and legs are affected first and lordosis and a waddling gait usually result.
3. *Facioscapulohumeral type (Mendelian dominant).* Onset is between 7 and 20 years of age with slow progression. The facial muscles are affected first; expression becomes flat and masklike. The muscles of the shoulder girdle are next affected with appearance of the "winged" scapula and later weakness and atrophy of the muscles of the upper arm. Late involvement of the spinal muscles with lordosis and scoliosis is evident.

There is no specific treatment for this condition. Intensive physical therapy, with the aim of strengthening and improving the function of the unaffected muscles, is usually advised.

POLIOMYELITIS

Poliomyelitis is a condition caused by a virus of the spinal cord and brain stem which in severe form leads to neuron destruction and irreversible muscular paralysis. There are five basic types of polio. However, only two would be of interest from an orthopedic or severe central nervous system involvement. Paralytic poliomyelitis (spinal type) is the type in which paralysis occurs; muscle tightness and pain on stretching may cause malfunctioning of the limb. Bulbar polioencephalitis involves the cranial nerves and the brain system; paralysis occurs. The best treatment for this condition is prevention. Oral vaccine (live virus vaccine) is recommended for persons up to 18 years of age regardless of the number of doses of Salk (inactivated) vaccine they may have already received.

COLLAGEN DISEASES

These diseases comprise a group of disorders characterized by damage to the intercellular ground substance of connective tissue and changes in the collagen fibrils. While connective tissues of all organ systems are usually affected, small blood vessels frequently are also involved. The conditions that we primarily hear of in children falling in this category are rheumatic fever and rheumatoid arthritis.

Juvenile rheumatoid arthritis (Still's disease) may occur insidiously or have a severe onset. The child usually has high fever and polyarthritis. The knee is most often affected. Prevention of deformities is perhaps the most important.

Management may include a range of motion exercises, hot moist packs or hot baths as well as drug therapy. Drug therapy may include use of analgesics, anti-inflammatory drugs, corticosteroids and gold. Side effects of the drugs may be gastro-intestinal disturbances, acid-base imbalance, hypersensitivity, fluid retention, constipation, excessive perspiration, palpitations, Cushingoid changes, easy bruising, and hypertension, to name a few. The side effects of the gold therapy are thought to affect kidneys and blood.

Sometimes these children have to wear braces to aid in immobilizing the involved part. Therapy is aimed at preventing deformity.

Arthritis may be influenced to great extent by emotional factors. Children with arthritis may show marked disturbance in mood and are unable to express their feelings. Allowing these children to work out their hostilities through play and drawing may be very useful.

OTHER DISABILITIES

Conditions such as spina bifida, myelomeningocele, and so on as well as congenital amputations, club feet, congenital dislocation of the hip, scoliosis, and osteomyelitis could be discussed here. It is more important, however, in this book that the nurse be cognizant of assessing for an orthopedic problem and helping parents to manage the treatment.

ASSESSMENT AND MANAGEMENT

In assessing the child with or suspected of having an orthopedic impairment, the nurse should note the following signs:

1. *Posture* Posture of the young child may be a clue to muscle weakness, deformity, and so on.
2. *Body symmetry*
3. *Hips* In infants, dislocation of the hip may be picked up if there is limitation on abduction. In a unilateral dislocation the limb may be shorter than the unaffected limb.
4. *Gait* Balance may be noted. Observe heel-toe movement. Notation of how the shoes appear from wear may also give clues to possible abnormalities.
5. *Weakness of any limb* This may be indicated by limping, inability to grasp and hold articles.
6. *Range of motion of joints*
7. *Alignment of lower limbs*
8. *Any pain and tenderness of joints and limbs*

Management of orthopedic conditions depends on the needs of the child. Treatment is geared toward preventing further problems, enhancing function, and/or restoring function. Often the limb is immobilized so as to prevent further problems. Casts are one means of immobilizing a part. It is important that the cast is supported to prevent sharp angulation which may result in irritation near the edges of the cast. Irritation may be manifested first by discomfort, then by redness or blistering. Prevention of extreme pressure on the soft tissue is also important, as this may cause circulatory impairment. Numbness of a part, a tingling, burning sensation, cold, blanching, cyanosis, and swelling may be indicative of circulatory difficulty. Inability to move a part that previously could move may also be an indication of impaired circulation. Parents should be advised to report any of the above. The limb that is not casted should be protected and kept in good alignment. The physical therapist may prescribe a program and work with the parents. Exercises, gait-training, suggestions for positioning to facilitate normal reactions, and special training programs are the domain of the physical therapist. Prescriptions for drugs, braces, splints, special shoes, physical therapy training, and application of casts are the domain of the physician. The nurse may suggest special apparatus and behavior-modification programs for improving daily living skills. The nurse needs also to support the parents in carrying out a treatment plan prescribed. Many mothers, for example, become perturbed about using the splints because the infants often cry when they first wear them. Mothers need reassurance that the infant has to become used to wearing splints and that they may be uncomfortable initially.

The nurse may teach parents the purpose of and how to care for braces. According to Bloomberg (1964), braces are used for one of the following purposes:

1. To stabilize one or more joints temporarily or permanently.
2. To check motion beyond what the joint is capable of doing.
3. To substitute for the loss of muscle.
4. To prevent injury or abnormal mobility of joint.
5. To prevent further damage.
6. To retain a position obtained by manipulation or surgical procedure.
7. To suspend an extremity and avoid weight bearing.

Braces should be light and non-irritating. The joints should not be noisy and they should be kept clean to avoid obnoxious odors. Between the period when the child puts on braces and the next time he is to return to the brace clinic many things can happen. Saddle soap or any leather cleanser should be used to cleanse the leather portion; it may be necessary to use oil at screw parts of the braces. The canvas pads should be washed. Braces should be aerated when not in use. Since braces are used primarily as a corrective force or a stabilizing force in neuromuscularly disabled children, most parents can see the need for them.

To support parents, nurses often have to explain repeatedly the rationale for treatment. The nurse should be careful that her explanations do not conflict with those of the physician and physical therapist.

MULTIPLE DISABILITIES

Children with multiple physical disabilities are often referred to as the multiply handicapped. Any combination of physical disabilities may result: children with multiple disabilities and cerebral palsy or mental retardation, children with multiple disabilities and seizures, children with multiple disabilities and hearing or visual impairment, children who are deaf, blind, and so on. The rubella epidemic of 1964 which resulted in a number of severely disabled children points to the great need for preventing conditions which can bring about known congenital malformations. Prematurity is another causative factor which may result in multiple disabilities.

In working with families that have children with multiple disabilities the nurse must as always assess the child and determine what can be done to help the child develop his potential so that he can be as independent and fulfilled as is possible. The nurse should be guided by the following principles:

1. The child has the same basic needs as other children in addition to some that are unique because of his special problems.
2. Often multiply disabled children have some difficulty in manipulating and managing their environment because of their unique problems so that the environment must be adapted to meet their special problems as much as possible.
3. That the nurse is only one professional that will probably be involved in the care of these children.

The nurse might be the constant person who helps manage the services to the multiply disabled child and his family. The nurse should keep in mind that it is the child's parents who are the most important people to influence his care. It is essential that parents learn how to help their multiply disabled children develop. Management in the pre-school years should be geared toward ameliorating developmental lags created by slow neuro-motor development and enhancing sensory stimuli that may be minimal because of disabilities in the sensory areas. Management should be toward preparing the pre-school child for academic achievement in the school years. During the early school years the child should be learning the basic skills that will help him eventually prepare for a vocation.

The early years, however, seem to be critical ones. For it is here that the experiences that get the child on a proper course of development are needed. Parents should be encouraged to get these children involved in activities both in the home and out of the home. These children need social interaction and opportunities to move about in the physical world. Many have deficits in sensory experiences. These must be provided for in every way possible. Exploration in the sensory areas cannot be encouraged enough. Most of these children are homebound and have only their families for social interaction. The nurse can become a valuable person to the family if she can help parents plan stimulating programs for these children. The nurse can help parents with how best to manage the family's daily activities so that the multiply disabled child can get the stimulation he needs. Special techniques in such things as feeding, exercising, and social and intellectual stimulation can best assist the parents.

Finally, the nurse needs to understand how the child and his family copes with a physical disability. She should be cognizant of threats to the child's image of himself. The nurse must help the child and his family develop a wholesome concept about the child's body. The nurse needs to know what the child's feelings about himself are as well as how his parents feel about him. Support in this area cannot be minimized.

REFERENCES

1. Ansell, Barbara M. "Rheumatoid Arthritis-Medical Management." Nursing Mirror Sept. 1971 p. 23.
2. Barnett, H. L. Pediatrics, 14th ed. New York, Appleton, 1968, Chap. 18.
3. Bradley, R. C. The Education of Exceptional Children. Wolfe City, Tex., The University Press, 1970.
4. Brewer, Earl J. Juvenile Rheumatoid Arthritis. Philadelphia, Saunders, 1970.
5. Clements, S. D., Lehtinen, L. E., and Lukens, J. E. Children with Minimal Brain Injury. Chicago, Illinois. National Easter Seal Society for Cripple Children and Adults.

6. Cruickshank, W. M. A study of the relation of physical disability to social adjustment. Am J Occup Ther 6:100, 1952.
7. Dave, M. T., and Neil, G. Clumsy children: A disorder of perception and motor organization. Dev Med Child Neurol 12:178, 1970.
8. Geist, H. The Psychological Aspects of Rheumatoid Arthritis. Springfield, Ill., Charles C. Thomas, 1966.
9. Geller, M., and Christoff, N. Diazepam in the treatment of childhood epilepsy. JAMA 215:2087, 1971.
10. Gibson, J. The Senses Considered as Perceptual Systems. Boston, Houghton Mifflin, 1966.
11. Grossman, H. Therapy of childhood seizures. Curr Psychiatr Ther 10:11, 1970.
12. Hahn, E. Problems in tongue behavior of children. Calif, State Dent Assoc., 1966.
13. Haverkamp, L. J. Brain injured children and the school nurse. Sch Health 40:228, 1970.
14. Hebb, D. O. The Organization of Behavior. New York, Wiley, 1949.
15. Kerr, Alice. Orthopedic Nursing Procedures. New York, Springer Pub. Co., 1969.
16. Lewis, R. S. The Brain Injured Child. Chicago, Easter Seal, 1963.
17. Lewis, R. S. Helpful Hints for the Child Who Does Not Chew or Swallow Easily. Santa Fe, N. M., Department of Public Health, Child Development Center, New Mexico.
18. Libo, S., Palmer, C., and Archibald, D. Family group therapy for children with self-induced seizures. Am J Orthopsychiatry 41:506, 1971.
19. Livingston, S. Breath holding spells in children: Differentiation from epileptic attacks. JAMA 212:2231, 1970.
20. McCarthy, M., and McCarthy, J. Learning Disabilities. Boston, Allyn and Bacon, 1971.
21. Mueller, H. A. Pre-speech Evaluation and Therapy. Zurich, Switzerland, 1967 (unpublished paper).
22. Pennfield, W., and Rasmussen, T. The Cerebral Cortex of Man. New York, Macmillan, 1950.
23. Piaget, J. The Origins of Intelligence in Children. Margaret Cook, trans. New York, International, 1952.
24. Pinkerton, P. Parental acceptance of the handicapped child. Dev Med Child Neurol 12:207, 1970.
25. Zieman, H. F. The neurologically handicapped child. Am J Nurs 69:2621, 1969.

9

CHILDREN WHO ARE EMOTIONALLY DISTURBED

LORETTA DENMAN

INTRODUCTION

In the context of this book it becomes necessary to define the term "emotionally disturbed child" since we are discussing in various chapters exceptional children, some of whom may have emotional disturbances associated with their problems. A child is emotionally disturbed when responses to life situations are unsatisfactory to him and inappropriate to his peers and adults. In discussing nursing management of the emotionally disturbed child, references may be made to collaborative roles and therapy in such instances. For the purposes of this chapter, however, the major focus will be on children whose major problems are emotional ones and who may be referred for psychiatric diagnosis and/or therapy to some individual or agency, sometimes by nurses in the community.

Theoretical approaches in child psychiatry are as many and diverse as in adult psychiatry. It is not the purpose of this chapter to explore these in detail. The professional nurse will find employment in a treatment setting which encompasses the philosophy of care to which she can subscribe and implement her specific philosophies in nursing practice. The nurse carrying out the nursing process with disturbed children and/or their significant others should be able to carry out her independent nursing functions just as other professionals do while exercising her dependent functions within the theoretical treatment framework.

Currently the settings in which the child psychiatric nurse functions include residential treatment centers, either schools or hospitals, day care centers, and mental health clinics. A few nurses are in private practice. There are other settings such as public schools or well child clinics in which the child psychiatric nurse specialist may function as a consultant. Nurses in acute care general hospital settings and in the community become involved in the care of emotionally disturbed children also.

The latest diagnostic and statistical manual of mental disorders published by the American Psychiatric Association lists three categories of mental illnesses specifically related to children. The first of these is schizophrenia — childhood type; the second, transient situational disorders or adjustment reactions; and the third, behavioral disorders of childhood. In addition, children may be diagnosed as psychoneurotic. These might be referred to as the legal labels which are applied to disturbed children. Nurses work with the children in terms of presenting behaviors. Rather than discuss each type of disturbance as a separate entity, the developmental periods will be followed, and the disturbed behaviors which might occur and the diagnostic labels under which these behaviors might fall will be identified. The interventions utilized by the nurse in working with the children will be discussed.

Among the factors which the nurse will consider in planning interventions for disturbed children are the constitutional factors which are operating in relation to the child, the experiences the child has had to date in his development, and the social milieu in which the child is developing. Recent genetic studies have shown increasing evidence of the influence of heredity on the behavioral aspects of the organism's functioning. Other psychosocial studies show the importance of the environment in determining the behavioral functioning of the human organism. It becomes important, then, for the nurse to make a complete assessment of the child and his family in order to understand the implications for nursing care in the specific situation.

PREVALENCE

In the foreword of the report, "The Mental Health of the Child", Bertram Brown points out that over half the population of the

United States is under 25 years of age. An estimated 10 percent or more of these require mental health services. While the numbers of adult patients in mental hospitals decline, the first admissions and resident child populations have been increasing steadily. He further points out that only 40 percent of 268,000 children under 18 seen in child guidance clinics actually received treatment; the other 60 percent were merely diagnosed.

The 1966 edition of the Department of Health, Education and Welfare's report, Patients in Mental Institutions, reported 2.6 children under 18 per 100,000 residents in private institutions and 16.9 per 100,000 in state and county institutions, a total of 19.5 children per 100,000. Dr. Brown's report, discussed earlier, implies that this figure is conservative for today's rate. No further figures on out-patient care and/or clinic care for emotionally disturbed children were found.

ETIOLOGY

Most of the studies in etiology have to do with childhood schizophrenia. To date it has been identified that there is no one etiological pattern of development. In fact there is a range of etiology for the differing groups of behaviors exhibited in the childhood schizophrenias. Goldfarb (1961, 1966), in his study of disturbed children, points out that disturbed children with normal neurologic findings have disturbed family situations, while those with neurologic problems tend to have fairly well-adjusted family environments. This is one of the etiological factors of the relationship of neurologic disturbances to schizophrenia as opposed to the environmental influences on the development of childhood schizophrenia.

There are other research reports which suggest that the neurologic disturbances may have a more important causal role than environment in childhood schizophrenia. Research is also being carried on in relation to some of the biochemical factors in schizophrenia. One of the problems in relation to this research is the wide variation of samples and controls which exist, as well as the actual diagnostic methodologies involved. It is difficult to attempt to see any real correlations among the studies underway. Steps are being taken at the Center for Schizophrenia at the National Institute for Mental Health to develop some standards for research which may help to advance the reliability of the studies in the future. Long-term genetic studies, particularly on twins, have been reported from time to time. Here again the variation in procedure does not lend itself to generalizations. There is further genetic research being done, particularly in the structure of genes. Most of these etiological factors now being studied may have influence for the lesser disturbances of children — for instance, the transitional disturbances which occur at important developmental stages as well as the behavioral disturbances (discussed below).

Regardless of the etiological factors which are operating, the child responds as a total organism in a holistic way; and his response is manifested in the particular behaviors which are unique to him as a person. This is the factor which makes a common etiology difficult to presume.

INFANCY AND EARLY CHILDHOOD

One of the difficulties in identifying emotional problems of small infants is the wide variation of so-called baseline or normal behaviors expected at this time in the individual. Behaviors such as refusal to eat, sleeplessness, and crying have a wide range and may be called "normal" in infants. A mother may speak of her child as having been a quiet baby or an active baby or one who cried a lot — comments which in the majority of cases have no meaning in terms of emotional disturbance at a later time. On the other hand, some of these behaviors in retrospect are identified as the beginnings of more severe behavior problems which blossom around the age of 2 or after.

For the young age group, the skill and alertness of the pediatrician and the pediatric nurse clinician, who see infants early and can utilize specific assessment devices available to them, may identify early symptoms of "autistic behavior" or "symbiotic behavior." These behaviors may become more evident later on in the child's life. The most common behavior problems which occur — feeding, sleep disturbances, and crying — may be related to some emotional factors in the mother. Senn (1971) lists a number of such relationships which once recognized can be dealt with and the child's disturbances alleviated. Many of these can be categorized as transient situational disorders of mother and infant.

The child who does not grow and develop within the expected growth pattern may be labeled as a "failure-to-thrive" child. The child is measured against himself and not necessarily compared to other normative standards, except for establishing a baseline for comparing how far the child is from the norm. The child may have delayed skeletal maturation and retarded psychomotor development.

If no physiologic reasons can be determined for the condition, then psychosocial reasons are suspected. Most nurses think of failure to thrive as occurring only in the infant. Senn (1968) points out that it can appear at any age from early infancy to the preschool period. Failure to thrive may also occur in any socio-economic group.

The child who is not developing and growing as he should may be identified before he ends up on a hospital unit. The nurse who sees the child in the clinic or home should pay close attention to how the mother talks about the child and how she handles him. Benedek (1952) discusses the importance of adequate mothering and some of the problems women experience that prevent it. Rhymes (1966) reports on experiences mothers have during the prenatal period that may be factors in their inability to adequately mother. Senn (1968) states that the mother of the "failure-to-thrive" child may have physical and mental health problems herself. Further, she may have been deprived of good nurturing in her childhood because of a chaotic home situation.

Parrish (1971) finds that mothers of infants who were diagnosed as failure to thrive had unclear perception of their infants. Their attitudes were mixed — overprotection, overindulgence, rejection, and acceptance.

Whitten (1972) notes that the relationship between delayed psychologic and emotional development and the lack of maternal stimulation is now firmly established. He states, "Treatment of the mother is as important as treatment of the child."

Mothers who are have difficulty adapting to their infants see them as unattractive, perceive their odor as revolting, hold them away from their bodies, let their heads dangle without support or concern, are disgusted by their sucking sounds, and so on. The mother may be immature or have a stressful situation that she is unable to cope with adequately. The nurse should observe patterns of behavior in the infant and the mother. How does the mother communicate with the infant and feed him? Is she sensitive to the infant's needs? How much body contact exists between mother and infant?

Is the father present? What role does he assume with the infant? Does the mother seem to derive pleasure from the infant and understand his affective states? The father may be minimally involved in the family, and the mother may feel that she has little or no support from him. She may feel burdened and has to cope alone. The part-time or absent father has been evident in several cases of failure-to-thrive infants. Part-time fathers are those who are salesmen or businessmen and make frequent trips out of town. In the latter cases, many of the pregnancies are unexplained and unwanted; in some instances there is marital discord. In cases of the absent fathers in the armed services or serving time in penal institutions, the children are illegitimate.

Financial stress, unemployment, impoverished circumstances, and poor health of the parents are other factors that may be considered in precipitating this condition. Children who are cared for by disinterested servants rather than their parents may not be adequately stimulated; consequently they may fail to mature.

The nurse's role is primarily one of support to the mother. The nurse should encourage the mother to talk about herself and her feelings toward the child. The nurse should praise the mother for the duties she does well. She should suggest that the mother talk to, hold, bathe, and cuddle the child, but the nurse should be prepared to do these also so the mother can see how it is done.

> An infant of a 29-year-old unwed mother was admitted to the nursery and diagnosed as a failure to thrive. This young mother was afraid to hold the baby for fear that she would hurt him.

Many mothers are uncertain about feeding their infants; some underfeed and some overfeed. The infant may respond by being a difficult eater. Mothers need to understand that they are important to the baby and that the baby needs contact with a caring human being. The nurse, says Rhymes, "is usually more effective if she avoids the role of the expert or authority figure and instead engages in a friendly, informal relationship with the mother as an ally or collaborator in the care of the baby. If, in effect, she says to the mother, 'Look, your baby is indeed difficult to feed and comfort, but let's put our heads together and see what we can do to make him happier.' "

The prognosis of the child who fails to thrive is excellent if the parents are able to make the necessary changes in their management. The mother who is mentally ill, however, must be placed under the care of a psychiatrist and the infant's care taken over by a competent individual.

> Janice, a 3-year-old, had no intelligible speech and climbed on people as if they were inanimate objects when she needed to get to an object she wanted. On a home visit Janice was seen sitting in a corner looking up at an unusual light in the family room, smiling. Her mother explained that Janice enjoyed the light and a large ball. The child was diagnosed as being mentally retarded in one child development clinic and as autistic in another.

Behaviorally, autistic children are characterized by extreme withdrawal; they seem to have no interest in people. There is poor interaction with other humans, preoccupation with self, and poor or no verbalization. Echolalia is not uncommon in the preschool autistic child, though many are mute. Parents often report that their autistic child rocks or bangs his head and seems to enjoy rhythmic body movements. The child seems to relate skillfully to objects and has a particular affinity for mechanical objects. Autistic children are often thought of as mentally deficient.

Some believe that autistic children have suffered brain damage, since their behavior is often similar to that of some brain-damaged children. Lack of psychologic stimulation from parents is another theory. Bender (1969) reports on her long-term study of autistic children and describes her concept of "maturational lag" in development. She also points out that a variety of factors produce the behavior and must be taken into account in therapy.

Behavior modification may be one possible way of managing these children in that it will allow for consistency, structure, and a reward system. Rewards should be in the form of physical contact such as a pat, words of approval, and smiles, as well as an opportunity to play with a favorite toy.

Speech should be encouraged by describing things to the child and rewarding his attempts at speech. The autistic child must develop confidence in humans and feel it is worthwhile to have a trusting relationship with them.

Peplau (1967) compares two theoretical approaches to infantile autism, one stressing behavior therapy and the other psychoanalytic theory. She identifies commonalities as well as differences. Pothier (1967) describes her nursing intervention with an autistic child, stressing the analytic approach and delineating the phases of therapeutic interaction.

While there is some divergence of opinion, it seems that the majority of psychiatrists believe that infantile autism is one form of childhood schizophrenia. As the infant grows older he develops additional behavioral characteristics which make it difficult for those who are around him. The autistic child, it has been pointed out, needs structure and consistency in his environment and sometimes sets up rituals which may create problems for the persons with whom he lives. Furniture must be in particular places and certain routines must be observed in relation to eating, sleeping, and daily living.

Schizophrenic children withdraw from the realities surrounding them and participate in fantasy life almost completely. They may or may not be verbal. Some develop their own language which has meaning for them but is unintelligible to others. Schizophrenic children may be impulsive, aggressive, and sometimes self-destructive. Some, however, may simply withdraw and live in their fantasy world without too much acting-out behavior which might be harmful to themselves or others.

Some schizophrenic children, particularly autistic children, have great difficulty in perceiving more than one object at a time. A number of studies have been done on this subject (Ornitz et al., 1970; Senn, 1971).

In the older schizophrenic child, behavior resembles that of the adult schizophrenic. Treatment involves attempting to help the child to return to the real world. This has been done in several ways. In some instances children are seen regularly in the home by a therapist and the parents are guided in terms of handling the behavior of the child.

Behavioral therapy is one of the more promising therapies which is being used more often. The nurse becomes an important person in helping the parents to carry out this type of therapy, in reinforcing appropriate behavior, and using some form of negative reinforcement to attempt to eliminate the unacceptable behaviors. This therapy has been discussed in detail in other chapters of this book.

Nursing has assumed a prominent role in utilizing parents and explaining and supporting them in carrying on such activity. In some instances residential schools and/or hospitals use the same type of therapeutic approach. In addition, most residential schools have special education programs for schizophrenic children, and nursing may be an important factor in helping to control the therapeutic milieu of the institution. The psychiatric nurse specialist may be a major member of the therapeutic team in the overall conduct of the total program.

OTHER PSYCHOTIC BEHAVIOR

Little is reported on other types of psychotic behavior, such as manic-depressive psychosis, as a childhood illness. Some depressive reactions are described at the maturational crisis periods. Psychoneurotic behaviors are evidenced in children. Very often they may not become causes for psychiatric therapy, particularly if the child is able to maintain a fair adjustment in terms of schools and other activities of daily living. However, pediatricians, as well as nurses in hospital settings, may identify neurotic behavior in such children and may need to deal with the behaviors presented. Psychosomatic symptoms are generally identified in these cases.

HYPERKINETIC BEHAVIOR

As the child grows older, behavior patterns become more differentiated; and it is possible to classify behaviors in a more specific way. Jenkins (1969) summarizes the various behavioral disturbances of children which are not psychotic behaviors but which may require therapeutic intervention. He describes hyperkinetic behavior patterns which include muscular overactivity, restlessness, distractibility, mischievous behavior, impulsive behavior, excitability, and a lack of control. Hyperkinetic behavior may be identified in early childhood and continue to occur fairly strongly up to the age of 8 and then gradually lessen so that by the time the child reaches the midteens his hyperactivity has disappeared.

The etiology of this condition has been attributed to constitutional inheritance, social environment, or a combination of both. An organic cause has been postulated because the child simulates the activity of a brain-damaged child. The fact that the condition lessens and disappears makes this diagnosis questionable. The management of this type of child requires a home that is stable, a good deal of parental understanding, and the ability to remain firm and consistent. Rather than to attempt to reduce the activity, it is wise to channel the energy into constructive activity wherever possible to lessen stimulating situations. The nurse can provide support and understanding to parents during this period of activity. Working with the child in a therapeutic environment, she can be instrumental in planning ways to challenge his energy and in providing the consistency and firmness which he needs. Very often, as these children reach school age, they are brought to the attention of the therapist because they become problems in school. In some instances, however, teachers are able to effectively deal with the behavior with the help of the school nurse or a consultant in psychiatry.

WITHDRAWAL PATTERNS OF BEHAVIOR

We have discussed the extreme psychotic withdrawal of schizophrenia. Children, however, particularly between the ages of 5 and 7, may develop a reaction pattern of withdrawal which is not as severe and perhaps not as enduring as schizophrenia. It may affect their behavior to some degree as adults. These children may demonstrate a great deal of shyness and timidity; they may appear rather listless and withdraw from difficult situations; they evidence a good deal of daydreaming and fantasy life and tend to be seclusive, apathetic, and unable to develop the friendships which are common at this age level.

Jenkins points out that these children cannot be defined as autistic. They may, in times of hurt and frustration, turn to this type of thinking as a way of detaching themselves from a situation. Usually this behavior occurs when the child has unsatisfactory relationships with his parents. Perhaps the mother may be ill and the father indifferent; there may be no consistency in the household. If it is a temporary situation, the child may improve as the situation clears up. If the child can be provided an opportunity to develop a relationship through which he can be drawn back to reality and learn to deal effectively with the real world, the prognosis is optimistic. The alternative is that the withdrawal pattern may continue and the child may become a full-blown schizophrenic.

The mental health nurse may be involved in such a family for other reasons. For instance, if there is marital discord, an alcoholic father or mother, or some other health problem, the family may be referred to the community mental health clinic. The nurse should recognize the pattern of withdrawal evident in the child and help through proper intervention at this time. Unfortunately, in such disturbed families the withdrawn child may be overlooked until the withdrawal pattern is firmly fixed. The nurse working with the child can provide a stable, warm, and consistent relationship as a substitute mother figure. Sometimes, if the major problem lies with the child's relationship to his father, a male therapist can provide the type of support and guidance which will help the child to establish a firmer hold on reality and learn to deal with his future problems in a more overt way.

OVERANXIOUS BEHAVIOR PROBLEMS

Children with overanxious patterns of behavior constitute a relatively large group of emotionally disturbed children. The behaviors may include chronic states of anxiety, excessive unrealistic fears, nightmares, sleeplessness, conforming behavior, and approval-seeking behaviors.

A major illustration of this pattern of reaction is the phobic behavior of the school-age child. Some 6-year-olds develop school phobia and are unable to attend school. The anxiety may be that of the mother or father; it may occur particularly in children of middle-class families where the parents are ambitious and have high expectations of their children in terms of behavior and achievement. The child may have the feeling that in order to secure the love and affection of his parents he must meet certain standards and conform. He may have an overdependent attitude in relation to them and may be always trying to please, as this is his main source of security. The coping patterns which the child utilizes in dealing with his anxiety may form the basis for the development of a psychoneurotic reaction pattern later unless, through therapeutic intervention, he is helped to learn new ways of dealing with his problems.

The more severe anxiety reaction may be expressed also through psychosomatic behaviors. Children in extreme anxiety may suffer diarrhea, nausea, headaches, and a variety of other somatic complaints which are expressions of their anxiety in stressful situations.

Recently, at a dancing school recital, one anxious child had an attack of nausea and vomiting at the moment she was to dance out on to the stage. Later, in the same program, another child developed diarrhea. In each instance fond parents were in the audience and expected a high level of performance from their children. These behaviors were fairly consistent reaction patterns which the children exhibited. The parents were asked about the type of help they were receiving for their children. One set of parents said they had been told that the child needed help; it had been recommended that they seek help from the local mental health clinic, which they had rejected. The other couple had not considered the possibility of severe emotional disturbance, but welcomed the idea of seeking help for their child.

Many behaviors characterizing anxiety reactions of children are not so severe that the child is institutionalized. The treatment process may be one of individual psychotherapy, or in some cases therapy through a mental health clinic where the nurse may be the major therapist involved. In either event, the parents will also need counseling. This may become the nurse's function. When we speak of treatment for emotionally disturbed children, we will talk about family therapy as a means of intervention in these disturbances.

RUNAWAY BEHAVIOR

Jenkins describes a group of behaviors in children with emotional disturbances which he labels the "runaway" reaction. He talks about children who are rejected by parents, sometimes even before birth, who are living in inconsistent, harsh family situations in which they are intensely unhappy. They appear apathetic and seclusive; they may be rather furtive and inclined to steal. The pattern may be for the child to steal money in the home and then run away and stay out all night. These behaviors cause them only more unhappiness and discouragement. The treatment by the parents becomes more severe and the family situation becomes increasingly hostile.

In order to treat these children, family therapy is indicated. It may be difficult to initiate therapy. Sometimes the child must be removed from the home. This may entail relatively long placement and treatment in a foster home setting or perhaps an institution. One of the difficulties is that children with a history of running away or stealing are difficult to place in foster homes. However, the runaway child has neither the physical stature nor the temperamental aggressiveness to become an overt delinquent or aggressive child. Jenkins indicates that often they may be the "hangers-on" of a group of delinquents rather than active participants in delinquent or socially unacceptable aggressive behavior.

UNSOCIALIZED AGGRESSIVE BEHAVIOR

Other children rejected by parents may demonstrate unsocialized aggressive behavior such as hostile disobedience, quarrelsomeness, verbal or physical aggressive behavior, destructiveness, and sometimes sexual aggressiveness. There seems to be a lag or lack of socialization and a high frustration response in these children. Studies have found that the parents of such children are unstable and frustrated in their marital relationships and that there has been no consistent acceptance or affection within the family. The child may realize that he was never wanted and has not learned to trust any adult. Because of the marital instability, he is likely to have a step-parent and be an only child.

We cannot discuss emotional disturbances in children without talking about parental behaviors as well. Aggressive children are often somewhat overprotected by their parents. The mother may seek to demonstrate to the public her maternal qualities but actually present it in a way which restricts the child, then frequently shields the child from the natural consequences of his aggressive and delinquent behaviors to protect herself more than to protect the child. Inconsistent punishment of variable severity occurs, which reflects the parents' feelings more than the actual behavior being punished. The parents use various means to control their children by alternating bribery with punishment. There is probably little agreement on discipline within the family.

A common problem among children with aggressive behavior patterns is persistent enuresis. The enuresis is felt to be one of the expressions of hostile frustration of the child against his parents. This may be exacerbated by the parents' punishing reactions to continual bedwetting by the child.

Treatment of the aggressive behavior reaction pattern should be instituted early if it is to be successful. Such behaviors may not be brought to the attention of therapists or be recognized by the family as an emotional disturbance until the patterns are well established. The family reaction to the behaviors is well ingrained so there is an abnormal behavior pattern continually recurring. Treatment involves managing the child in an entirely new way and working with the parents. The mother, who may be very unhappy in her marriage, will need a great deal of emotional support and guidance in order to change her behavior. Sometimes this is not possible and the child may be institutionalized in a hospital or in another type of treatment setting, perhaps a foster home; therapy may be instituted with the parents.

In dealing with the institutionalized child, the nurse must be firm, accepting, and warm, and set limits and demonstrate to the patient that one cannot be bullied by aggressiveness. The limits set on the child's behavior must be explained so that he can understand and accept the fact that discipline is stressed out of concern for him and not as a punishment. If treatment is not instituted or is unsuccessful, the extreme of the behavior may be the psychopathic personality.

LATE CHILDHOOD AND EARLY ADOLESCENCE

Most of the emotional disturbances of early childhood which we have discussed may be carried over to late childhood and adolescence. In addition, we see a great deal more neurotic reactions, phobic behavior patterns in adolescence, aggressive patterns, and delinquent behavior, which we have not discussed in detail. Delinquent behaviors such as gang delinquency, stealing, truancy, and drug abuse will be discussed in the chapter on social disability.

Many problems which we have discussed may become more prominent or may continue into adolescence. Bender (1968) points out, for instance, that only about one-quarter of the childhood schizophrenics are able to progress to the point where they seem to be leading adequate social lives in a community. The others are described as living in the community but poorly adjusted, or living in residential treatment centers or other institutions. While the adolescent in his earlier childhood may have had behavioral problems, they may not have been of such severity as to require therapy. The stress of adolescence and the identity crisis which occurs at this time may exaggerate the symptoms so that they require psychiatric intervention. During this period, schizophrenic reactions may occur or emotional disturbances may take the form of full-blown psychosomatic reactions. There is a good deal of sexual acting-out behavior, and various delinquency problems are common. The latter are discussed in the chapter on social disability.

Adolescence is the time of heterosexual confusion for a great many children. It would appear that this uneasiness is greatly compounded by some of today's happenings in relation to sexuality — for instance, the Gay-Lib Movement and the transexual surgery which is becoming more and more publicized throughout the country.

DRUG ABUSE

Drug abuse is found largely in the adolescent group; however, there is also evidence that younger children are testing out the use of drugs and some have become pushers. This is discussed further in the chapter on social disability.

Another major problem in adolescence is suicide. In the past decade the number of suicides among adolescents has increased by 60 per cent, and recent figures show that there is an increasing number of suicides in the younger age group as well.

Mattson et al. (1970) report that of 170 child psychiatric emergencies seen at University Hospital Clinics in Cleveland, 75 were due to suicidal behavior — 70 of them between the ages of 12 and 18. Major precipitating factors for the suicidal behaviors were conflict with parental figures, grief reactions, school conflicts, sexual conflicts, and pregnancy. Depression signs had been evidenced for some weeks prior to the attempts in most cases. The authors suggested that community educational efforts toward early identification of potentially self-destructive children and adolescents be initiated.

TREATMENT OF EMOTIONAL DISTURBANCES

INTENSIVE PSYCHOTHERAPY AND RESIDENTIAL TREATMENT

Shaw and Lucas (1970) list psychotherapy and intensive residential treatment as the major therapy modalities for emotionally disturbed children. They indicate, however, that in their setting less than 10 per cent of the patients seen become in-patients and about 20 per cent receive out-patient care. Disposition of other cases through referral to other treatment settings is common.

The child who is seen in intensive psychotherapy is one out of ten, and the one being seen is usually selected in terms of his willingness and his capability for engaging in this type of interaction. Therapists who are frankly selective vary in the criteria which they use. The type of psychotherapy may also vary from therapist to therapist, but almost universely "play therapy" has become a part of the psychotherapeutic interaction. Here again it may vary according to the therapist. Some use only dolls and allow the child to play and manipulate the dolls as he desires. Others may want to structure the type of play the child is engaging in. Still others use a variety of games and toys and may or may not structure the activity with these. Nurses have used this technique successfully in working with disturbed children.

Individual psychotherapy may be a part of the treatment in the intensive residential unit for the child or it may be done on an out-patient basis. While originally it was felt that only psychiatrists and perhaps clinical psychologists were capable of doing psychotherapy, persons engaging in such activity now include social workers and well-prepared and experienced psychiatric nurses. They follow essentially the same techniques used by psychiatrists and function in residential settings, out-patient clinics, mental health clinics, and other facilities. They, too, may be selective of their patients as are the psychiatrists in working with behavioral problems in which they intervene according to their skill and experiences. The intensive residential treatment unit usually operates on the concept of therapeutic milieu (Shaw, 1970) in which all of the personnel are considered part of the patient's therapy. Very often, group therapy may be employed; individual psychotherapy, play therapy, and a variety of other treatment techniques are utilized within the context of the therapeutic environment, with people acting consistently for and with the patient.

Units utilizing behavior-modification techniques have trained personnel in this technique. When this form of therapy is utilized, the family must be helped to learn patterns of positive and negative reinforcement so that they can carry on the therapy when the child returns to the family. Schaefer and Martin (1969) have developed a rather complete discussion of behavioral therapy in a very practical way. There are a number of other articles which describe some of the particular ways in which behavioral therapy and behavioral modification is carried on.

TREATMENT OF THE CHILD WHO REMAINS AT HOME

As was noted, only three out of ten children may receive individual psychotherapy or in-patient care in intensive settings. After diagnosis many children are returned to the home environment and a treatment program is developed for them within that context. If they are unable to attend regular school sessions, plans may be made for placing them in special public school classes. This is not always possible, and current reports indicate that existing programs are often inadequate for many types of emotionally disturbed children. Progress has been made in terms of special classes for mentally retarded children, but children with other disturbances find great difficulty in obtaining adequate learning experiences. Special tutoring is another form of education which may be utilized. This is expensive for some individuals. Day schools such as the League School in Brooklyn are being organized, which contribute greatly to the therapy of disturbed children.

Kysar (1968) believes that mental health professionals generalize that pathologic parent-child relationships have brought about the child's emotional disturbance and that only removal of the child from the home will help. Kysar, the father of a severely disturbed child himself, and other parents have established a private day school for disturbed children as an alternative to continuous institutionalization. He cites the success of the League School as a precedent.

When the child remains home, the family is going to need a great deal of support and therapy. This is provided in a variety of ways. When there is a nurse available, she can counsel parents, particularly in terms of helping them to learn ways of dealing with their children. If behavior therapy is used, she can demonstrate ways of instituting the treatment and can support the parents in carrying it out. Parents may engage in group psychotherapy through a clinic, hospital, or with private therapists.

TREATMENT IN OTHER TYPES OF INSTITUTIONS

The child who is removed from the home, if not placed in an intensive residential treatment center, may be institutionalized in a private or public mental hospital, a juvenile detention center in certain cases, or in a boarding home or school. Treatment may vary in intensity, and in some cases custodial care may be the focus. The institutional stay may be lengthy, often permanent.

FAMILY THERAPY

Ackerman (1972) defines family therapy as a dimension of family healing, which has been going on for centuries, and describes the status of the treatment today. He lists ten forms of therapy and indicates his belief that the future of this form of treatment holds much promise.

Zilback et al. (1972) believe that the young child should be included in family therapy. They point out ways in which his participation may be facilitated. They suggest three guiding principles: (1) the child must be respected as a person, (2) no one is obliged to answer any questions, and (3) the language is kept simple so the child understands. Play activities for the child (or children) are made available to further facilitate participation and to lessen the child's anxiety. Ferber and Ranz (1972) have described treatment of a family by way of a case study highlighting the major events in the ongoing therapy. The complete volume, edited by Sager and Kaplan, presents some of the latest concepts, theories, and findings regarding group and family therapy. Getty and Shannon (1967), Bulbulyan (1969), and Smith and Mills (1969) have written of their experiences as family therapists and have demonstrated that nurses can be effective in this form of therapeutic intervention.

Ostendorf (1967) describes the nurse's role in the treatment of a schizophrenic child in the home, particularly in helping the family accept him and his illness. Coffman (1969) has discussed the significance of anger on the part of the nurse in a children's residential treatment center, indicating the importance of demonstrating to the child that the nurse is affected by his actions and concerned by them.

DRUG THERAPY

In most therapeutic regimes for disturbed behavior, drug therapy is an important aspect of treatment. Tranquilizers and mood elevators have been beneficial in reducing disturbing behaviors to levels which can be more effectively managed through other therapeutic techniques.

Eisenberg (1964) studied the effect of psychoactive drugs and/or brief psychotherapy on neurotic and hyperkinetic children. Brief psychotherapy seems more effective with neurotics, while stimulating drugs seem to be more effective in reducing hyperkinetic behavior.

One of the dangers in the use of drugs with children is that side effects may cause undue harm if they are not identified and dealt with. Nurses working with children undergoing such therapy must be well versed in the nature of drug effects and be responsive to the children's reactions. If the children are at home, parents will need help in interpreting their children's responses to drugs.

The nursing aspects specifically directed toward the emotional disturbances under consideration have been discussed. It is not to be construed that the problems of daily living and the normal developmental needs of such children are neglected. The total needs of the patients and their families, which are within the province of nursing care, are assumed to be a part of the nursing care plan which the nurse develops and implements.

To this writer, the best intervention and treatment for any emotionally disturbed child is prevention. With great emphasis on the nurse as the primary care agent, it appears that opportunity for detection of early signs pointing toward emotional disturbances are an important nursing function. There is a growing amount of information on family dynamics, mental health, normal growth, and development for both professional and lay people. Community mental health centers are providing educational programs to community groups, schools, and individuals.

REFERENCES

1. Ackerman, N. The growing edge of family therapy. In Sager and Kaplan, eds. Progress on Group and Family Therapy. New York, Brunner/Mazed, 1972, pp. 440-456.
2. Bender, L. Childhood schizophrenia: A review. Psychiat 5:211, 1968.
3. Bender, L. A longitudinal study of schizophrenic children with autism. Hosp Community Psychiatry Aug., 1969.
4. Benedek, T. Mothering and nuturing. School of Nursing, University of Pittsburgh. (unpublished paper.)
5. Benedek, T. Psychosexual Functions in Women. New York, Ronald, 1952.
6. Bernard, B. When a child's distress is a family affair. Nurs Clin N Am S:677, 1970. Brown, B. The Mental Health of the Child. National Institute of Mental Health, Rockville, Maryland, June, 1971, p. viii.
7. Bulbulyan, A. A. The psychiatric nurse as family therapist. Perspect Psychiatr Care, 7:2:58-68, 1969.
8. Coffman, J. A. Anger: Its significance for nurses who work with emotionally disturbed children. Perspect Psychiatr Care 7(3):104, 1969.
9. Department of Health, Education, and Welfare. Patients in Mental Institutions. Washington, D.C., 1966.
10. Eisenberg, L. Role of drugs in treating disturbed children. Child 5, 1964.
11. Ferber, A., and Range, J. How to succeed in family therapy. In Sager and Kaplan, eds. Progress on Group and Family Therapy. New York, Brunner/Mazed, 1972, pp. 346-375.
12. Getty, C., and Shannon, A. M. Nurses as co-therapists in a family therapy setting. Perspect Psychiatr Care 5(1):36, 1967.
13. Goldfarb, W. Childhood Schizophrenia. Cambridge, Harvard, 1961.
14. Goldfarb, W. et al. Treatment of childhood schizophrenia: A three year comparison of day and residential treatment. Arch Gen Psychiatry, 1966.
15. Harris, F. G. A psychiatric nursing experience with a troubled child in the community. Perspect Psychiatr Care 5(2):92, 1967.
16. Jackson, D. Etiology of Schizophrenia. New York, Basic Books, 1959.
17. Jenkins, R. L. Classification of behavior problems of children. Am J Psychiatry, Feb., pp. 125-28, 1969.

18. Johnson, K. Hyperkinetic syndrome in children. Nurs Mirror 128:21, 1969.
19. Kanner, L. Child Psychiatry, 3rd ed. Springfield, Ill., Charles C Thomas, 1957.
20. Kysar, J. E. Reactions of professionals to disturbed children and their parents. Arch Gen Psychiatry 19, 1968.
21. Masserman, J. H., ed. Individual and Family Dynamics. New York, Grune & Stratton, 1959.
22. Mattson, A. et al. Suicidal behavior as a child psychiatric emergency. In Chess and Thomas, eds. Annual Progress in Child Psychiatry and Child Development, New York, Brunner/Mazed Inc., 1970.
23. Mayer, G., and Hoover, M. When Children Need Special Help with Emotional Problems. New York, Child Study, 1967.
24. Montanari, A. J. A community-based residential program for disturbed children. Hosp Community Psychiatry, Apr., 1969.
25. Mosher, L., and Feinsilver, D. Special Report: Schizophrenia. Rockville, Md., U.S. Department Health, Education, and Welfare, 1971.
26. Ornitz, E. et al. Environmental modification of autistic behavior. Arch Gen Psychiatry, 22:560, 1970.
27. Ostendorf, M. J. The public health nurse's role in helping a family to cope with mental health problems. Perspect Psychiatr Care 5:5, 1967.
28. Parent-Child Relationship's Role of the Nurse. New Jersey, Rutgers, 1968.
29. Parrish, B. An Exploratory Study To Examine Concepts and Attitudes of Mothers Who Have Infants with a Diagnosis of Failure to Thrive. Lexington, Kent. University of Kentucky, College of Nursing, 1971 (Unpublished master's paper.)
30. Peplau, L. Infantile autism. Perspect Psychiatr Care 5:3, 1967.
31. Pothier, P. C. Individual therapy with a mute autistic child. Perspect Psychiatr Care 5:3, 1967.
32. Rhymes, J. P. Working with mothers and babies who fail to thrive. Am J Nurs 66:1972, 1966.
33. Robison, O. L., Dahgleish, K. B., and Egan, M. H. The treatment of school phobic children and their families. Perspect Psychiatr Care 5(5):219, 1967.
34. Sager, C. J., and Kaplan, H. S., eds. Progress in Group and Family Therapy. New York, Brunner/Mazed, 1972.
35. Schaefer, H. H., and Martin, P. L. Behavioral Therapy. New York, McGraw-Hill, 1969.
36. Segal, J., ed. The Mental Health of the Child. Rockville, Md. National Institute of Health, 1971.
37. Senn, M. Infantile Autism. Conference Presentation, University of Kentucky, College of Medicine, April, 1971.
38. Senn, M., and Solnit, A. J. Problems in Child Behavior and Development. Philadelphia, Lea & Febiger, 1968.
39. Shaw, C. R., and Lucas, A. The Psychiatric Disorders of Childhood, 2nd ed. New York, Appleton, 1970.
40. Smith, L. E., and Mills, B. L. Intervention techniques and unhealthy family patterns. Perspect Psychiatr Care 7:3, 1969.
41. Troffert, D. A. Epidemology of infantile autism. Arch Gen Psychiatr 22:431, 1970.
42. Whitten, C. F. T.L.C. and the hungry child. Nurt Today 7:10, 1972.
43. Williams, F. Intervention in maturational crises. Perspect Psychiatr Care 9:6, 1971.
44. Zilbach, J. J., Bergel, E., and Gass, C. The role of the young child in family therapy. In Sager and Kaplan, eds. Progress on Group and Family Therapy. New York, Brunner/Mazed, 1972, pp. 385-399.

10

CHILDREN WITH SOCIAL DISABILITY

DAVID A. SABATINO

Central to the function of nursing is the recognition of the patient's specific disability or disabilities. Awareness that a patient has a definitive handicap, chronic illness, or acute problem that needs immediate attention alters the type of nursing service provided for that individual. The problem in discussing social maladjustment is to acquaint the nurse with the means of identifying the socially disturbed child and youth, while showing the differences between this group and children who exhibit normal adjustment reactions. The critical question with which a nurse is faced when a child displays hostility, extreme aggressiveness, or withdrawn behavioral symptoms is a determination of the child's adjustment processes. No two individuals, when confronted by stress, react similarly. The normal process of adjusting to life, especially in a developing child, includes reactions that are frequently magnified out of proportion according to the standards of the adult world. Hospitalization, preparation for surgery, and convalescence are unique experiences to most children. They can be quite stressful, overwhelming the child with the fear of threat to his personal or emotional well-being.

Any situation which is threat-producing to a child poses a possible danger to his physical or emotional well-being. The child entering the hospital for surgery may feel no threat from the fear of separation from his mother for the first time. However, a child may feel a real threat to his other emotional supporting structures, such as his home, his person, or his feelings, and this imagined threat can result in an emotional reaction. This emotional reaction is itself an adjustment process. Adjustment implies that a child is interacting in a satisfactory manner to a particular environment or environmental situation in which he finds himself. Within a given period of time, all of us adjust or readjust to constant environmental changes. For the majority of children, maladjustment is a temporary process which will pass with the time that it takes to remove the threat and residual anxiety.

Children seem to survive and even grow emotionally from interactions in situations where they may express emotionality. The rules which govern behavior in our society sometimes provide situations in which a person may exhibit anger, fear, affective warmth, or hostility and still be seen as showing normal adaptive mechanisms. The particular situation is all important. A soldier may display extreme emotionality under wartime conditions and still be considered as showing normal behavior. However, the same reaction by the same man in a peacetime office situation in which the stress may be equally as great would be evidencing maladaptive behavior under society's rules.

SOCIAL VS. EMOTIONAL MALADJUSTMENT

There seem to be two important yet different concepts involved in this situation: emotional and social maladjustment. For the sake of clarity, we may generally distinguish social maladjustment from emotional maladjustment by examining the interaction of the individual under stress in a situation.

Basically, an emotionally maladjusted child lives with total disregard for most social-environmental situational interactions. Such children are inhibited from adjusting to a given social situation by faulty operating adjustment mechanisms expressed in extremes of overt behavior, ranging from aggressive destruction of self or others, to total withdrawal from people and things. Emotional maladjustment is neither temporal nor related to the immediate situation or environment.

Social maladjustment or adjustment, on the other hand, tends to be ephemeral and dependent upon, or interrelated with, the context of the immediate environment. It is generally regarded as a difficulty in interpreting societal rules and an inability or unwillingness to adapt to a particular environmental situation. Such children are unable to control overt observable behavior such as aggressiveness, withdrawal, and other attention-getting behaviors. The most common example of social maladjustment is seen in delinquent acts committed by juveniles. One description of this concept is discussed by Pate (1963).

> *Socially maladjusted* children are chronic juvenile offenders who regularly disregard broader social values and rules as a matter of course, substituting in their stead the values and rules of their peer group. They make up delinquent gangs who are constantly in trouble with the law. Their accepted code of conduct is truancy, fighting, and defiance against constituted authority. Socially maladjusted children are handicapped by their provincial patterns of social values. *(p. 240)*

The nurse must recognize that psychosocial adaptation of a given individual to his environment represents a total adjustment process. That is, each person is influenced by how well he thinks he feels, what is happening in his immediate family and vocational life, as well as his ability to use psychologic adjustment mechanisms. Any one of the major systems that influence the way we feel mentally and how we adjust psychologically will, in turn, promote or inhibit that adjustment process. Equally important, the overt or observable behaviors are not always what they seem. The *pseudoadjustment phenomena* are real. Such phenomena are associated with the attempt to project the state of being well adjusted and happy when, in fact, one is troubled to some degree. But even more prevalent is the substitution of socially acceptable physical symptoms, selected from established patterns of illness, to cover feelings that the patient senses he cannot express. The hidden feelings, or covert behavioral expressions, are much more serious since they represent some aspect of his life that needs help or assistance. The nurse, interested in interacting with the total person, must be concerned with this process of total adjustment. She must realize that the reason that feelings are being hidden is that the patient thinks he cannot be accepted for how he feels. His social adjustment must be good, so he may safely evidence health problems. The process takes shape even in the adjustment patterns of young children; if little boys get physically hurt, they are expected "not to cry." Therefore, nurses must be willing to develop some systematic way of looking at human adjustment and raising questions about how each aspect is interacting to promote or inhibit that process. One approach is to examine such major components of psychosocial adaptation as biologic, sociocultural, and psychologic concerns. Figure 10.1 attempts to describe some of these and indicates the importance of each one in that total, ongoing process called psychosocial adaptation.

The adaptation of man to his environment is dependent upon several identifiable features or variables. The biologic factor includes

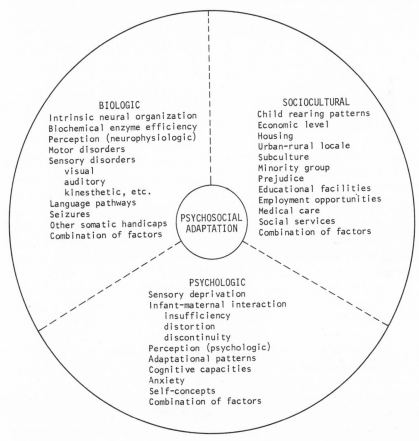

FIG. 1. Major components of psychosocial adaptation. (From Richmond. J.A.M.A. 191:3, 1965. Courtesy of the author and the American Medical Association.)

how his body performs, the absence or presence of physical pain, and his sensory function. These are basic to his view of self and, consequently, his view of the world. Not all children want to be football players but some would like to be, feeling the need for the same social recognition that football players receive. Physically, a boy may not have the size or endurance to play. Therefore, he must adapt to the situation or else enter a nonadjusted phase of living. The type of environment he grows up in and the abilities he has or lacks render him more or less adjusted to societal pressures. More importantly, however, is the total interaction of the biologic, sociocultural, and psychologic factors into a combined complexity which represents adaptation. Thus, the boy who wants to play football displays these three broad concerns.

The high school senior girl, wanting to be a nurse, may have been reared in a rural setting devoid of the cultural characteristics that promote vocabulary development. She enters school with a poorly developed speech and language pattern and consequently may become a poor reader. Frequently the poor reader dislikes reading and school. Her elementary grades deprive her of the opportunity to take algebra, physics, and chemistry. As a senior, her applications for nurse's education are rejected. This result is due to several biologic, sociocultural, and psychologic variables interacting together. Now, at 18 years of age, she must readjust her dreams and her life style or suffer frustration. Whether she can readjust to being a nurse's aid or accepting a position in the kitchen of a hospital depends upon the strength and balance of the psycho-social adaptive mechanisms.

The astute nurse begins to organize human behavior into patterns that may be associated with varying difficulties in any one area. She will better understand human behavior by perceiving some systematic relationship in the psychosocial adaptation process.

TYPES OF SOCIAL MALADJUSTMENT

Social maladjustment is generally related to social values and how or if these values have been learned. The three classifying conditions are known as *asocial*, *dysocial*, and *antisocial*.

Asocial means without knowledge of social rules or morals and is evidenced in the example of a 5-year-old child in a hospital outpatient clinic for a preschool examination. He has little language except vulgarities, grunts, and gestures. His overt behavior is filled with gross, aggressive acts of hitting, biting, and kicking. His social adjustment is comparable to the "negativism" characteristic of a 2-year-old, and yet he has a performance (nonlanguage) of normal intelligence on several commonly used standardized tests. The case history shows that he had been in seven different homes, never knew his father, and had multiple mothering as a result of living with various women for short periods of time (no longer than 14 months). In short, he does not know how to act appropriately. He is without knowledge of the rules of society, even those normally incorporated into the working repertoire of a normal 5-year-old child.

The next societal conflict is referred to as *dysocial*, in which the person is presented with two positions of equal importance reflecting different values. The child learns that a given rule is never to be broken. That is, he should never steal from others. Upon entrance to school, he finds that the children from other homes steal; and these children have regard for one rule only — that it is wrong to be caught. The child in question is now confronted with dysocial values, that is, two opposing views which seemingly apply to the same social situation.

The third type, or *antisocial* condition, is more characteristic of how most delinquents, who are brought to the attention of the court, are viewed by the public. The antisocial youth has learned from some source a value consistent with those taught by society. But as a result of gang or personal pressure, he violates that value, resulting in confrontation with societal norms and the law.

Two other diagnostic categories associated with social disability are *character disorders* and *transient situational personality disorders.*

Character disorders are manifested as habitual types of behaviors which generally draw unfavorable attention to the person. They are not representative of either mental retardation or psychopathology; the person is not mentally disturbed. Character disorders may be more accurately described as an individual's possession of some behavioral characteristic that disturbs others. An example is the child described as having a "mean streak"; he bullies smaller children. He does not have a mental disorder in that his behavior is driven by neurotic anxieties. He seemingly likes to boss, direct, and influence weak and smaller children, perhaps because he cannot express this personal need with children his own age.

The following example distinguishes the character disorder from the psychopathologic personality disorder. One child expresses aggressive, hostile behavior in a socially disapproved manner by bullying smaller children. Another child tends to withdraw, unable to express his frustrations and hostility openly, and displays such behavior as building and lighting fires in homes. The former displays a character disorder while the latter exhibits a more serious personality disorder.

There is a large grey boundary between the child who recognizes that he should not "pick on" children smaller than he and the withdrawn child whose anxiety drives him to express feelings that he cannot explain and seemingly has no power to control. Between the character disorder and acute personality disorder is the area of *transient situational personality disorder*. It falls under the heading of social maladjustment and not emotional maladjustment because of its transient nature. The most important characteristic of the transient situational personality disorder is that the child frequently displays the more severe manifestation associated with neurotic anxieties, but the resulting overt behaviors can be explained in rational terms by the child (as contrasted to an emotional rationale) and understood by the nurse when the pieces of information are brought together.

WITHDRAWAL-AGGRESSION CONTINUUM

A general rule of thumb in the management of a child's reaction to a stressful situation (such as hospitalization or leaving his mother) is to isolate the triggering mechanism. Once the situational pressure is understood and manipulated by both the nurse and the child a relationship can be established that will reduce the feelings involved and promote a security base from which the child can further reduce other stresses. If this does not happen, then the child will attempt to manipulate and test the situation more and more to determine the points from which the pressures originate. This type of transient situational maladjustment is frequently associated with passive-aggressive and passive-withdrawn personality disorders. The child expressing a passive-aggressive personality is under repeated anxiety attacks, well controlled for the most part, but he defends against these anxiety attacks by seeking a more passive state which contrasts with the aggressive behavior he displays when anxiety-ridden. To offset a buildup of anxiety he finds an outlet for his frustration at selected times: In the presence of the school principal he breaks a window for reasons not apparent to him; on a child twice his size he displays physical force in the restroom after recess for no apparent reason. In the hospital he may be the perfect patient for 3 days; the afternoon before he is to return to a stress-filled home he resumes his antisocial behavior. While he seems tense, but able to express himself and talk about various problems, he suddenly manifests an aggressive or withdrawn act for which he seemingly wants punishment.

This series of behaviors is caused in part by his inability to understand and isolate his anxiety-inducing problem, which is real and has a situational base. At the same time he has foreboding fears of another anxiety buildup which may not have any basis in reality. This combination results in the transient passing of behavior from a passive state to an overt withdrawn or overt aggressive state.

Most children with such problems constantly draw attention to themselves in schools, hospitals, and society in general. It is difficult to generalize about the etiology of such pathology, but several of the more common reasons are rejection by parents, inability to meet parental expectancy, fears promoted by unsuccessful social interaction, academic or athletic failure, and fears instilled by peers or parents. The problem in treating such a child is the simultaneous needs he imposes for acceptance, punishment, and a consistent structure to guide his life's activities.

JUVENILE DELINQUENCY

One of the major categories of social disability is juvenile delinquency. Social cultural problems are so closely related to delinquency that "delinquency appears most frequently in areas where there is poverty, adult crime, or a constellation of community values that are grouped under the names of 'anomie' or 'social disorganization.' " (Eisner, 1969) Susceptibility to the influences of physical and intellectual capability or family background could determine the degree of delinquency or conformity. There have been attempts to reconcile apparent inconsistencies in the vast amount of research on the individual delinquent, his social group, and his community. Explanations on how these forces interact generally tend to caution us that neither sociologic nor psychologic explanations of delinquency are complete by themselves. Personality and social pressures are also important determinants of delinquency behavior.

The tendency of societies to "label" human behavior presents a number of problems in actually discerning "who is a delinquent, who is not, and what should be done about it." (Kvaraceus, 1964) Pointing to the legality of the term delinquency, Quay (1965) believes that "it is the most sensible, useful, and independent definition of the behavior to which the word refers, and should maintain a focus upon the legal sense of its meaning." By his definition:

> The delinquent, then, would be a person whose misbehavior is a relatively serious legal offense, which is inappropriate to his level of development; is not committed as a result of extremely low intellect, intracranial organic pathology, or severe mental or metabolic dysfunction; and is alien to the culture in which he has been reared. Whether or not the individual is apprehended or legally adjudicated is not crucial. *(Page 12)*

Delinquency is related to misbehavior, but not all misbehavior is delinquency, even when considered inappropriate for the age of the individual. Both the quality of the behavior and the degree of social deviance are factors in judging an act delinquent or trivial on the one hand, or delinquent or psychopathologic on the other. In essence, Quay prefers to use the term delinquent on a universal basis to eliminate any ambiguity when discussing such behavior.

IMPORTANT CONSIDERATIONS IN DELINQUENCY

Sex. In most western countries the ratio of male delinquents to female delinquents assumes a standard rate of 6:1, while in other countries it rises as high as 10:1. Parsons (1947) has written that the sex ratio illustrates the most demonstrative difference in societies' role assignment for the sexes. For example, in some situations it is quite possible for a society to look favorably on adventurous male activities such as stealing and "joy-riding" in a stolen car. It may be an assertion of masculinity to commit such acts, while to feel obedient and display good behavior are feminine qualities inculcated in women. This is true of boys' feelings toward their mothers at puberty. The stronger the mother's control, the stronger the act of breaking it. Consequently, many crimes are committed by children from low socio-economic areas, since the father image is usually absent and the mother "assumes" the dominant role. Generally the type of crime committed by a lower class girl is quite different from that of a boy from the same socio-economic milieu.

Age. The age at which the individual commits his primary deviant act is most important. In their classic study, Glueck and Glueck (1956) found that, on the whole, if the acts of delinquency begin very early in life they are abandoned at relatively early stages of adulthood. Conversely, they also found if such acts begin later they may be abandoned later provided the natural processes of maturation are not interfered with by a treatment agency, school, nurse, etc. These two statements are generalities, and exceptions can by expected. In most western countries, delinquency has decreased in mean age. In fact, in the industrial countries adult crime has decreased, while juvenile crime has increased. The incidence of delinquency is highest in most countries during early adolescence, ages 14 to 16. In fact, a mean age of 14 years is common to many countries. By age 21 the amount of criminal activity decreases quite substantially; however, the severity of the crime usually increases with age.

Social Class. Social class, subclass, or subculture influences what we learn to accept as socially correct. Cohen (1965) writes, "What we see when we look at the delinquent subcultures . . . is that it is nonutilitarian, malicious, and negative (p. 25)." It is defined by its "negative polarity" to the norms of "respectable society." What happens in the delinquent subcultures is that they take their norms from the culture at large, reversing these values until what was good, according to society, is now bad. The delinquent's conduct is normal by the values of his subculture, yet these values are wrong according to the larger culture. In short, the basic values of a delinquent may represent an entirely different set of norms than those which are standard in the conventional society.

Delinquency or any form of antisocial behavior is seemingly the result of sociologic and familial influences. The home represents the primary social subcultural environment in which the parents, by their presence or absence, establish the tone and conditions. The individuality of the interaction between a child and his immediate environment should convince us of the difficulty of discussing any such "generalization" or "categorization" of people or conditions. The difference between delinquent children and a delinquent child is that the latter can be discussed in the light of the particular events that have interacted to produce the resulting behavior which society has labeled as inappropriate. This is precisely what many researchers caution about generalizing from data on groups of children. To speak with some knowledge about a particular individual, or a particular act at a specific time committed by him, precise observations must be made in reference to the causative factors, time, events, and place that the behavior occurred.

In studies of children from the same high-risk neighborhood in various cities, many probation officers and case workers have observed that brothers in the same family were equally divided in regard to their respect for social values. Frequently, a policeman, minister, and hardened criminal came from the same family. The obvious fact is that no two people are alike genetically. Therefore, if it were possible to cast an ideal environment within the home and school, it could not be ideal for more than one person. The mother who works to treat all her children alike, denying one a birthday party because his brother does not want one, has not treated her children as individuals, but has denied one the very consideration that would have promoted his social growth. On the other hand, to force both brothers to have birthday parties would be just as inequitable, especially if one brother were as socially retiring as the other is socially outgoing.

Family breakdowns are occurring with increasing regularity as evidenced by the rise in divorce rate, changes in role relationships among family members, and the social disorganization of advancing urbanization. Delinquency is also increasing steadily, which may suggest a relationship in the antecedent factors related to both family stability and the social adjustment of children. Except for Orientals and blacks, delinquency occurs about twice as frequently among the children of immigrants as among those of native-born parents (Conger and Miller, 1966). Parental prestige, the foreign language factor, and the change from a simple rural to a complex urban environment are all contributing factors. First-generation parents may themselves have difficulty adapting to the new environment. Parental inability to guide their children, due to their own limited experience in a new cultural setting, may itself contribute to a role model deficiency. A middle-class culture frequently restricts boys from lower classes in the achievement of material possession; Cloward and Ohlin (1960) considered this matter. They noted that delinquents repeatedly wanted "big cars," "flashy clothes," and "swell dames."

> These symbols of success, framed primarily in economic terms rather than in terms of middle-class life styles, suggest . . . that the participants in delinquency subcultures are seeking higher status within their own cultural milieu. If legitimate paths to higher status become restricted, then the delinquent subculture provides alternative avenues. *(Page 96)*

Other studies have shown delinquents to be either highly motivated to obtain material possessions and comforts (Cartwright, Howard, and Short, 1966) or frustrated by a lack of economic and social status. They cite the emphasis in gang membership among lower class youths as one way of meeting the needs for feelings of personal worth and peer acceptance to overcome what they feel are deficiencies in material possessions and social position.

INCIDENCE OF SOCIAL MALADJUSTMENT

The purpose of examining delinquency in some detail was to acquaint the reader with the factors that are associated with it. However, there are many socially troubled youths who do not violate society's values but who are presented with problems that interfere with their own adjustment.

In 1954, MacFarlane, Allen, and Honzik reported data collected longitudinally since 1929 on 252 children who were part of a Berkeley survey. The survey drew its sample from one of every three children born between January 1, 1928, and June 30, 1929. Eighty-six children were available for study in their fourteenth year, enabling the investigators to sample 46 possible problem areas. The results showed that problems of speech, elimination, fears, thumb-sucking, overactivity, destructiveness, and temper declined with age. Nailbiting was the only problem to increase with age, subsiding by age 14. Problems such as insufficient appetite and telling lies rose to a peak and then subsided. Several problem areas showed a twin peak-ing effect, one occurring at the time of entrance to school and the other at adolescence. These were evidently situational problems that are prone to appear when a child is under stress. Included in this group are restless sleep, disturbing dreams, physical timidity, irritability, demanding attention, overdependence, somberness, and jealousy. Table 10.1 shows the areas of problem behaviors occurring for one-third or more of the boys and girls at each age level.

The only problem which had no evident relationship to age was that of oversensitivity, which was maintained by girls throughout the years of the study, but dropped dramatically in boys after age 11. Oversensitivity is an observable behavior, frequently displayed as a reaction to a fear or threat-producing situation in which the real fear is that of meeting expectancy (measuring up to what others think). The early adolescent girl may fear social situations such as parties, etc. simply because she has facial acne; or she may have too timid a voice to receive a part in the Junior play, while she can scream all night at a Friday football game. Her soft voice, or stage fear, is a product of the fear of embarrassment that she might forget her "lines."

TABLE 10.1. Behavior Problems Shown by One-Third or More of the Boys and Girls at Each Age Level[a]

Behavior		1¾	3	3½	4	5	6	7	8	9	10	11	12	13	14
Enuresis	B	+													
(diurnal and nocturnal)	G	+													
Soiling	B														
	G														
Disturbing dreams	B									+					
	G						+				+	+			
Restless sleep	B	+													
	G														
Insufficient appetite	B														
	G						+								
Food finickiness	B		+												
	G	+	+	+			+								
Excessive modesty	B														
	G														
Nailbiting	B												+		+
	G								+	+					
Thumbsucking	B														
	G	+	+												
Overactivity	B		+	+	+	+		+	+	+					
	G		+	+	+	+									
Speech	B														
	G														
Lying	B		+	+	+	+		+							
	G			+	+	+	+								
Destructiveness	B														
	G														
Overdependence	B														
	G														
Attention demanding	B														
	G														
Oversensitiveness	B			+	+	+		+	+	+	+		+		
	G			+	+	+	+	+	+	+	+	+	+	+	+
Physical timidity	B														
	G			+		+									
Specific fears	B	+	+	+	+	+	+	+	+		+				
	G	+	+	+	+	+	+	+	+		+			+	
Mood swings	B										+	+	+		
	G						−	−	−	−	−		+		
Shyness[b]	B	−	−	−	−	−	−	−	−	−					
	G											+			
Somberness	B					+									
	G							+							
Negativism	B			+		+									
	G				+										
Irritability	B														
	G														
Tempers	B	+	+	+	+	+	+	+	+	+	+		+	+	+
	G	+	+	+	+	+	+	+					+		
Jealousy	B					+		+		+					
	G				+	+	+		+						
Excessive reserve[b]	B	−	−	−	−	+				+	+				
	G				+	+	+		+	+	+	+		+	+

[a]From MacFarland et. al.[28] Originally published by the University of California Press; reprinted by permission of The Regents of the University of California.

[b]—Data not obtained.

Another major finding in this study was the differing patterns in sibling birth order. First-born boys were more withdrawn and tended to internalize their problem much more than those occupying another position in the birth order. Younger children were seen to be more aggressive and competitive than their older siblings. First-born girls appeared to have more problems and difficulty in coping with stress situations. Of all the findings presented by MacFarlane and co-workers (1954), the most important one was that most problem behaviors did not persist throughout the age range. Children seem to enter periods when several problems are manifest around 5 to 7 years of age and subside by 11 to 12. The most frequently occurring problems were overdependence, somberness, and irritability, all of which tend to begin and end between the ages of 5 and 14. The authors concluded with a rather concise statement:

> May we pay our respect to the adaptive capacity of the human organism, born in a very unfinished and singular dependent state into a highly complex and not too sensible world. Unless handicapped by inadequate structure and health, and impossible and capricious learning situations, he treads his way to some measure of stable and characteristic patterning. *(Page 154)*

Another study of maladjustment (Lapouse and Monk, 1959) used the survey technique to study a sample of 482 children in Buffalo, New York, between 6 and 12 years of age by interviewing mothers in their homes. They found more intense and higher incidence of worries and fears in lower socio-economic children, younger children, and blacks. An examination of the characteristics covered by the survey suggests that most of the concerns manifested by children were more normal than clinical.

Children live under many stress situations, a stress situation being defined as one that denies comfort and tends to promote threat. A trip to the family physician may be a pleasant visit for an adult, but for the child it may produce fears and worries that result in many inappropriate and attention-getting behaviors. The overt behaviors listed in Table 10.2 may not have any relationship with the real fears or worries that may produce them. They may, in fact, be only symptomatic representations of a real problem or no problem at all. Child *A* may bite his fingernails to alleviate anxiety produced from the fear of failing to achieve his parent's expectancies. Child *B* may bite his fingernails to remove irritating dirt. Fingernail biting is a symptom; the point is, of what?

The relativity of problem behaviors, or at least troublesome behaviors or misbehaviors, are reflected in Zeitlein's (1957) report that as high as 41 per cent of the entire student-age school population

TABLE 10.2. The Prevalence of Some Behavior Characteristics in a Weighted Representative Sample of 482 Children Aged 6 to 12 as Reported by Mothers[a]

	Characteristic	Percentage
1.	Fears and worries, seven or more present	43
2.	Bedwetting within the past year	
	All frequencies	17
	Once a month or more	8
3.	Nightmares	28
4.	Food intake	
	Less than "normal"	20
	More than "normal"	16
5.	Temper loss	
	Once a month or more	80
	Twice a week or more	48
	Once a day or more	11
6.	Overactivity	49
7.	Restlessness	30
8.	Stuttering	4
9.	Unusual movements, twitching, or jerking (tics)	12
10.	Nailbiting	
	All intensities	27
	Nails bitten down (more severe)	17
11.	Grinding teeth	14
12.	Sucking thumb or fingers	
	All frequencies	10
	"Almost all the time"	2
13.	Biting, sucking, or chewing clothing or other objects	16
14.	Picking nose	26
15.	Picking sores	16
16.	Chewing or sucking lips or tongue or biting inside of mouth	11

[a]From Lapouse and Monk. Am. J. Orthopsychiatr. 29:803, 1959. Copyright, the American Orthopsychiatric Association, Inc. Reproduced by permission.

were cited once or more for misbehaving during the school year. Of the misbehaviors reported, 82 per cent involved problems of disturbance, disobedience, and disrespect. Boys were more frequent offenders than girls. It was also surmised in this study that children from higher socio-economic homes, with higher IQs, did better academically in school; and children with greater popularity were better adjusted than children who lacked these attributes.

Incidents of problems in delinquent youth were reported in a study by Eisner (1969). He analyzed data from San Francisco, dividing the children according to several variables. Separate tabulations were made for boys and girls, and, as previously found in other studies, boys showed delinquent behaviors averaging six times higher than girls. The ratio varied in different city census tracts, the lowest ratio being 3½:1. In one San Francisco census tract the boys' rate was nine times that of the girls.

The next primary divisions of the individual groups of boys and girls was by race and age, and compared four age divisions among the five racial groups. The problem of delinquency for each sex and race at each age is shown in Table 10.3.

TABLE 10.3. Delinquency Rates (1960) by Sex, Race, and Age[a]

Age (in years)	Males				Females			
	8-10	11-13	14-16	17	8-10	11-13	14-16	17
All interactions								
White	10	47	167	210	1	6	28	27
White-Spanish	18	62	251	444	2	9	36	33
Negro	35	146	381	575	5	39	86	60
Chinese	8	26	54	72	0	1	10	3
Other	3	82	189	310	0	20	54	46
Juvenile court cases								
White	8	33	84	86	0	6	22	10
White-Spanish	13	36	99	173	2	9	31	13
Negro	29	118	252	295	5	37	78	36
Chinese	5	20	40	46	0	1	10	3
Other	2	67	124	184	0	18	49	22

[a]From The Delinquency Label, by Victor Eisner. Copyright ©1969 by Random House Inc. Reprinted by permission of the publisher.

The data in Table 10.3 indicate that delinquency rates varied considerably with race. The lowest delinquency rates for both boys and girls were among Chinese youths, a fact that was true at all ages except for the very youngest boys (8 to 10 years old). In order of increasing delinquency rates, the racial breakdown showed a progression from Chinese to white, "other," white-Spanish, and black. The highest rates for both sexes at all ages were for blacks.

The black group displayed rates about 2½ to 3½ times as high as the average Chinese. Seventeen-year-old boys, in fact, had an average delinquency rate of 575 per 100; over half were either warned by the police or sent to juvenile court in the course of a year. The rate of juvenile court citation for the Black group was 295 per 1000.

Table 10.4 represents the number of delinquents by race, sex and family income. Unexpectedly, the highest numbers did not appear in the lowest income groups, except for black girls. Girls of all the other races, and white, white-Spanish, and "other" boys were in maximum family income levels between $2,500 and $5,000. The highest number of delinquents were black and Chinese boys in the $5,000 and $10,000 parent-earning bracket. The findings that maximum numbers of delinquents were in middle-income groups was true for this study and does not agree with many studies which frequently report most delinquents to be in the lower income groups.

	Males				Females			
Income	0- $2,500	$2,500- 5,000	$5,000- 10,000	Over $10,000	0- $2,500	$2,500- 5,000	$5,000- 10,000	Over $10,000
Race								
White	20	70	20	3	8	19	3	0
White- Spanish	18	62	11	2	9	13	3	0
Negro	81	104	121	3	30	22	9	0
Chinese	3	11	14	2	0	2	2	0
Other	6	63	21	0	12	18	4	0

[a]From The Delinquency Label, by Victor Eisner. Copyright © 1969 by Random House Inc. Reprinted by permission of the publisher.

Table 10.5 takes into account the number of parents in the home. This factor did not produce consistent effects. The presence of two parents in the homes was associated with low delinquency rates. The highest rates were found when there was only one parent; but there were exceptions in the case of Chinese girls and "other" girls. However, the pattern seems clear. Juveniles who have no parents in their homes have delinquency rates slightly above those who have both parents. Older children with delinquency rates were also more likely to come from broken families. The preliminary results showed that the numbers of parents in the home was a factor that affected delinquency labeling.

Eisner (1969) contends that both definition and statistics need overhauling. The common statistic that 4 per cent of the 10-to-17-year-old group are apprehended by policemen in a year is misleading.

> The delinquency rates of high-risk groups are sufficient, I believe, to force a complete re-evaluation of the usual concept that delinquents are deviants, that is, that they differ in their attributes from the "normal" boys of the community. If three out of four 17-year-old Negro boys in two large districts of San Francisco are recorded as delinquent in the course of a year, I submit that the deviant in this group is the one boy in four who does not become delinquent. But if delinquency is not due to deviant members of the group, one is driven to the conclusion that the entire group, at least by police standards, must live a life that is opposed by the rest of the community. We should speak of deviant groups, not deviant individuals. The delinquent in this group is the normal member of his society. Psychotherapy will not cure his delinquency, and a cure of delinquency will not help him to get along in his

society — indeed, it may very well alienate him from his friends and associates. *(Page 43)*

TABLE 10.5. Juvenile Court Delinquency Rates (1960) by Sex, Race, and Number of Parents in Home[a]

Number of Parents	Males			Females		
	2	1	0	2	1	0
Race						
White	20	65	23	3	18	10
White-Spanish	19	64	28	5	15	6
Negro	44	100	47	11	31	14
Chinese	9	15	22	1	3	0
Other	27	34	35	10	9	14

[a]From The Delinquency Label, by Victor Eisner. Copyright ©1969 by Random House Inc. Reprinted by permission of the publisher.

The citizenry of the great middle-class culture have many status needs, but they frequently fail to recognize the status needs of delinquent youth who reside in a different subculture. There is not stock society; the society we know is the particular subculture we live in. Why, then, do we repeatedly ask others to join our society when we fail to understand theirs?

SOCIAL MALADJUSTMENT AND OTHER HANDICAPS

Earlier in this chapter the discussion of delinquency was related to all types of social, family, and economic conditions. However, the discussion did not relate it to other handicaps, as few studies have been conducted to interrelate the variable of social disability and other handicaps.

Children with social maladjustments are generally thought to have normal mental and physical capabilities. Some are handicapped, however, with multiple handicaps, encompassed by social maladjustment as one type of disability in addition to another physical or mental deficit. If at birth both these conditions are present, the child may be mentally as well as physically handicapped. However, the handicapped child with a social maladjustment is not usually multihandicapped because the social disorder is secondary to the primary mental or physical handicap. A primary handicap is a disability or handicap unrelated to any other handicap. A secondary handicap, for example, social maladjustment, is an overlay and is related to some other primary mental or physical handicap. It is important that the nurse make a distinction between a secondary and primary social maladjustment evidenced by the handicapped child if she is to provide realistic care. An 8-year-old child may become difficult to manage upon admission to the hospital and separation from his mother. The cause could be the child's desire to obtain attention, and he may have learned that he can achieve this by demonstrating aggressive and distinctive behavior. On the other hand, these behaviors could be secondary to a primary condition of mental retardation. The aggressive behaviors displayed by the child can be a secondary reaction, or a social emotional overlay, reflecting the limited mental development and adaptive behavior level more appropriate to the child's mental than chronological age.

The so-called "defective delinquent" is a child with mental retardation and delinquency. In 1951 Westwell reported that a committee of members from the American Association on Mental Deficiency (AAMD) met to study the problems of the defective delinquent. They concluded:

> A mentally defective delinquent is any person affected with intellectual impairment from birth, or from an early age, to such an extent that he is incapable of managing himself and his affairs; who is charged with, arraigned for, or convicted of a criminal offense; and who for his own welfare, the welfare of others in the community, requires supervision, control or care, and who is not insane or of unsound mind to such an extent as to require his commitment to an institution for the insane. *(Page 285)*

There seems to be no real relationship between the degree of intelligence and delinquency. Kvaraceus (1964) has interpreted defective delinquency in terms of Dollard's theory that frustration leads, in turn, to aggression. This is borne out in the retarded delinquent, because he has less tolerance for frustration. This is not to say that there are more delinquents in the retarded range of intelligence, because this is not true. The mentally retarded are seemingly more easily apprehended by the police, whether or not they had a major or minor role in the delinquent act performed. The most significant attribute between IQ and delinquency is the variable of social-cultural influences. These range from poor home conditions and parental training to mistreatment within a poor nonunderstanding community environment. Blackhurst (1968) reviewed information on various aspects of mental retardation and delinquency and reported on 12 alternative hypotheses to account for the relationship between delinquency and retardation other than low IQ:

1. There is a "relatively higher incidence of mental retardation among the socially, economically, and culturally deprived segment of our population, which also produces the proportion of prison inmates." *(Allen, 1966; page 4)*

2. When negative correlations between intelligence and delinquency are found, they can be attributed "to the association with delinquency of that constellation of cultural factors which adversely affect the test score." *(Woodward, 1955; page 282)*

3. There are more commitments and fewer paroles for mentally retarded individuals accused of crimes *(Glueck, 1935)*; thus, one might expect the incarcerated population to be lower in intelligence.

4. Many times, retarded individuals are used as pawns by more intelligent ring leaders and are apprehended more easily. *(Wallace, 1929)*

5. Delinquent individuals from good homes, and who have high IQ scores, are often returned to their homes, if it appears that the parents are able and willing to provide adequate control. *(Mann and Mann, 1939)*

6. The retarded often make more mistakes while committing crimes and are not clever in eluding pursuit. *(Wallace, 1929)*

7. Very often, delinquency is accompanied by emotional instability, which can result in lower scores on intelligence tests. *(Burt, 1923)*

8. Retarded females who engage in illicit sexual activities are more frequently apprehended than normal females who engage in similar acts. *(Wallace, 1929)*

9. Criminals often score lower on tests of intellectual ability because of errors of a specific sort; they disobey instructions and are more impulsive in the testing situation. This is characteristic of extroverts; and there are more extroverts in the delinquent than in the normal population. *(Payne, 1961)*

10. Often, the retarded do not have sufficient funds to provide for adequate defense counsel and are subsequently convicted. *(Wallace, 1929)*

11. Delinquents may have low educational attainment, thus handicapping them on verbal test items. For example, one group of delinquents had mean verbal IQ scores of 82, but mean performance IQ scores of 98 on the WISC. *(Payne, 1961)*

12. Many times, mental retardation in the criminal population has been determined by using as a criterion a mental age score of 11 or 12 years. Wallin (1922) indicates that with this as a criterion, 47 per cent (44,556,000) of whites and 89 per cent (9,309,400) of Negroes would have been classified as mentally retarded in 1922 (based on World War I army records). It is apparent that using norms established for children is an unacceptable practice

when testing adults and would lead to inflated estimates of lowered intelligence in the criminal population. *(Zeleny, 1933; pages 381-82)*

Mulligan (1969) wrote concerning the origin and characteristics of dyslexia (reading disability) and concomitant delinquency problems, and confirmed earlier studies in illiteracy and its association with antisocial behaviors. He found that 60 per cent of most known delinquents were youths with 2 or more years of academic reading retardation. He also described the need for closer diagnostic study of delinquent nonreaders to determine if both conditions could have a common antecedent. A criminologist (Keldgord, 1969) attempted to establish brain damage as that common antecedent of delinquency and other observable problems in a study of apprehended youths. Taylor (1969) reviewed the literature and reported on 100 epileptic children. He concluded that aggressiveness in these patients was less likely to be a result of present interference in brain structures and more a result of early brain damage to learning control structures. His findings suggest that to prevent learned behavior problems, parental management and special training considerations are needed early.

Sabatino and Cramblett (1968) reported on the behavioral sequelae of California encephalitis virus infection in children. The purpose of the study was to examine the personality and behavioral sequelae of 14 children between 7 months and 2 years after their initial admission to the hospital. At the time of their assessment they ranged in age from 5 to 14 years.

The children they examined, upon release from the hospital, had previously become suddenly ill during the summer months due to an arborvirus carried primarily by mosquitos. The children were hospitalized from 4 to 15 days with a median duration of 7 days, and the maximum temperature for each child ranged from 91 to 105° F. During hospitalization 12 of the subjects complained of severe headaches; nine had their first seizures. Five were comatose and three semicomatose. Three of the children were disoriented for period of up to 3 days.

The EEG findings were abnormal in eight out of nine patients during the acute phase of their illness. Subsequent EEGs, obtained 1 to 10 months after the acute illness, were normal in three and borderline in six patients. Only one tracing showed a focal lesion; the others were all interpreted as generalized cerebral dysfunctions.

Quay's (1965) inventory was used to describe the behavior and personality of each child. In the result, the clinic personnel, teachers, and parents agreed that all the children showed some postillness sequelae in personality and behavior following hospitalization. A cluster analysis of the behavioral sequelae observed by the subjects' parents showed these patients to be typically nervous, hyperactive, restless, disruptive, distractable, easily frustrated, tense, preoccupied with self, and irritable (Table 10.6). Two of the children were reported to be enuretic, and six had headaches or other somatic symptoms following the illness. None of the children reported these complaints before the illness.

When the behavioral corollaries resulting from CEV infection in 14 children were examined within 2 years from the onset of the illness, the children seemed to have difficulty in receiving consistenly meaningful basic visual and auditory perceptual information. They seemed to find no difficulty in the higher language functions or in the conceptual skills associated with verbal intellectual function. The personalities of these children also seemed to fit the "organic" hyperkinetic syndrome. The result was a behavior pattern seemingly associated with specific learning disorders.

The importance of the Sabatino and Cramblett study to the nurse is that the children were discharged from the hospital with little thought that any serious long-term problem existed. Yet, they showed severe learning, behavioral, and adjustment difficulties routinely at home and school.

A nurse's job is wide-ranging in that pathogenesis is only one portion of her role. Providing medical supervision, being able to perceive deviant behavior, making suggestions to parents, and initiating referrals to other appropriate disciplines and agencies are also important functions. The social-emotional concern for a patient must be as great as any other care she would provide, for in the body of her patient reside old and new feelings, as well as fears and hopes that need expression and sympathy. The idea of a total treatment environment is not a new one, but the concept that such a milieu should focus on the patient as a person with feelings, as well as a biologic being, has been verbally expressed but seldom practiced.

Believing that the handicapped must be recognized as people, Gruhn and Krause (1968) examined the psychologic and social adjustment of 35 female and 38 male vocational high school students with significant handicaps of all types by means of sociometric procedure and standardized questionnaires completed by students and teachers. In comparing these handicapped individuals to a non-handicapped group, both showed similar (nonsignificant) adjustment

TABLE 10.6. Quay's Checklist of Problem Behaviors
Denoting Frequency of Cases where Agreement between Teacher, Parent, and Psychologist Was Established[a]

Frequency	Behavior
Behaviors rated as no problem (seldom observed)	
12	Oddness, bizarre behavior
12	Attention-seeking, show-off behavior
12	Fixed expression; lack of emotional reactivity
9	Self-consciousness; easily embarrassed
11	Crying over minor annoyances and hurts
11	Preoccupation; "in a world of his own"
13	Shyness, bashfulness
13	Jealousy over attention paid other children
13	Repetitive speech
13	Fighting
12	Loyal to delinquent friends
10	Excessive daydreaming
14	Masturbation
11	Has bad companions
13	Depression, chronic sadness
9	Uncooperativeness in group situations
12	Aloofness, social reserve
10	Passivity, suggestibility; easily led by others
11	Clumsiness, awkwardness, poor muscular coordination
8	Destructiveness in regard to his own and/or others' property
9	Negativism, tendency to do the opposite of what is requested
14	Sluggishness, lethargy
14	Drowsiness
11	Enuresis, bed-wetting
Behavior rated as mild problem (occasionally observed)	
7	Lack of self-confidence
6	Anxiety, chronic general fearfulness
5	Disobedience, difficulty in disciplinary control
6	Often has physical complaints — e.g., headaches, stomachaches
Behavior rated as moderate problem (frequently observed)	
11	Restlessness, inability to sit still
9	Disruptiveness; tendency to annoy and bother others
7	Short attention span
9	Inattentiveness to what others say
8	Temper tantrums
9	Hypersensitivity; feelings easily hurt
9	Tension, inability to relax
12	Hyperactivity; 'always on the go'
11	Distractibility
8	Nervousness, jitteriness, jumpiness; easily startled
7	Irritability; hot-tempered, easily aroused to anger

[a]From Paine and Oppe. Clinics in Developmental Medicine, 1966. Courtesy of Spastics International Medical Publications.

on the sociometric scale, self-concept, and teacher evaluation with controls. The handicapped had a far greater need for friends, were rigid in view of self, and had a significantly reduced level of aspiration. Can you hypothesize why these findings occurred?

Mitchell (1970) investigated differences in "barrier" scores between groups assessed as either high or low in their adjustment to the stress induced by severe physical disability. The barrier score was an index of adjustment to reality indicated by positive social and vocational goals. The subjects were 48 paraplegics and 48 quadraplegics. The high- and low-scoring paraplegics were significantly different on various social, adaptive, and personality measures. There was no significant difference between quadraplegic groups who scored high and low. The study indicated that the amount of physical involvement does not critically interfere with adjustment until that point where the lack of physical function interferes with personal and vocational success and, therefore, independence.

Ossowski (1969) found that the motivation of blind youth to respond to stress, consisting of heightened emotional tension, action to satisfy primary drives, or basic needs was determined by the types of stress, perception of stress, self-appraisal capabilities, resistance to stress, and whether one's disability might be exposed by counteracting stress. Their choice of actions was motivated by:

1. Fear of being juxtaposed with the public
2. Fear of being made aware of one's handicap
3. Striving to show that blindness is not the worst handicap

Nihiro, Foster, and Spencer (1968) established the need to understand the basic parameters of coping behaviors, which in the retarded vary considerably in nature and content, according to the level of retardation. Even if a physical impairment should cease, it may be especially hard for a normal social reaction to occur, because the disability seemingly attracts enough attention to detract from an interpersonal relationship between the handicapped and the physically normal person. Davis (1969) found that the interaction between the physically impaired and the "normal" was characterized by an overcompensation of the normal person for the handicapped, limiting the relationship so that the behavior was rigid and even the sentences were short.

It is useful for the nurse to understand how the normal person reacts to physical impairment in others. Such "aesthetic aversion" can be seen in the reactions of normal children to physical deviance (impairment) in other children (Barker, 1964). For example, groups of 10-to-12-year-old children (N = over 600) consistently ranked (from most to least liked) children's pictures according to their liking of them in the following order: a normal child, a child with crutches and a leg brace, a child in a wheel chair, a child with a left forearm amputation, a child with a slight facial disfigurement, and an obese child (Richardson and Royce, 1968). The same ordering was found using a social distance technique with drawings in a high school sample. The obese child, who had an aesthetic impairment, was the least liked by girls, and the forearm amputee, who had a functional impairment, was the least liked by boys in both age groups (Matthews and Westie, 1966). Racial variables made no difference in the rank ordering (Richardson and Royce, 1968).

Unfortunately, children's negative attitudes seem to increase with age (Billings, 1963) and are not overcome by social contact with the deviant (Richardson, 1969). Shears and Jensema (1969) suggested, on the basis of 94 young adults' social distance evaluations and rankings of 10 anomalies with respect to desirability in a friend and as a self-affliction, that six dimensions combine and interact to form attitudes toward deviants: visibility, communication, social stigma, reversibility, degree of incapacity, and difficulty in daily living. Perhaps children are more critical of visibility and social stigma in their consistently high rejection of the obviously handicapped child. This possibility is suggested by 186 high school students' responses to 12 exceptionalities, using a paired comparison questionnaire (Jones, Gottfried, and Owens, 1966). In this study, more visible disabilities led to greater rejection regardless of the social context described; but the ordering of less visible anomalies interacted with social context.

The nature of social interaction and social status relates closely to emotional adjustment, whether judged by self-concept (Wylie, 1967) or by personality traits (Coopersmith, 1967). In study after study the social acceptability of children, from preschool to college age, has been found to relate significantly and positively to personality or emotional adjustment and negatively to anxiety. The criteria for adjustment included teachers' ratings (Kwall, Smith, and Lackner, 1967); degree of initiation of verbal interaction with peers; independence from adults; responses to projective techniques such as the Rorschach (Northway and Wigdor, 1947); creative thinking (Yamamoto, Lembright, and Corrigan, 1966); and responses to anxiety scales (Ueda, 1964). Usually, however, researchers have examined responses to self-concept and/or social-personal adjustment on questionnaires. Whether the relationship found is cause, effect, or the result of an intervening variable is unknown, but a slight positive relationship occurs quite consistently, regardless of the size, sex, socio-economic status, or heterogeneity of the sample, in the criteria of social acceptability and adjustment in the experimental setting.

Therefore, one would expect socially unaccepted children, such as physical deviates, to show poorer emotional adjustment than more accepted children.

> In view of the generally negative public reception and of the "looking-glass" nature of self-concepts, it is no wonder that those calssified as deviant are inclined to be frustrated, unhappy, and often hostile. Even after their stigmata have become clearly visible, the individuals will attempt to "cover" them; the extra "performance" required (Goffman, 1959) drains the deviants' energy and many inevitable slips tend to discourage them. *(Yamamoto, 1969)*

In conjunction with Yamamoto's opinion is the finding that self-descriptions of 107 9- to 11-year-old handicapped children, when compared to those of nonhandicapped children, showed more expression of personal inadequacy and uncertainty and more general self-depreciation (Richardson, Hastorf, and Dornbusch, 1964).

DRUG ABUSE

In previous years an introductory chapter on social disability would not have contained a section on drug abuse. The problem has become a current one, with such far-reaching implications for society, that it is a major social disability issue. The nurse will encounter the drug problem from several standpoints. Frequently, she will be responsible for drug controls in institutions; she may be in a position to recognize the symptoms, alert other professional persons, and refer the family and/or the patient for corrective measures. In addition, she will be educating the general public to the issues that appear to be poorly understood as viewed in the broad social spectra.

Leech and Jordan (1968) have prepared an easily read book on the drug problem. They differentiate drug-takers from those "addicted" to drugs. The difference between addiction and dependence can be set in a biologic-psychologic balance. Addiction occurs when there is both a biologic need and a psychologic dependence; dependence is present when there is no biologic need, but a definite psychologic one.

A committee set up by the British Government to advise on drugs liable to cause addiction issued the following definition:

Drug addiction is a state of periodic or chronic intoxication produced by the repeated consumption of a drug (natural or synthetic); its characteristics include:

1. An overpowering desire or need (compulsion) to continue taking the drug and to obtain it by any means
2. A tendency to increase the dose, though some patients may remain indefinitely on a stationary dose
3. A psychologic and physical dependence on the effects of the drug
4. The appearance of a characteristic "abstinence syndrome"* in a subject from whom the drug is withdrawn
5. An effect detrimental to the individual and to society

In 1965 the same committee thought fit to define an addict as:

a person who, as the result of repeated administration, has become dependent upon drugs controlled under the Dangerous Drugs Act and has an overpowering desire for its continuance, but who does not require it for the relief of organic disease.

This definition covers addiction not only to heroine and cocaine, but to all the drugs mentioned in the Dangerous Drugs Act, which includes morphine, pethidine, methadone, and codeine.

There are two types of dependence on drugs; one is a combined physical and psychologic dependence, and the other is a psychologic one only. The former is produced by the addictive drugs, particularly the narcotics† and barbiturates, producing a physical *tolerance*. This condition is evident when drugs are taken to the point that they are needed in order for the person to function at a level tolerable to the user. The user is compelled to increase the dosage in order to stave off withdrawal symptoms. Stoppage of the drug could cause severe and painful repercussions and, in some cases, death. Withdrawal or abstinence syndrome is produced when these drugs are abruptly discontinued. However, the physical dependence created by alcohol and the barbiturates differs from that of the narcotics. Small doses of alcohol and barbiturates can be taken regularly over long periods without producing noticeable physical dependence. The sustained use of even small doses of the narcotics always leads to physical dependence.

*Abstinence syndrome means the pattern of physical and mental symptoms and behavior which occurs when the patient/addict "abstains" from, or does not have, the drug he is addicted to.

†Scientifically, narcotic means all tranquillizers, sedatives, sleeping pills, etc.; but it is generally used in international law to refer to any potentially harmful or addicting drug.

Cocaine produces no troublesome physical dependence; but is harmful to its users, because they tend to imagine they must protect themselves from unrealistic or other grave dangers (paranoid schizophrenia).

The psychologic dependence on drugs occurs when the addicted person places psychologic meaning on the use of the drugs and their effects. Its characteristics are:

1. A desire (but not compulsion) to continue taking the drug for the sense of improved well-being which it engenders
2. Little or no tendency to increase the dose
3. Some degree of psychologic dependence on the effect of the drug, but absence of physical dependence and hence of abstinence syndrome
4. Detrimental effects, if any, primarily on the individual.

Psyhologic dependence on drugs is difficult to define. Drugs cause a change of mood or "personality" and, although there is no medical reason for taking the drug, the user feels the drugs offer a means of escaping from an unpleasant emotional situation. The adolescent suffering from chronic fatigue may take pep pills at the expense of ignoring his body's message telling him to "ease up."

When a healthy individual becomes dependent on drugs in order to effect a change of personality, there is obviously something wrong which needs professional attention. If a drug is used to escape from boredom it is only a temporary relief, and the reason for being bored is only lost in the dependency on drugs.

Hager, Vener, and Stewart (1971) examined the sex, age, and school differences associated with drugs by eighth to twelfth grade students in white, nonmetropolitan, noncollege communities of the midwest. They found drug use to be present by age 13. The younger users had experience primarily with marijuana and other nonhard drugs. For this reason they believe drug education must begin in the elementary schools.

The large increase in percent of users of soft drugs (marijuana, hallucinogens, and amphetamines) occurs in the 15-to-16 age bracket. Once again, this seems to represent a need for adolescents to be accepted by an established peer group — to be on the in-side — even if the group is on the outside of general society. Most adolescent drug users are insecure and lack academic, athletic, or social competence.

At age 16 a leveling off of the use of soft drugs occurs. Adult-status-seeking adolescents see drug use as nonresponsible, delinquent-subculture-bond behavior; others, a small number, move to the hard drugs and become integrated into the drug subculture. Trends in hard drug use of the adolescent are not yet fully established because of the limited number who do become addicts.

Randall (1970) reported on the rising incident of drug usage in the Los Angeles City schools, showing figures of 925 reported arrests of school-age youths in the period 1956-to-1957 to 6,216 in 1968. The increase in number of apprehensions among elementary school pupils during the years rose from 7 cases in 1957 to 24 cases in 1966. The major type of drug abuse in elementary-age children was sniffing glue and injesting aerosol materials and other inhalants. According to Randall, children have been taking drugs and mixing them into what they term a "fruit salad," and sampling the resulting concoction. Twenty "paint thinner" addicts were reported during a 1-year period from among 75,000 Stockholm school children. The rapid increase in the rise of drugs centers around the family medicine cabinet, which may contain, on an average, 30 different medications, some of which are 20 years old.

Soloman (1968) classified drug abuse according to the reasons for such use. He proposed that the system of social, neurotic, or psychotic causes explains why the problem is initiated and persists. He also proposed that the proper management of each is distinctly different, as shown in Table 10.7.

TABLE 10.7. Type of Drug Dependence and their Characteristics[a]

Type of Drug Dependence	Basic Symptom Subserved by Drug-Taking	Patient's Fear	Goal of Drug-Taking	Chief Treatment	Danger
Social	Dissatisfaction	Unfulfillment, rejection	Identity, status pleasure	Educational	Waste, crime
Neurotic	Anxiety	Suffering	Relief	Psychologic	Addiction
Psychotic	Horror	Annihilation	Escape	Medical	Suicide, murder

[a]From Soloman. J.A.M.A. 206:1522, 1968. Courtesy of the author and the American Medical Association.

While views like this seem to predominate, recent research has suggested that the personalities of marijuana smokers may be more complex. Hogan, Mankin, Conway, and Fox (1970) studied the personality correlates of four levels of marijuana use at two universities. The sample was divided into frequent users, occasional users, nonusers, and principled nonusers. The groups differed significantly on 10 of 19 scales of the California Psychological Inventory (Gough, 1957) and four questionnaire items. According to their data, users in their groups were socially poised, open to experience, and concerned with the feelings of others. Conversely, they also seemed impulsive, pleasure-seeking, and rebellious. In contrast, nonusers were responsible and rule-abiding; however, they also tended to be inflexible, conventional, and narrow in their interests.

Berg's (1970) report on the patterns of nonmedical use of Dangerous Drugs discusses the type of user:

> Among secondary school students in San Mateo County, California (1969), the proportion of marijuana users increases as frequency of marijuana use increases. This pattern is also the same for Utah high school dropouts (1969), hippies in San Francisco (Shick et al., 1968), and working youth in the Boston area (Boston Globe, 1970). The following patterns also emerge from the frequency statistics of other drugs:
>
> 1. *LSD and other hallucinogens* — The proportion of users decreases as frequency of use increases.
> 2. *Amphetamines* — These stimulants are second only to marijuana in use, but rates of use of the amphetamines are well below rates of marijuana use. Only a small proportion of those reporting amphetamine use said that they were frequent or regular users. Among hippies in Haight-Ashbury (1968), oral use of amphetamines was extremely high, but even among this group the proportion of users decreased drastically as frequency of use increased.
> 3. *Barbiturates and tranquilizers* — While use of these drugs appear to be increasing, few statistics on patterns of use are available. The data, however, suggest that only a small proportion of persons use these drugs without prescription on a frequent or regular basis.
> 4. *Opiates* — Survey statistics are not available on patterns of use of this class of drugs.
> 5. *Special or "exotic" substances* — Survey statistics are not available on patterns of use of these substances. *(Page 16)*

Many drug users reported that they used more than one drug. Some marijuana users report that they have used one or more drugs in addition to marijuana. King (1969) found that about 4 per cent of the respondents reported using both marijuana and LSD. College students in the Denver-Boulder metropolitan area reported the following multiple drug use: marijuana and amphetamine use, 6 per cent; marijuana and LSD use, 1 per cent; marijuana, amphetamine, and LSD use, 4 per cent.

School officials are aware that drug use may be as serious a problem at the secondary level. Concern over effective remedial and preventive measures is growing more and more evident among parents, teachers, law enforcement officials, and numerous professional groups. While many have argued for or against the use of various drugs, the impact of their statements has been diminished by a lack of supportive empirical data. Research on both the physiologic and psychologic effects of different drugs and on the characteristics of drug users is limited.

Dearden (1971), however, the coordinator of Drug Education at Griffin Hospital, Derby, Connecticut, has listed the following points as important on the recognition of the drug cult:

1. Drug use among students is a social phenomenon.
2. The need for recognition and acceptance is high among drug-using students, and their verbal activity and occasional aggressiveness in small groups is one means of gaining the attention they seek.
3. Drug users as a subgroup tend to be cohesive and supportive of each other, thereby providing an atmosphere in which the individual can feel secure, cared about, and important as a human being. The group cohesiveness is helped along by the sharing of a common experience, i.e., the use of drugs. Factual knowledge is less among nonusers. Knowledge about drugs among drug users, however, is primarily experiential and "grapevine" information, which is frequently distorted or incomplete.
4. Many students who use drugs share their drugs and do not "push" them. In addition, they do not actively promote or sell the idea of using drugs to those students who do not use them.
5. Students have shown a reduction in the use of drugs or a discontinuance of their use when made to feel accepted and respected. *(Page 10)*

This discussion on drug abuse is not designed to be a complete review of this problem. Rather, it is to acquaint the nurse with the social problems that the drug misuse can cause, some factors in recognizing the frequent user, and something about his management. To provide comprehensive coverage of the topic for nurses, two sections would need to be prepared: one, relating the problems of acute addiction as seen in children in the hospital situation, and a second on what might be described as the "drug culture" to the public health nurse, nurse in a private physician's office, or in an out-patient department.*

*The reader, interested in greater depth on this topic, is encouraged to read Dorothy Berg's recent publications: Illicit Use of Dangerous Drugs in the United States, (A Compilation of Studies, Surveys, and Polls), and The Non-Medical Use of Dangerous Drugs in the United States (A Comprehensive View). Both of these papers can be obtained from the Drug Science Division, Office of Science and Drug Abuse Prevention, Bureau of Narcotics and Dangerous Drugs, United States Department of Justice, Washington, D.C.

THE NURSE AND THE SOCIALLY DISABLED CHILD

The nurse, or student nurse, reading this chapter, will probably find the ambiguity of social disability somewhat baffling. She will agree that, as a nurse, she has a role in the care and management of the socially deviant child, but her natural inclination to wonder just how far she may go in being all things to all people is justifiable. More important than any other point made is the serious personal feeling or consideration for disability of any type and how the professional person reacts to disability. Far too frequently the nurse reacts to medical pathogenesis of the child with a social disability as if the care and management of that child resides solely in medical treatment. The nurse may believe that parents, who may themselves need help, should discipline him; that he should be seen by a psychiatrist or psychologist; and that he should be medically treated or referred to the juvenile officer for probation. Any or all of these could be true. Equally so, they can be active types of the nurse's own personal wish to remain uninvolved with the patient on any level except to bathe him, smile sweetly, and administer medication cheerfully. If the nurse, as a member of a medical management team, identifies the child as a social deviant but interacts with that child as she would with a normal child instead of accommodating him with special treatment she may be aggravating his social handicap. If, however, she can provide that child with a realistic view of self and a basis for establishing interaction with the real world, she may aid him towards a "normal" life. It is impossible to interact therapeutically with a person unless one first views him as a being equal to all others, with dignity and worth. Belittling, negating, or returning the patient's abuse will reinforce the behavior currently being displayed.

The inability to leave the nursing station for any activity, except to deliver a medication, limits the involvement of the nurse with that particular patient. The inability of the public health nurse to see past the physical chaos in a home and render personal-emotional support to the people that comprise that family limits her effectiveness in reducing that chaos. Medical settings are sterile, as reflected by the use of white uniforms. That same white uniform can be a barrier between the nurse and a child who fears the pain associated with it;

it is the person in the white uniform who gives him a "shot." Pediatric settings where uniforms have been removed, as well as in state and private institutions for exceptional children or individuals, have reduced the medical environment, have substituted a more homelike atmosphere, and have shown definite changes in the attitudes of their patients. It may be just as important to life to hear what a person says emotionally, and to attempt to feel what he describes, as it is to know his heartbeat and other vital signs. The serious student will find many good texts on counseling techniques, and, as many other nurses have done, will develop these skills of interacting with people. The extra effort required to establish a relationship with a child and his family may be a demanding one, and its rewards may never be fully known or appreciated. To gain insight into the lives of others, the nurse should be able to relate to the patient as a person and be sensitive to feelings and his emotionality.

The nurse occupies a position which permits her to gain a great deal of information and observation about people. She needs to become more aware that this information should be communicated to appropriate people. Frequently, the hospital record reads, "quiet P.M., morning B.M." It is more significant that a 12-year-old patient, for example, tried to read, became frustrated, and regressed to doll play or social isolation. So, if the physician who reads a record does not clearly understand the importance of the nurse's observation of behavior, she should discuss it with him.

The nurse needs to view her role as central to that of patient management. Frequently, she will discover that she is in a position to coordinate activities for the patient. Two of the most important of these are (1) the referral of the child with a suspected problem, and (2) the follow up through to see that the parents and the child keep the appointment or see its importance. If, for example, the nurse, having established a relationship with a child, breaks the ice by taking the child to the psychologist's office in the hospital and introduces him, she has assisted another professional peer. She may even remain for some introductory conversation.

As a member of society and an authority figure, the nurse occupies a special role as a trusted figure to many socially deviant children. Positive gains can be made if the nurse can do some or all of the following:

1. Establish for the child a healthy experience with an authority figure.
2. Make use of behavioral limits to define acceptable behaviors, and recognize the socially deviant child's limit-testing behavior, or his reasons for breaking the rules.

3. Increase social interaction and provide a catalytic base for parents and the patient, other children, and other adults; in short, increase the child's social experience.
4. Initiate the patient's self-examination, the discussion of feelings — even those thought to be forbidden — counseling, and the connecting of relevant experiences.
5. Encourage the patient's realistic self-appraisal, expression of thought and feelings, shared feelings and experiences, and concrete action to show trust and true friendship.

THE NURSE AND THE DRUG ABUSER

As with the socially disabled patient, the nurse plays an equally important role in working with drug abusers. Recognition of the problem is not critical to the alert nurse who only needs to increase her list of toxic states to include drug abuse as she systematically reviews records or prepares patients for examinations, hospitalizations, or sees them in regard to public health concern. The management of the drug abuser must be considered in at least three stages. First, the problem of addiction is generally related to other sound and psychologic factors, which means the nurse must view drug abuse as an interdisciplinary management team, of which she is one member. Second, the nurse is frequently the professional who can provide early detection of drug abuse, relating her observations to those with whom she works. Third, the cure for drug addiction is at best painful, expecially as it influences the psychologic development of children. Prevention is the real cure, and must begin with education on drugs. The public health and school nurse may well be the professional person in a good position to undertake the transmission of this vital information.

REFERENCES

1. Barker, D. G. Concepts of disabilities. Personnel Guidance 43:371, 1964.
2. Berg, D. F. Illicit Use of Dangerous Drugs in the U.S.: A Compilation of Studies, Surveys and Polls. Drug Sciences Division, Office of Science and Drug Abuse Prevention, Bureau of Narcotics and Dangerous Drugs, United States Department of Justice, Washington, D.C., 1970.
3. Berg, D. F. The Non-Medical Use of Dangerous Drugs in the U.S.: A Comprehensive View. Drug Control Division, Bureau of Narcotics and

Dangerous Drugs, U.S. Department of Justice, Washington, D.C., 1970.
4. Billings, H. K. An exploratory study of the attitudes of noncrippled children toward crippled children in three selected elementary schools. J Exp Educ 31:381, 1963.
5. Blackhurst, A. E. Mental retardation and delinquency. J Spec Educ 2:379, 1968.
6. Brain, R. The report of the interdepartmental committee on drug addiction. B J Addict, July, 1961, pp. 81-103.
7. Cartwright, D. S., Howard, K. I., and Short, J. F., Sr. The Motivation of Delinquency, 1966. (Unpublished manuscript)
8. Cloward, R. A., and Ohlin, L. E. Delinquency and Opportunity: A Theory of Delinquent Gangs. Glencoe, Ill., Free Press, 1960.
9. Cohen, A. Delinquent Boys. Glencoe, Ill., Free Press, 1955.
10. Conger, J. J., and Miller, W. C. Personality, Social Class, and Delinquency. New York, Wiley, 1966.
11. Coopersmith, S. The Antecedents of Self-Esteem. San Francisco, Freeman, 1967.
12. Davis, F. Deviance disavowal: The management of strained interaction by the visibly handicapped. Soc Prob 9:120, 1961.
13. Dearden, M. H. Observations about student use of drugs. Sch Manag 15:10, 1971.
14. Eisner, V. The Delinquency Label: The Epistemology of Juvenile Delinquency. New York, Random House, 1969.
15. Glueck, S., and Glueck, E. Physique and Delinquency. New York, Harper & Row, 1956.
16. Gough, H. G. The California Psychological Inventory. Palo Alto, Calif., Consulting Psychologists, 1957.
17. Gruhn, H., and Krause, S. On the social behavior of physically handicapped children and teenagers. Probl Ergeb Psychol 23:73, 1968.
18. Hager, D. L., Vener, A. M., and Stewart, C. S. Patterns of adolescet drug use in middle America. J Counsel Psychol 18:292, 1971.
19. Hogan, R. T., Mankin, D., Conway, J., and Fox, S. Personality correlates of undergraduate marijuana use. J Consult Clin Psychol, 1970. 35:58-63, 1970.
20. Jones, R., Gottfried, N. W., and Owens, A. The social distance of the exceptional: A study at the high school level. Exceptional Child 32:551, 1966.
21. Kelgord, R. E. Brain damage and delinquency: A question and a challenge. Acad Ther 4:93, 1969.
22. Kvaraceus, W. C. Juvenile Delinquency: A problem for the Modern World, Paris, UNESCO, 1964.
23. Kvaraceus, W. C., and Mental retardation and norm violation. J Educ 147:17, 1964.
24. Kwall, D. S., Smith, J. T., Jr., and Lackner, F. M. Functional relationship between sociometric status and teacher ratings, expiration level, academic, and parent-child variables. Proc 75 Ann Conv APA, 2:285, 1967.
25. Lachenmeyer, C. W. Systematic socialization: Observations on a programmed environment for the rehabilitation of anti-social retardates. Psychol Rec 19:247, 1969.
26. Lapouse, R. and Monk, M. A. Fears and worries in a representative sample of children. Am J Orthopsychiatry 29:803, 1959.
27. Leech, K., and Jordon, B. Drugs for Young People — Their Use and Misuse. Oxford, England, Religious Education Press, 1968.
28. MacFarlane, J. W., Allen, L., and Honzik, M. P. A Developmental Study of the Behavior Problems of Normal Children Between Twenty-one Months and Fourteen Years. Berkely, Calif. University of California Press, 1954.
29. Matthews, V., and Westie, C. A preferred method for obtaining rankings: Reactions to physical handicaps. Am Sociol Rev 31:851, 1966.

30. Mitchell, K. R. The body image barrier variable and level of adjustment to stress induced by severe physical disability. J Clin Psychol 26:49, 1970.
31. Mulligan, W. Study of dyslexia and delinquency. Acad Ther 4:177, 1969.
32. Nihiro, K., Foster, R., and Spencer, L. Measurement of adaptive behaviors: A descriptive system of mental retardates. Am J Orthopsychiatry 31:381, 1968.
33. Northway, M. L., and Wigdor, B. T. Rorscharch patterns related to sociometric status of school children. Sociometry 10:186, 1947.
34. Ossowski, R. Behavior of blind youth under stress. Przegl Psychol 18:85, 1969.
35. Parsons, T. Certain primary sources and patterns of aggression in the social structure of the western world. Psychiatry 10:167, 1947.
36. Pate, J. E. Exceptional Children in the Schools. Lloyd M. Dunn, ed. New York, Holt, Rinehart and Winston, Inc., 1963.
37. Quay, H. C. Juvenile Delinquency. Princeton, N.J. Van Nostrand, 1965.
38. Randall, H. B. Patterns of drug use in school-age children. J Sch Health 11:296, 1970.
39. Richardson, S. A. The effect of physical disability on the socialization of a child. In D. A. Goslin, ed. Handbook of Socialization Theory and Research. Chicago, Rand McNally, 1969, pp. 1047-1064.
40. Richardson, S. A., Hastorf, A. H., and Dornbusch, S. M. Effects of physical disability on a child's description of himself. Child Dev 35:893, 1964.
41. Richardson, S. A., and Royce, J. Race and physical handicap in children's preference for other children. Child Dev 39:467, 1968.
42. Sabatino, D. and Cramblett, H. Behavioral sequelae of California encephalitis virus infection in children. Dev Med Child Neurol 10:331, 1968.
43. Shears, L., and Jensema, C. J. Social acceptability of anomalous persons. Exceptional Child 36:91, 1969.
44. Sheldon, W. J. The Varieties of Human Physique. New York, Harper & Row, 1940.
45. Soloman, P. Medical management of drug dependence. JAMA 206:1521, 1968.
46. Taylor, D. C. Aggression and epilepsy. J Psychosom Res 13:229, 1969.
47. Ueda, T. A study of the stability of sociometric status among elementary school children: On the stability of choice received. J Nara Gakugei Univ 12:135, 1964.
48. Westwell, A. E. The defective delinquent. Am J Ment Defic 56:283, 1951.
49. Wylie, R. C. The Self Concept. Lincoln, Neb., University of Nebraska Press, 1967.
50. Yamamoto, K. To Be Different. Lecture presented at the Pennsylvania State University, University Park, Pa., 1969. (Unpublished)
51. Yamamoto, K., Lembright, M. L., and Corrigan, A. M. Intelligence, creative thinking and sociometric choice among 5th grade children. J Exp Educ 34:83, 1966.
52. Zeitlin, H. Phoenix reports on high school misbehavior. Personnel Guidance J 35:384, 1957.

COMMUNITY RESOURCES

Community responsibility for exceptional children is delivered in programs that either consider education of professionals and the public, research, or clinical services. Clinical services have four important phases: case finding, diagnosis, treatment, and follow-up. In many states there are day programs, residential programs, as well as special education programs in public schools. Most states have some type of directory of services for children.

Often, nurses are asked about resources in the community for exceptional children. It is not expected that the nurse would be able to recall all the agencies in the community. She does need, however, to have a general knowledge of voluntary and governmental agencies on the national, state, and local levels that she can advise parents of and that she as a professional can use to aid in advising parents of exceptional children. In many communities, church groups, women's groups, and civic groups, such as the Lions Club, Jaycees, and Kiwanis Club, offer services to exceptional children and their families. Nurses may be involved in community action programs that would be geared toward assessing the community for needs of services. The nurse involved in the care of exceptional children might be a valuable consultant in helping communities plan for services. The nurse can document problems that families have with existing services or because of the lack of resources. It might be wise for the nurse who works with exceptional children to compile information about formal and informal resources in the community she serves.

If the nurse is unsure of community agencies she can always contact the state or local health department to begin to obtain information. The Department of Welfare and the Department of Education are other potential starting points to begin to get information about programs for exceptional children.

Since many parents worry about what will happen to their exceptional child who has limited intellectual ability, nurses should make them aware of the Social Security Administration service to disabled children over age 18 of retired, disabled, or deceased workers. These children are eligible for benefits. Dependent exceptional children of military personnel may also be able to receive certain benefits. There are many voluntary and several governmental agencies that have programs of education, research, or services.

Listed below are some agencies that the nurse might use to get information for helping exceptional children and their families.

Alexander Graham Bell Association for Deaf, Inc.
1537 35th Street
Washington, D.C.

American Association for Gifted Children, Inc.
Trinity University
San Antonio, Texas

American Association of Mental Deficiency
5201 Connecticut Avenue N.W.
Washington, D.C.

American Association of Workers for the Blind, Inc.
1511 K Street, N.W.
Washington, D.C.

American Foundations for the Blind, Inc.
15 West 16th Street
New York, New York

American Phsyical Therapy Association
1740 Broadway
New York, New York

American Printing House for the Blind
1839 Frankfurt Avenue
Louisville, Kentucky

American Speech and Hearing Society
9030 Old Georgetown Road
Washington, D.C.

Association of Children with Learning Disabilities
2200 Brownsville Road
Pittsburgh, Pennsylvania

Association for Education of the Visually Handicapped
Virginia School for Deaf and Blind
Staunton, Virginia

Association for Education of the Visually Handicapped
711 14th Street NW
Washington, D.C.

Boy Scouts of America
Route 1
New Brunswick, New Jersey

Child Welfare League of America, Inc.
44 East 23rd Street
New York, New York

Council for Exceptional Children
1201 16th Street, N.W.
Washington, D.C.

Epilepsy Information Center
319 Longwood Avenue
Boston, Massachusetts

Girls Scouts of America
830 3rd Avenue
New York, New York

Goodwill Industries of America, Inc.
9200 Wisconsin Avenue
Washington, D.C.

Information Center
Recreation for the Handicapped
Southern Illinois University
Carbondale, Illinois

Institute of Child Health and Human Development
with the National Institutes of Health
National Institute of Health
Bethesda, Maryland

Joseph P. Kennedy Foundation
719 13th Street NW
Washington, D.C.

Muscular Dystrophy Association
1790 Broadway
New York, New York

National Association for Gifted Children
8080 Spring Valley Drive
Cincinnati, Ohio

National Association for Mental Health
10 Columbus Circle
New York, New York

National Association for Retarded Children, Inc.
420 Lexington Avenue
New York, New York

National Easter Seal Society for Cripple Children & Adults
2023 West Ogden Avenue
Chicago, Illinois

National Epilespy League, Inc.
203 North Walbash Avenue
Chicago, Illinois

National Rehabilitation Association, Inc.
1522 K Street, N.W.
Washington, D.C.

National Society for the Prevention of Blindness, Inc.
79 Madison Avenue
New York, New York

United Cerebral Palsy Associations, Inc.
31 West 44 Street
New York, New York

The author recognizes that this list is incomplete. A more complete list might be found in the Council for Exceptional Children's Publication of April 3, 1969.

Index

Page numbers in *italics* refer to figures and tables.

Brain (cont.)
  development, evaluation of,
      123
  disorders, diagnosis of, 124-25
  feedback systems, defined, 121
  haptic system, defined, 123
  pyramidal tract damage, 129,
      136
  reticular stem formation, 65,
      121-22
  speech development and, 96
  taste-smell system, 123. *See also*
      Nerves, cranial; Reflexes.
Brain-damaged children
  behavior patterns of, 125
  body movement in, 127
  sensory disturbances in, 129
  skill development in, 70. *See
      also* Mental retardation; Per-
      ceptually impaired.

Calcium, 125
Carbon monoxide, 39
Cataracts, 82
Cerebral palsy, 49, 135-37
  speech and, 96
  type II behavior, 125
Children *see* Adolescents; Gifted
      children; Infant; Preschool
      children; School age chil-
      dren
Chromosome count test, 124-25
Class
  child-rearing attitudes and, 17-
      18
  disadvantaged, familial charac-
      teristics of, 50
  exceptional children and, 16-
      19
  juvenile delinquency and, 175,
      182
  mental retardation and, 38
  neighborhood, exceptional
      children and, 19
Cleft lip, 96, 97
Cleft palate, 96, 97
Club foot, 137
Cocaine, 193
Collagen diseases, 140-41
Communication, 110
  in gifted children, 77
  as infant stimulation, 65
  retardates and, 37, 53-54. *See
      also* Language; Speech.
Conditioning, free operant, 24,
      25-30

Contingency management, de-
      fined, 25
Convulsions, generalized, 130
Critical periods, concept of, 64,
      66
Cystic fibrosis, 138
Cytomegalic inclusion disease, 39

Deafness
  diagnosis of, 99
  parent counseling in, 103-4
  peripheral, *52-53*
Delinquency, juvenile
  age and, 174-75, *178-79, 181*
  defined, 173-74
  multi-handicapped and, 183-
      91,
  sex and, 174, *178-79, 181*
Destructiveness, *178*
Dexedrine, 133
Diabetes
  orthopedic impairment and, 138
  vision and, 83
Diazepam, 131
Dilantin, 131
Discipline, of exceptional chil-
      dren, 3-4
Down's syndrome *see* Mongolism
Dreams, disturbing, *178*
Dressing, 62
Drug abuse, 159-60
  addiction, defined, 191-92
  incidence of, 194
  psychologic dependence, de-
      fined, 193, *194*
Drug therapy, 163-64
Dyslexia, defined, 126, 186
Dysphasis, defined, 99

Echolalia
  autism and, 152
  treatment of, 133
EEG *see* Electroencephalogram
Electrodiagnostic tests, use of,
      125
Electroencephalogram, 124
Encephalitis
  behavior, effect on, 186-87
  measle, 50
Enuresis, 158, *178*
Epilepsy *see* Seizures
Esotropia, 83, 84
Eupholia, 29
Exotropia, defined, 83

Family
  activity, exceptional children
      and, 15
  affectional relationships in, 11-
      12
  child-centered, characterized
      12
  emotional development and,
      150-51
  guilt, 21
  health, exceptional children
      and, 20
  juvenile delinquency and, 174,
      175-77, 182-83
  mother-child interactions, *68-
      69, 70-71*
  organization, types of, 13-15
  role fulfillment in, 10-12
  size, exceptional children and,
      12-13
  types of, 10, 13-14
  values, 15-16
Fear, 6-7
Feeding, 70
  in cerebral palsy, 136-37
  disorders, *178*
  as infant stimulation, 65
  retardates, 61
Fibroplasia, retrolental, 83
Figure-ground, as perceptual mo-
      tor deficit, 127-28
Finger agnosia, defined, 128

Galactosemia, 40
Gifted children, 76-79
Glaucoma, vision and, 83
Grand mal *see* Seizures
Guilt, exceptional children and,
      6-7

Hallucinogens, use of, 193, 195
Harelip *see* Cleft lip
Health services
  care-by-parent unit, 22
  child, 119
  exceptional child, 7-8
  hearing services, 108
  respite care, 71
Hearing
  acuity, measurement of, 102,
      103
  auditory stimulation, 70
  deficiency, defined, 101
  development, 104-7

Hearing (cont.)
  disorders, classified, 102-3
  minimal brain damage and, 127
  sound perception and, 102
  speech development and, 96.
      See also Deafness.
Heroin, 39
Hospitalization
  behavior, effect on, 186-97
  speech development and, 96
Hygiene, 50
  feminine, functional age and,
      26
Hyperactivity *see* Hyperkinesis
Hyperkinesis, 132, 133, 154-55
  as sense modality impairment,
      127, *178*
Hyperopia, 82

Idioglossia, 111, 114-15
Imitation, 26
Impulsivity, minimal brain dam-
      age and, 132, 133
Individual differences, concept of,
      64, 66
Infant
  blind, management of, 88
  development, normal, *68*
  emotional problems of, diag-
      nosis of, 149
  hearing testing in, 104-5, 106
  seizures, 130
  visual problems of, 86
Intelligence
  delinquency and, 184-86
  development of, 122
  orthopedic impairment and,
      138
  in perceptually impaired chil-
      dren, 126-27
Irritability, *178*

Jealousy, *178*

Keratitis, vision and, 83
Klinefelter's syndrome, 40, *41, 45*

Language
  blindness and, 85
  defined, 109
  descriptive, class and, 113

Language (cont.)
McGinnis method of teaching, 100
and minimal brain damage, 127
nonstandard systems of, 100. *See also* Speech.
Laterality, defined, 128
Lead, 39
poisoning, neonatal, 50
Learning, associative, 25
Librium, 133
Listening, as parental working technique, 22
LSD, 39
Lying, *178*

Malnutrition, 50
Marijuana, users of, 193, 194-95
Maturational lag, concept of, 152
Memory, minimal brain damage and, 127
Meningitis, 50, 103
Mental retardation
aggression tolerance in, 184
attention span in, 53
characterisitics of, 37-38
counseling in, 72
cultural-familial retardates, 50
defined, 36-37
diagnosis of, 99
familial, 53
genetics and, 40-47
mild, characteristics of, 49, 51-57
moderate, 57-58
nature of, 38-39
negative reinforcement in, 27-29
perinatal causes of, 39-40, 50-51
prevention of, 63-71
profound, 63
seizure-induced, 130
sensory deprivation and, 65
severe, 58-63
six-hour, defined, 53
speech development and, 95
Mime, 63
Modesty, *178*
Mongolism, 40, *44, 48*
Moodiness, *178*
Multiple disabilities, 143-44
Mumps, 103
Muscular dystrophy, 138, 139-40
Myelomeningocoele, 141

Myopia, 82
Mysoline, 131

Nailbiting, *178*
Narcotics, 192
Nerves, cranial
perceptual-motor difficulties and, 128
vision and, 84
Nurturance, 64, 66
child development and, *68-69*
Nutrition, neurologic disorders and, 123

Object-loss, concept of, 21
Orthopedic impairment, 137-43
braces, use in, 142-43
diagnosis of, 124-25
Otolaryngologist, role of, 107
Otologist, role of, 107

Palsy, kinds of, 136
Perceptually impaired
coordination problems of, 128-32
described, 125-26
management of, 133-35
Perseveration, defined, 128
Petit mal *see* Seizures
Phenobarbital, 131
Phenylketonuria, 40
seizures and, 130
Phosphorous, 125
Photophobia, 84
Pneumoencephalogram, 124
Poliomyelitis, 138, 140
Prematurity, 49
hearing and, 103
speech development and, 95
Prenatal care, importance of, 118
Preschool children
blind, management of, 88
hearing testing in, 105-7
normal development of, 59, *69*
stimulation of, programs for, 65
training of, 56-57
Psychologically disturbed
at-home therapy, 161-62
diagnosis of, 99
family counseling, 57-58
family therapy, 162-63
manic-depressive psychosis, 154

Vision (cont.)
in minimal brain damage, 127
partial, 81, 85, 87
refraction, errors of, 82, *83*
restricted, defined, 80-81
Snellen chart rating of, *80*
stimulation of, 70
systems, defined, 123
testing, 86-87. *See also* Blindness.
Vistaril, 133

Walking, as infant stimulation, 65
Withdrawal behavior, 155-56
aggression continuum, 172-73
passive-withdrawn disorders, 172-73
as social adjustment, 168. *See also* Aggression.
Writing, 110

X-rays, neurologic diagnosis by, 124